"I am really excited about *A Good a* reader in as if it were a novel. It is acc full of stories and illustrations. Moreover, the amount of research and breadth of topics covered are impressive. While this book will make apologetics accessible to a broad Christian audience, its main purpose is achieved with excellence: to have an honest, thoughtful conversation with an unbeliever so he or she will have to consider the credentials of Christianity. This is now the best book to give to an unbelieving friend or relative. I loved reading this book, and so will you."

—**J. P. Moreland**, distinguished professor of philosophy, Talbot School of Theology, Biola University; author of *A Simple Guide to Miracles*

"In his wonderfully engaging style, Gould takes the reader on a grand expedition in search of the cosmic narrative that best explains the human experience of the world. As a well-seasoned trail guide, he leads the reader past majestic vistas and through rocky terrain, pointing out the signposts that are crucial to the journey. With remarkable clarity, he maps out a narrative that, unlike nontheistic alternatives, is intellectually and spiritually satisfying—a glorious, humane story that gives each of us an objectively meaningful identity, legitimizes our yearning for the transcendent, and offers ultimate hope."

—**Melissa Cain Travis**, distinguished fellow of great books and philosophy, Southeastern University; author of *Science and the Mind of the Maker*

"Aristotle said that philosophy begins with wonder. We human beings are all philosophers; each of us has a philosophy of life. But does my philosophy of life satisfactorily address the wide range of fundamental questions each worldview must answer? Paul Gould is a seasoned guide for the reader who is curious about the world and its workings, the nature of our humanity as well as one's personal identity, the 'pursuit of happiness,' and what's behind it all—the source of purpose, meaning, and healing for our brokenness. Indeed, there is one story to rule them all, to make the best sense of the way things are and ought to be. Gould's well-crafted book points us to a God of love who appears in Jesus of Nazareth to rescue us, to unite us to our Creator, and to restore us to what we were meant to be."

—**Paul Copan**, Pledger Family Chair of Philosophy and Ethics, Palm Beach Atlantic University; author of *Loving Wisdom: A Guide to Philosophy and Christian Faith*

"Gould's *A Good and True Story* invites the reader to sojourn with him through the human experience. His narrative-driven exploration of this life—from the eye-opening scientific facts to the wonder of beauty—provides a unique opportunity to wander into life's deepest questions. Gould's work is an accessible, relatable, and humorous quest to discover our personal story in and through the story of the world."

—**Mary Jo Sharp**, assistant professor of apologetics, Houston Baptist University

"For many of us, Paul Gould has been a primary voice pointing to a proper embrace of Christian faith as true, good, and beautiful. Seeing the gospel as a blend of reason and romance is paradigmatically Gouldian. In this book, he walks with us as our guide—along with other guides, such as Ladies Nature and Philosophy, Lewis, Chesterton, Pascal, and a wonderful variety of movies, plays, and literature—leading us on the journey to see the Christian story as the greatest possible story. Be careful: If you read this book, you may just find your true name."

—**Travis Dickinson**, professor of philosophy, Dallas Baptist University

A
GOOD
AND TRUE
STORY

OTHER BOOKS BY PAUL M. GOULD

Cultural Apologetics: Renewing the Christian Voice, Conscience and Imagination in a Disenchanted World

Stand Firm: Apologetics and the Brilliance of the Gospel (with Travis Dickinson and R. Keith Loftin)

Philosophy: A Christian Introduction (with James K. Dew Jr.)

The Outrageous Idea of the Missional Professor

A GOOD AND TRUE STORY

Eleven Clues to Understanding Our Universe and Your Place in It

PAUL M. GOULD

BrazosPress
a division of Baker Publishing Group
Grand Rapids, Michigan

To all fellow travelers,
then and now, . . .
and to my family.
The journey is better together.

Published by Brazos Press
a division of Baker Publishing Group
PO Box 6287, Grand Rapids, MI 49516-6287
www.brazospress.com

Printed in the United States of America

Library of Congress Cataloging-in-Publication Data
Names: Gould, Paul M., 1971– author.
Title: A good and true story : eleven clues to understand our universe and your place in it / Paul M. Gould.
Description: Grand Rapids, Michigan : Brazos Press, a division of Baker Publishing Group, [2022] | Includes bibliographical references and index.
Identifiers: LCCN 2022008630 | ISBN 9781587435195 (paperback) | ISBN 9781587435874 (casebound) | ISBN 9781493438440 (ebook) | ISBN 9781493438457 (pdf)
Subjects: LCSH: Apologetics. | Theology. | Christianity—Philosophy. | Identity (Psychology)—Religious aspects—Christianity.
Classification: LCC BT1103 .G68 2022 | DDC 296.3/5—dc23/eng/20220322
LC record available at https://lccn.loc.gov/2022008630

Baker Publishing Group publications use paper produced from sustainable forestry practices and post-consumer waste whenever possible.

22   23   24   25   26   27   28   7   6   5   4   3   2   1

Contents

Introduction

The Search

Magic Mirror on the wall, who is the fairest of them all?

—The Evil Queen in *Snow White
and the Seven Dwarfs*

It's a dangerous business, Frodo, going out your door. . . . You step into the Road, and if you don't keep your feet, there is no knowing where you might be swept off to.

—J. R. R. Tolkien, *The Lord of the Rings*

Who am I? Have you ever asked, really asked, this question? What is your identity? What is your essence? How might we go about answering questions like this?

In fairy stories, talking mirrors can help. In the real world, normal mirrors reveal some things—hair color, personal style, tattoo placement. But what makes you uniquely you? Your social-media feed? Your success in school, sports, or a job?

Perhaps we can start with seemingly easier questions, like, Where am I? I'll speak for myself. Possible answers include my office, my house, Jupiter Farms, Jupiter, Florida, the United States, the Northern Hemisphere, Earth, the Milky Way Galaxy, the universe, the Mind of God.[1]

1

Let's try another question, maybe a bit closer to the question of identity: What am I? Possible answers include husband, father, son, professor, writer, my Facebook feed and profile, a thinker, a feeler, a dreamer, a man, a human being, a happy accident, a creature. Let's play it safe: I'm a human being who has many roles and is in relationship with many others. That seems to cover the important terrain. I'm a human being sitting in my office in Florida writing. A human *doing*. Does any of this help us answer our fundamental question about identity? Have we struck gold yet? I don't think so. In fact, I'm leading you down a dead end.

Dead ends can be instructive, though. Especially if we turn around and try a different path in search of answers. In fact, *you cannot answer the question of identity until you answer the question of story*. Our identity is wrapped up with the story of our lives: the story we tell, the story we live in. The philosopher Hannah Arendt notes that "the moment we want to say *who* somebody is, our very vocabulary leads us astray into saying *what* he is; we get entangled in a description of qualities he necessarily shares with others like him; we begin to describe a type of 'character' in the old meaning of the word, with the result that his specific uniqueness escapes us."[2] Arendt says the only way to escape this is through story: "*Who* somebody is or was we can know only by knowing the story of which he is himself the hero—his biography, in other words; everything else we know of him, including the work he may have produced and left behind, tells us only *what* he is or was."[3] Discover the story you inhabit, and you'll find yourself too.

Let's not take Arendt's word as final. Consider your own experience. What do you find? I'll report my own intuition and experience and encourage you to do the same. Here is my sense of things: I came into this world as part of an ongoing story. (For me, this ongoing story includes parents who became business leaders and educators, grandparents who spun tales of walking to their one-room schoolhouse in the snow uphill both ways, and a few skeletons in the proverbial family closet.) I envision myself as the main

2

character, the hero, as I take my place as part of this ongoing story. My story has a telos, a purpose, an end. I'm headed somewhere.

This is an important discovery. My sense is that life is a journey. We are on a quest. Each of us lives on stories and lives a storied life. We are the main character, but of course, not the only character. We're headed somewhere. But where? It all depends on the story in which we find ourself.

Time for another bold claim: to correctly answer the question of identity, *you must locate your life in the true story of the world.* Before you check out or cry foul, let me set a worry aside. I'm not here to pontificate. I do think there is truth to be found; I do think there is a true story of the world, a story alive and alluring. I'm a fellow traveler. I'm not going to just up and tell it to you. Rather, I want to invite you to join me, and many of the guides I've found helpful, on a journey of discovery. It's your journey, after all, so you need to walk it yourself. But you needn't, and really shouldn't, walk alone. Let's go together.

There are many stories "out there," stories that compete for your allegiance and invite your participation. Chief storytellers shout (or whisper, depending on their mood), "Follow me, and you'll find your authentic self, you'll find your purpose, your meaning, [*insert Darth Vader voice*] your destiny." Yet many stories conflict with each other, so they can't all be true. So how do we know which one is the true story of the world?

I have a proposal. Let's embark together on a journey of discovery. I have friends (guides, if you will)—philosophers, scientists, artists—who will join us on the way. These escorts will lead us down paths of reason and romance, head and heart. It shouldn't surprise us, upon reflection, that there are multiple converging paths that must be trodden on our quest: we long for a story that is both true to the way the world *is* and true to the way the world *ought* to be. In other words, the deep longing of the human heart is for a story that is both *true* and *satisfying*. We want a story that is true (for truth is of supreme importance; we want to be rightly related to reality), but also good and beautiful. I'll introduce you

3

to our first guide at the end of this introduction. She'll walk with us for a while before we invite others.

But first let's simplify our project. There are two basic stories, and we'll use these as our foil on our journey of discovery. The first one, prominent among the modern intelligentsia and said to have the authority of science as its chief backer, we'll call, for lack of a better name, the *nonreligious story*. The second basic story, prominent throughout most of human history and still alive in many quarters today, we'll call the *religious story*. We'll fill in details as we go, but for now, let's offer a brief sketch of our two basic stories of the world.

The Nonreligious Story

Stories are dramatic. They have a plot, a narrative arc, that brings together events and ideas and agents into some coherent whole. All stories have a beginning, a middle, and an end: an origin, a quest, and a destiny. How might we chart the basic plotline of the nonreligious story? Here's one way to capture its narrative arc:

matter—vulnerable selves—buffered selves

Let's unpack this a bit. In the beginning, if there is a beginning at all, there was *matter*. All that exists are atoms and collections of atoms in the shape of cells, aardvarks, dogs, humans, mountains, stars, and so on. Minds (or brains) appear late in this story, but once they have arrived, they take center stage. Humans are *vulnerable* to the ravages of nature and of each other. So, they begin to work together to understand the world and to protect themselves—to *buffer* their vulnerable selves from harm, from pain, from death. Along the way, they also enjoy the gifts of nature: pleasure, warmth, and discovery.

Five philosophical ideas support the nonreligious story: scientism, materialism, reductionism, atheism, and nihilism. *Scientism* is the dominant theory of knowledge that drives this story. In its strongest form, scientism is the idea that all our knowledge comes from the sciences. Thus, the men and women in lab coats, surrounded by instruments of discovery, are the priests and priestesses of this story, telling the rest of us the truth about the world. If science is the only source of knowledge, and the sciences explore the material world, then it follows that the only kinds of things that we can with surety say exist are material things. This is *materialism*.

Reductionism is closely related to but distinct from materialism. Here's how reductionism goes: Consider the universe, the sum of all material reality. We can view the universe as a series of hierarchies of material things: galaxies, planets, biological species, chemical compounds, atoms, and sub-atomic particles. According to reductionism, the basic building blocks of the universe are whatever physics identifies as the fundamental particles. Everything else is "nothing but" collections of these particles. Thus, sociology reduces to anthropology, which reduces to biology, which reduces to chemistry, which reduces to physics. Once we hit rock bottom, we are plumbing the "real" or really existent things.

Since, on the nonreligious story, science is the only source of knowledge, and since science tells us that there are only material things, *atheism* naturally follows too. (We could opt for an agnosticism, the view that we don't know either way on the question of God's existence, and leave open the possibility that science will confirm the existence of nonmaterial realities, including God. But then, that would be another story, and we'd not know whether it was a religious or nonreligious story. I'll set it aside to keep the options simple—and binary—for now.) On atheism, there is no God; there is nothing beyond the material world. Since there is no God, there is no meaning to the world either; hence, *nihilism* follows. (In chapter 6, I'll consider a more hopeful version of the nonreligious story that seeks to avoid nihilism.) Each person is free to find some purpose, some meaning, some identity for himself or herself, but this meaning, purpose, and identity pass away when they do.

Where does this leave us? What are humans, according to the nonreligoius story? How does it answer our question of identity? Humans are "star-dust brought to life,"[4] "blobs of organized mud."[5] We are the happy accident of evolution. Humans are cosmic orphans on a vast sea of nothingness. That is, according to this story, *who* you are. Atheists view their story quite differently. Some, for example, think this is a bad story, a rather boring story. The playwright George Bernard Shaw reportedly describes the nonreligious story as a "tragedy" in which "nothing ever happens and dullness kills us."[6] Others, such as the atheist cosmologist Lawrence Krauss, think the nonreligious story is the most amazing story ever.[7] Let's try to refrain from making a value judgment about this story yet. Let's just note the following: if this is the true story of the world, then so be it. Let's embrace the spirit of one of the great atheists of the twentieth century, Bertrand Russell, who argues that even though people are "the product of causes which had no prevision of the end they were achieving" and "the outcome of accidental collocations of atoms," still we must live with courage "on the firm foundation of unyielding despair."[8] Let's face it with courage. And let's get on with the business of our lives.

The Religious Story

The religious story begins and ends with God. There is considerable debate among philosophers and theologians about what God, if God exists, is like. Is God personal (as the theist claims) or impersonal (as the pantheist claims)? In other words, is God distinct from the universe or part of it? Does God have a gender? Is God perfect? Does he, she, or it care about us?

In order to get the discussion moving, I'm going to stipulate a definition of God. We'll test and refine it along the way. We'll also need to discover whether there is a being that satisfies our definition of God. In other words, it is one thing to define the term *God*, but it is quite another to discover that such a being exists. I define God as an *immaterial personal being that is worthy of worship*. There are three things I want you to notice about my stipulated definition. First, I'm suggesting that our prephilosophical idea of God includes personhood. In other words, our intuition (or again, I'll speak for myself and invite you to plumb your own intuitions) is that God, if he exists, is personal.[9] I think there is another way we can arrive at a basic, first-pass definition of God. The medieval philosopher and theologian Anselm defined God as the greatest conceivable being.[10] This is a good start. But why add, as I did, the bit about being personal? Consider: Is it better to be personal or nonpersonal? Intuitively, it is better to be personal. Then God, as the greatest conceivable being, will possess or have personhood. My intuition regarding God as personal could be wrong, and you might not share my intuition (and not buy the argument I gave to motivate it). That's okay. We are free, as we embark on our journey of discovery, to work with a different conception of God if we find reasons from science or philosophy for rejecting the concept that God is personal. But I submit that it is at least a natural place to begin our investigation of the divine. If God is personal, that means he is the kind of being that has an intellect and a will. God knows things and does things.

Second, the idea of being worship-worthy does a lot of work. If we come to find out that our existence is a result of brute chance or that we are part of a computer simulation or that we are just brains in a vat being poked and prodded by some evil scientist, it doesn't follow that chance or the computer or the scientist is God; rather, it follows that God doesn't exist. To be worthy of our worship, one must possess certain metaphysical, moral, and aesthetic qualities. In other words, to satisfy the concept of deity, a divine being must be ultimate or supreme as well as wholly good, maximally powerful, and exhaustively knowledgeable. That's quite a high bar. It would be a big deal to discover that such a being exists. It would shape everything else. Finally, it's important to remember that I've only defined what God is *like*, if he exists. I've said nothing about who God *is*. To learn God's identity, we'll need to discover the true story of the world.

The basic outline of the religious story, as a kind of generic theism, can also be understood as a three-act play:

God—alienation—union

In this story, *God* exists and, out of sheer goodness and love, creates a world full of unity and diversity, order and abundance, beauty and delight. According to this story, humanity is a unique creation endowed with capacities enabling us to relate to God, such as moral and aesthetic awareness and volitional freedom. Free choice is the power of alternatives, and as the story goes, humans choose the alternative to God—autonomy. And what follows autonomy is *alienation*—alienation from ourselves, others, the environment, and God. But God has done something about this deep alienation. The details differ depending on which religion is in view, but the idea is that on the religious story, genuine reconciliation is possible. Humans can become whole again; *union* with deity is possible. This story, like the nonreligious story, is woefully imprecise at the moment, but it will serve as a helpful starting point on our journey to discover the true story of the world.

There are also five philosophical ideas that support the religious story (at least as I envision it; other philosophers will quibble): particularism, dualism, teleology, antireductionism, and supernaturalism. *Particularism* is the view that we can know things without knowing how we know them.[11] In other words, I can know that I exist, that this is a hand, and that $2 + 2 = 4$ without first identifying some criterion for what counts as knowledge. The upshot is this: the particularist has a healthy respect for empirical facts without limiting knowledge to empirical facts. There are other potential sources of knowledge, including moral, rational, spiritual, and aesthetic sources. On the religious story, God—an immaterial personal being that is worthy of worship—exists. This entails that there is more to reality than material reality. There is an immaterial part too. Thus, *dualism* follows. It is an open question how far this material/immaterial dualism extends. There could be, in addition to God, other immaterial parts to reality such as the souls of finite creatures, mental properties or entities such as thoughts or minds, abstract objects such as numbers, and so on.

Teleology is the idea that there is design or purpose or end-state-directed processes. Many have pointed out that there seem to be two kinds of teleology found in the world: a teleology that belongs to some "parts" of the universe and a teleology that belongs to the universe as a whole. Let's begin with the teleology found in "parts" of the universe. For many creatures, we find a kind of ideal end state: acorns mature into oak trees, zygotes mature into adult humans, and tadpoles mature into frogs. There is an internal principle, a nature that determines what a thing is and guides its development toward a specific end (its telos). In addition to this teleology found in "parts" of the universe, many have noted a kind of teleology that guides the *whole* universe. The idea is that everything seems to fit together into a well-ordered unity. The universe itself is headed somewhere—it has a purpose—and as we'll see in a later chapter, it seems as if the universe was designed with humans in mind.

Antireductionism is the view that there are fundamental things "above" or "higher up from" the base of the hierarchy of material reality. Thus, living things—bacteria, bulldogs, baboons—are more than just the sum of their parts; they are fundamental wholes with natures, and their parts (eyes, hands, atoms, etc.) depend on and get their identity from the whole in which they find themselves. Finally, *supernaturalism* is the idea that there is meaning to be found in this world because God exists and created the world for a purpose. At this point, we don't have much of an idea what that purpose is and thus what meaning there is to be found, but we begin with the philosophical idea that there is a meaning and it is our job to discover it.

To summarize, our identity is tied to our narrative; our narratival choice at the highest, most abstract level is, generally speaking, of two orders: the nonreligious and the religious. You probably have, at this very moment, a propensity toward one or the other.

Open to Transcendence

A couple summers ago, my teenage son, Travis, and I set out to summit not one but two fourteen-thousand-foot peaks (known among the locals as "Fourteeners") in a single hike: Challenger

Point and Kit Carson Peak in the Sangre de Cristo Range of the Colorado Rocky Mountains. After a few days of preparatory hiking around Colorado, we arrived in the tiny mountain village of Crestone. It was full of mosquitoes as big as birds and as ubiquitous as the feral hogs in Texas. We checked into our hotel room and out of reality as we knew it. The town felt spooky—haunted, even. It was a mixture of the Wild West, hippy Berkeley, and New Age Sedona. The quaint and odd mountain town and the journey from it to the top of the mountains and back again supply a fitting metaphor for life. To convey it well, I first need to share about our attempt to summit these two alluring peaks.

Our alarms jolted us awake from an uneasy sleep at 2:45 a.m., and we jumped out of bed and got into our hiking gear. After a two-mile drive up a winding dirt road, we parked and hit the trailhead. Hiking the next two hours by flashlight, I yelled "switchback" at every turn partly to keep us awake, partly to keep away whatever critters watched us, or stalked us. As the sun rose, Kit Carson Peak and Challenger Point came into view. My soul soared as Travis and I enjoyed a moment of rest and drank in the beauty around us, eating stale donut holes in silence. After a few more hours of hiking we saw our first humans, a couple who had spent the night near a high-altitude lake. Hiking around the lake, we began the more technical ascent to the first summit, Challenger Point. There were only six of us on the mountain: Travis and me and two other couples. One couple chose the difficult but snow-free spine of scree (loose stones) to the left. I was well aware that earlier that week a hiker had gone missing on this very ascent. (Sadly, I found out later that day that a search and rescue team found his body about the same time we were climbing.) We followed the second couple to the right for the safer yet still snow-covered path to the summit. A half mile from the summit, the passage became too dangerous: as the snow deepened, the path vanished in a sea of white. Disappointed, we realized the summit was beyond our reach. After enjoying the view, we reluctantly turned back. Five hours later, we were safely back in our hotel room, tired but thankful for the shared experience.

While we have unfinished business with the mountain, I still consider this hike with my son a success. Compelled by our love for each other and our love for adventure, sustained by courage when the hike became harrowing and difficult, and guided by wisdom, humility, and openness to reality when the road became impassable, we enjoyed communion with each other and the world around us. We forged a bond of friendship and a memory that will nourish us for our journeys ahead. These same characteristics— love, courage, wisdom, humility, openness—are needed as we embark on our expedition to discover the true story of the world.

Our loves and longings drive us. They move us. We desire to find truth, to be nourished by goodness, and to be satisfied by beauty. We desire to be known and loved. These longings compel us; they set us on a quest. But this journey will require wisdom to know when to turn back and when to turn to the right or left. It will require courage too, especially the courage to follow clues wherever they might lead. Finally, this journey will require openness to reality. Herein lies a unique challenge, given the widespread disenchantment of our age.

The philosopher Antony Flew once argued that when we begin to explore the question of God, we ought to begin with a presumption of atheism.[12] The idea is this: Everyone already believes that the universe exists. The theist, however, has an extra burden of proof because she believes that in addition to the universe, there is also God. That's adding something more—a big something more—to the furniture of reality. To add such an extraordinary being to the inventory of things that exist requires extraordinary evidence. Thus, if one doesn't find that evidence, one is justified in being an atheist, since we should begin with that presumption anyway. I think this is a mistake. There is no special burden that the theist must shoulder in this quest to find the true story of the world. We all shoulder the same burden of proof—of the justification, through reason and experience, of our beliefs about God, the world, and our place within it. Moreover, there is a risk of overlooking key evidence for God if we begin with a presumption of atheism.

I encourage you to adopt a different posture toward the question of God. I encourage you to be genuinely open to the possibility that God exists.[13] Even more, I encourage you to be open to the possibility that God is better than you think, that God is better than you've been told. When Travis and I were hiking through boulder fields on our journey to Challenger Point, we followed cairns along the way. These rocks stacked by those who preceded us revealed the way when the path became obscure. What if cairns display the way forward on our journey in life too? These cairns could serve as guides to help us successfully discover the true story of the world. Now my biggest claim: *such cairns exist, and they beckon us forward.* I think these cairns, these physical and metaphysical pointers, show us the way to God; they lead us on the path to the true story of the world. Now you know where I'm coming from. You know what I think I've discovered. All I can do is point to those clues—the stones that I think reveal a transcendent reality—and then let you decide for yourself.

Here's my plan: I want to explore eleven features of the world to find out which of our two basic stories—the nonreligious or religious, the atheistic or theistic—provides the best fit to accommodate the nature of these features (first taken individually and then all together). I will argue that these eleven clues are signposts that point to something beyond concrete material reality. That "something" I shall argue is God, as defined above. As we stack those stones together and take a look at the whole, I shall argue that we are led to the author of the true story of the world. I invite you to follow the path I've walked, looking carefully at the clues I've found that reveal something beyond this world. Let's tread this path together with courage, wisdom, humility, openness, and most of all love. It's time to meet our first guide.

Cosmic Wonder and Lady Nature

I end this chapter with a final claim. *The quest to discover your authentic self begins in wonder—the wonder that there is anything at all and the wonder of individual objects and people seen in a new light.* How might we cultivate wonder as we embark on our quest to discover the true story of the world? We've already noted a posture, of openness to transcendence. All that is needed is a starting point for our journey and a new way of relating along the way. Let's select our starting point first. In fact, let's make it easy. We'll start with the natural world and its many denizens. Why start with nature? For two reasons. First, there is an ancient idea that "man" (as the ancients would have said) is a microcosm, a miniature picture of the cosmos as a whole. In other words, you can't know yourself until you know what kind of world you find yourself in. Second, there is a principle of reasoning I find impeccable: when seeking an answer to something that is unclear or puzzling or mysterious, begin with clear cases of knowledge and work from those to an answer to that which is initially unclear. Humans have learned a great deal about the natural world. What we know, as we shall see, leads to some startling discoveries.

But to cultivate wonder, we need a new way of relating. We need help to behold (and not merely see) the world and its denizens. So, I've enlisted our first guide, a guide prominent in many medieval travel stories: Lady Nature. In a medieval work by Alan of Lille called *Plaint of Nature*, Lady Nature descends from the immutable realm to answer the queries of a young poet undergoing inner turmoil. As she makes her appearance, all the creatures celebrate her arrival. Alan of Lille describes the scene: "Thus everything in the universe, swarming forth to pay court to the maiden, in a wondrous contest toiled to win her favor."[14] Perhaps as we begin, Lady Nature can spin her magic again. We need "everything in the universe" to come to her—to us—and "pay court" so that we might see the extraordinary within the mundane. Once wonder is aroused, inquiry can begin. I invite you to join with me, submitting to the "ordering stride"[15] of wonder and inquiry, awe and perplexity, adoration and participation, as we seek the true story of the world and an answer to our fundamental questions of identity, meaning, and purpose.

It turns out there is a mirror of sorts. It's not on a wall. But we find it by walking on the way.

1

The Universe

The universe that we observe has precisely the properties we should expect if there is, at bottom, no design, no purpose, no evil and no good, nothing but blind, pitiless indifference.

—Richard Dawkins, *River out of Eden*

The modern world, insofar as it is proposed to humankind as its habituation, is too small, too dull, too meager for us. After all, we are very remarkable. We alone among the creatures have learned a bit of the grammar of the universe.

—Marilynne Robinson, *What Are We Doing Here?*

In the science fiction comedy *The Hitchhiker's Guide to the Galaxy*, we meet "hyperintelligent pandimensional beings" who grow tired of bickering over life's meaning since it interrupted their favorite pastime: a game where they hit each other for no apparent reason and run away.[1] So they design "a stupendous super computer" named Deep Thought in order to find out, once and for all, the answer to "Life, the Universe, and Everything."[2] The idea of a computer discovering the answer to humanity's deepest questions might sound outrageous; after all, in this novel it is commonly thought that "the Quest for Ultimate Truth is quite clearly the inalienable prerogative of your working thinkers."[3] Deep Thought not only threatens to put philosophers out of a job; it also insults thinking creatures everywhere with the supposition that a machine could determine the answer to humanity's deepest questions. But Deep Thought has a solution to those problems: since it will take seven and a half million years to determine the answer to life's meaning, the philosophers have plenty of time to bicker over what answer the computer will come up with. Everyone is happy; there is still something for "working thinkers" to do.

After seven and a half million years, Deep Thought produces the answer to "Life, the Universe, and Everything." And the answer turns out to be the number forty-two.[4] Understandably, folks are a bit perplexed: "Forty-two. . . . Is that all you've got to show for seven and a half million years' work?"[5] The problem, according to Deep Thought, isn't the answer; rather, it's "that you've never actually known what the question is."[6] And unfortunately, even Deep Thought can't tell them what the question is. Rather, a future computer, superior to Deep Thought, will tell them what the question is—after another ten million years.[7]

Adams's absurdist novel highlights at least two challenges to discovering the answer to "Life, the Universe, and Everything." First, there is the challenge of disagreement. We "working thinkers" are rather poor at landing on answers to our perennial questions. Second, there is the challenge of asking the right questions. I don't think either of these challenges should detain us long. These questions are complex, even if they don't take seven and a half million years to answer. This should encourage humility as well as courage. As finite beings with limited perspective and knowledge, our job is to do our best to explore these questions with all the resources available to us (including evidence from sensory perception, reason, memory, testimony, introspection, and more) and to follow where the evidence leads. Other than some truths of logic and mathematics, very little in life can be known with absolute certainty. Still, we can know truths beyond a reasonable doubt.

When it comes to asking the right questions, that too is a skill we can develop. It could be that in order to discover the answers to "Life, the Universe, and Everything," we need to ask a series of preliminary questions that help us see clearly. In this chapter, with Lady Nature as our guide, I begin to ask some of those preliminary questions. We start our journey by exploring the universe itself, noting four features of the universe that awaken wonder and cry out for explanation: its contingency, finitude, immensity, and fine-tuning. We then ask three questions in order to discover an explanation of the universe: Why is there something rather than nothing? Did the universe begin to exist? Is the universe indifferent to humans? Let's see if we can do better than Deep Thought.

Contingency

You exist. You wouldn't be reading this book if you didn't. It wouldn't help to argue that you're hallucinating and therefore you don't exist. You still exist even if this book doesn't. You and your hallucination would exist. So, you exist. But you might not have existed. We can imagine many scenarios in which you do not exist. Maybe one of your parents was never born. Maybe your parents never met. Maybe your parents never had any children.

To say that you exist but might not have existed is to say that you are a contingent being. You are not self-made. The explanation and cause of your existence lies outside you. In this case, that explanation lies with your parents. But what about your parents? Are they self-made? A moment's reflection helps us see that they too are contingent. We could go on, of course: your parents' parents are not self-made, and their parents are not self-made. We've discovered something important about humans: we are contingent beings. But what about other living organisms: dogs and donkeys, oak trees and onions? Again, a moment's reflection reveals that all organisms are contingent. Animals and plants come into being and pass away just like humans do. Their existence is caused by another. But what about inorganic things: quarks, the Higgs field, rocks, water, sodium chloride, planets, stars, galaxies? Pick any material object in the universe, it doesn't matter which, and it too will be a contingent thing. (We'll challenge this claim below, but for now, we can at least admit that every material object *seems* to be a contingent thing.)

Contingent objects are dependent objects (since they are not self-made); thus every object in the universe is a dependent being. But what about the universe as a whole—is it a contingent, dependent being? The philosopher Joshua Rasmussen supplies the following principle: "Purely dependent things form dependent totals."[8] Just as you can only get a white floor from white tiles (and not a purple floor from white tiles), you can only get a contingent, dependent total from contingent, dependent parts. To argue that you can build an independent (and noncontingent) thing from dependent things is to commit, according to Rasmussen, a "construction error."[9] Since every material thing in the universe is a contingent, dependent thing, it follows that the universe as a whole is a contingent, dependent thing.

This contingency—our own and that of the universe—is a source of wonder. If the familiar objects of our everyday experience are all contingent, we may rightly wonder why there is anything at all. The contingency of our own lives cries out for explanation. This perception of our contingency begins in wonder, moves to puzzlement, and fuels inquiry and the search for answers. What explains my existence? What explains the universe's existence? One possible answer, as Lady Nature suggests in *Plaint of Nature*, is that God "decrees the existence of things."[10] God is the "architect of the universe" and the "golden constructor of a golden construction" who brought the universe into being "by the command of his deciding will alone."[11] The other option is that the universe exists without an explanation. It just exists as a brute, unexplainable fact. Before we decide which of these is more likely, let's consider some more features of the universe.

Finitude

For much of human history it was thought that the universe was eternal and static. The earth was considered to be the center of the universe. All change, motion, generation, and corruption were thought to take place in the earthly realm, governed by the various "sympathies" latent within the four elements (earth, air, fire, and water). Just above the moon, it was believed, was the eternal and immutable: the planets and the fixed stars. Much of this general picture of the world began to unravel beginning around the time of Copernicus in the sixteenth century. Still, the belief that the universe was eternal and static persisted until Albert Einstein published his work on the general theory of relativity in the early twentieth century.[12] As Einstein developed his gravitational field equations in 1917, he introduced a "fudge factor"—a move he later came to regret—to avoid a troubling implication of his newly discovered gravitational theory: the fact that the universe seemed to be expanding. Others, such as Alexander Friedmann and Georges Lemaître, were able to formulate solutions to Einstein's field equations. This led to the same conclusion, which they made no attempt to fudge: the universe is expanding. Since both sets of equations were empirically equivalent, a definitive answer to the question of the universe's temporal status (as eternal and static or expanding and temporally finite) would need to wait for physical evidence.

Scientists didn't wait long. Looking at the night sky through a giant telescope at the Mount Wilson Observatory near Los Angeles, astronomer Edwin Hubble discovered empirical evidence that would forever change our view of the cosmos. To understand the importance of his discovery, we need to understand a bit about light. Visible light travels through space as a wave, transporting energy (carried by wave-like particles called photons traveling at approximately 186,282 miles per second) from one location to another. If the light source is moving toward you, the wavelength shrinks, shifting to the blue end of the visible light spectrum. Alternatively, if the light source is moving away from you, the wavelength expands, shifting to the red of the visible light spectrum. Hubble discovered that the distant light from galaxies was shifted to the red end of the visible light spectrum. Hailed as "one of the great scientific discoveries of the twentieth century," the reality of the redshift of light implies that the universe is expanding.[13]

If the universe is expanding, that means we can extrapolate back in time to a moment when the universe began. Moreover, we can extrapolate back to a time when all the matter in the universe was together at a single point of infinite density called *the singularity*. The singularity represents the origin moment of the universe, a point from which all space, time, matter, and energy come into being *out of nothing*. As Princeton astrophysicist J. Richard Gott explains:

> Time began at the Big Bang. . . . What happened before the Big Bang? This question makes no sense in the context of general relativity, because time and space were created at the Big Bang. It's like asking what is south of the South Pole. If you go farther and farther south, you will eventually get to the South Pole. But you can't go farther south than the South Pole. Likewise, if you go farther and farther back in time, you will eventually get to the Big Bang. That is when time and space were created, so that's the earliest you can go.[14]

So what we learn from Hubble is that the universe is temporally finite. It does not exist from all eternity. Moreover, all time, space, matter, and energy came into being at the "moment" of the Big Bang out of nothing. This origin event is a source of wonder. It also raises an important question: What—or who—was responsible for bringing the universe into existence?

Immensity

"Space," according to *The Hitchhiker's Guide to the Galaxy*, "is big. Really big. You just won't believe how vastly hugely mind-bogglingly big it is."[15] *The Hitchhiker's Guide* is surely correct. The universe is huge; it is "mind-bogglingly big." How big? Let's start with some numbers we are familiar with and see if we can begin to comprehend the immensity of the universe.[16] Consider the number ten. We are personally acquainted with the number ten. We have ten toes and ten fingers. We first learned our numbers by counting to ten. We can easily work with ten: we can multiply and divide it; we can stack ten donuts on top of each other or ten dominoes next to each other. Football teams earn four more downs if they move the ball ten yards. The fastest among us (i.e., Usain Bolt) can run a hundred meters in under ten seconds. I just mentioned the number one hundred when referencing the hundred-meter run, and you didn't skip a beat. We are familiar with this number. It's one more than the ninety-nine bottles of beer on the wall that we sing about on long bus rides. For many of us, the biggest dollar bill we've seen or held is the hundred-dollar bill.

Let's move on. Skipping over a thousand, consider the number one million. We have some grasp of the immensity of this number. Here's a tasty fact: Hostess makes one million Twinkies every day.[17] Moving from Twinkies to money, many of us dream of becoming millionaires. We aspire to make millions so that we can enjoy the finer things in life (including, critically, Twinkies). Shifting focus to our humble planet, the surface area of the earth is 196 million square miles, and we stand 96 million miles away from our sun. Our sun, of course, is a star. How big is it? We can fit 1.3 million earths within its borders. That's big. But our sun is a rather ordinary-sized star. Consider the massive star Betelgeuse, located in the constellation Orion. That star is so big that you could fit 1.6 billion of our suns within its borders.

Let's consider how big the number one billion is by considering something more mundane and familiar: McDonald's hamburgers. McDonald's signs famously read BILLIONS AND BILLIONS SERVED. How many hamburgers has it served since its opening in 1955? Estimates are around 300 billion.[18] How many is that? If you laid 300 billion hamburgers (4 inches wide) from side to side, you'd cover the circumference of the earth 648 times. But you'd still have some hamburgers left over. How many? Enough to stack them on top of each other (2 inches tall) to the moon and back three times! Then you'd have finally used each of your 300 billion hamburgers. No wonder cows encourage us to eat more chicken![19]

Let's expand our horizon beyond the sun, moon, and stars within our galaxy. While estimates differ, there seem to be at least 100 billion galaxies in the universe, each containing roughly 100 billion stars. That is a big number! Written in exponential notation, this number is ten to the twenty-second power, or 10^{22}. At this point, these numbers, and the quantity of things (very big things), become mind-boggling. Even more amazing, each of these big things is composed of many smaller things. Here is one final number: 10^{80}. This is the number of atoms within the universe. Every material object we find in the universe is composed of atoms, which in turn are composed of still smaller parts.

A moment's reflection on these large numbers and the diverse scales found within the universe reveal two related features that invoke awe and wonder: the universe's interconnectedness and structure. The world is structured into a hierarchy of ascending and descending chains of material objects: subatomic particles compose into atoms, atoms compose into cells, cells compose into organisms, organisms compose into ecosystems, ecosystems into planets, planets into solar systems, solar systems into galaxies, and galaxies into clusters of galaxies. There truly is more to the universe than meets the eye; as the astronomer Martin Rees highlights, "Our universe covers a vast range of scales, and an immense variety of structures, stretching far larger, and far smaller, than the dimensions of everyday sensations."[20]

Do the immensity of the universe and the corresponding tininess of humans give us reason to think the universe is indifferent to our existence? On the face of it, it seems so. "Surely," concludes the atheist Victor Stenger, "it is ludicrous to think that humanity, which came along only about 100,000 years ago and will be lucky to last another 100,000 years, is the special creation of divinity that presides over this vast reality."[21] Lady Nature offers a different perspective, a perspective that seems a bit pompous and self-centered if uttered by us tiny humans: "man" is a microcosm of the cosmos. In turn, the cosmos is a picture, writ large, of man. "For I [i.e., Lady Nature] am the one who formed the nature of man according to the exemplar and likeness of the structure of the universe so that in him, as in a mirror of the universe itself, Nature's lineaments might be seen."[22] Who's right? Should the beauty, order, abundance, and diversity found in the universe be understood as a lavish gift from a Creator, or as a cosmic accident? Recent work on the fine-tuning of the universe, as we shall see, gives reason to think the universe is not as indifferent to humans as it might initially seem. Let's take a look.

Fine-Tuning

The universe is fine-tuned on a razor's edge for life. If the laws of physics, the initial conditions, or the constants of nature had been just a little bit different (I'll tighten the phrase "just a little bit different" shortly), life would not be possible. Now, it is one thing to claim that the universe is fine-tuned for life. It is quite another to claim that the universe is fine-tuned for life by a *fine-tuner*—that is, God. The latter claim involves a philosophical inference. In this section, we'll explore the empirical evidence for a finely tuned universe. In the concluding section of this chapter, we'll consider whether there are good reasons to think fine-tuning suggests a fine-tuner.

So, what is the evidence for a finely tuned universe? Consider the initial order, understood as usable free energy found at the beginning of the universe. We know, given the second law of thermodynamics, that for any closed system, the amount of usable free energy will dissipate over time. Applied to the universe, what the second law of thermodynamics tells us is that the universe is winding down. But it hasn't yet (thankfully) wound down! There is still plenty of usable free energy, and that energy fuels life's many

23

processes here on earth (and any other place in the universe where life might be found). Tracing the universe's supply of usable free energy back in time to the beginning of the universe, scientists can determine the amount of usable free energy that was "built into" the universe at the beginning. Surprisingly, the universe began in a low-entropy (i.e., highly ordered) state. Why is this surprising? Let's return to the numbers. Oxford physicist Roger Penrose has calculated the odds of a low-entropy initial state of the universe to be 1 in 10 to the power of 10^{123} (i.e., 1 chance in 1 followed by 10^{123} zeros).[23] This is the biggest number we've seen yet. The low-entropy initial state of the universe is highly improbable, "much greater than the precision that would be required to hit an individual proton if the entire visible universe were a dartboard!"[24] In the beginning, there was order! Other initial conditions of the universe that are finely tuned include the balance of matter to antimatter (one second after the Big Bang, there were a billion and one protons for every billion antiprotons), the cosmological constant that measures the acceleration of the universe (unaccountably fine-tuned to 1 part in 10^{120}), and the density of the universe (fine-tuned to 1 part in 10^{55} one second after the universe began).[25]

In addition to the initial conditions of the universe, the laws of nature and the constants found within nature are fine-tuned as well. Consider gravity, that "primary governor of the Universe,"[26] as described by Newton's law, $F = Gm_1m_2/r^2$. According to Newton's law, the force of attraction F between two spatially separated material objects is the product of the gravitational constant G and their masses divided by the square of the distance between them.[27] Gravity is the main organizing force of the universe.

What would happen if the gravitational force were nonexistent, weaker, or stronger? In a universe with no gravity, there would be no stars, no planets, no elements, and, thus, no life. Gravity is needed to clump matter together. If there had been no gravitational force to pull together the particles found in the early universe, stars would never have formed in the first place. Thus, there would have been "no long-term energy sources to sustain the evolution (or even existence) of highly complex life."[28] What if gravity were weaker than it is? While it's not clear that a weak-gravity universe could produce stars in the first place, suppose it could. What kind of universe would result? A rather boring—and lifeless—one. In order to produce stable stars, a weak-gravity universe's stars would need to be immense. These immense stars would simply burn through their fuel and die with "their essential elements locked away forever in their cores. The universe would remain a rather uninteresting sea of hydrogen and helium, dotted with only mildly more interesting dead and dying stars."[29] Finally, what if the gravitational force between objects were stronger? In a strong-gravity universe, stars would burn hotter and more rapidly, "emitting radiation that is lethal to life and dying in an even more energetic and dangerous supernova explosion."[30] In our real-world universe it seems that the strength of gravity is just right relative to the other fundamental forces of nature and the arbitrary physical quantities that govern them (i.e., the constants): gravity is not too weak or too strong, enabling the existence and evolution of stable stars, galaxies, and planets conducive for life.

From Cosmic Wonder to a Cosmic Cause

With Lady Nature as our guide, we've embarked on a cosmic tour, noting four features of the universe that are sources of wonder: (1) Everything in the universe depends for its existence on something else. (2) The universe had a beginning; there was a time when it was not. (3) It is more immense than the human mind can hold. (4) It is exquisitely fine-tuned for life. I posit that each of these four facts leads us toward one of two directions: that the universe just is, or that it was caused by something beyond itself.

We begin with the argument from contingency. Pick any existing thing: its existence is explained either through itself or through another. The universe's existence is not explained through itself (as we noted above, the universe, understood as the totality of contingent things, is itself contingent). Therefore, the universe is explained through another. Moreover, whatever explains the universe's existence cannot itself be a contingent thing; if it were, it too would need an explanation for its existence. Therefore, whatever explains the universe's existence is a necessary being. What does it mean to say that some being exists necessarily? A necessary being cannot fail to exist. It's part of its nature or essence to exist. Importantly, the existence of a necessary being is explained through itself. When it comes to necessary beings, or at least when it comes to the necessary being responsible for the universe, we don't look for a further explanation that explains it; we've reached explanatory bedrock. The argument from contingency leads to an important discovery: the universe exists because a necessary being exists. There is some being that exists, cannot not exist, is not "part" of the universe, and is the source or ground or explanation of all contingent reality.

Why not just stipulate that the universe doesn't have an explanation? Since explanation must stop somewhere, why not stop with the contingent totality? Here, I point to a modest principle, one that I think is self-evidently true: *anything that needs an explanation for its existence has an explanation for its existence.* I've argued that the universe, as a contingent totality, needs an explanation for its existence. Thus, the universe has an explanation for its existence.[31] We could arrive at the same conclusion with a still weaker principle: *anything that needs an explanation for its existence has either an explanation for its existence or an explanation for why it is a mistake to seek an explanation.*[32] According to this weaker principle, the burden of proof is on the atheist to explain why no explanation for the universe is needed. Moreover, given the intelligibility of the universe, we have good reason to think there is an explanation. Unless or until we have some reason to think the universe exists as a brute fact, it is more reasonable to conclude that the argument from contingency is successful. A necessary being is the fundamental *ground* or *explanation* of the universe.

The temporal finitude of the universe points to a fundamental *cause*. The argument runs as follows: Whatever begins to exist has a cause. The universe began to exist. Therefore, the universe has a cause. This is the *kalām* cosmological argument, and it moves from the total sequence of causes and effects *in* the universe to a First Cause of the sequence. If the singularity represents an absolute beginning, then there are good reasons to think (given the premise that whatever begins to exist has a cause, a premise that is eminently plausible) that the universe needs a First Cause that itself is not material (since all matter came into existence at the singularity), is uncaused (since otherwise it would need a cause too), and is personal (since there are only two kinds of causes—events and agents—and there was no event "before" the Big Bang that could cause the universe to come into being).

Most of the debate over the *kalām* cosmological argument centers on the question of the temporal finitude of the universe. Attempts to deny an absolute beginning focus on that moment of the early universe, prior to Planck time (the first 10^{-43} second after the Big Bang singularity), when the known laws of nature break down. This lack of knowledge of what the universe was like and how it unfolded for the first 10^{-43} second after the singularity has spawned a number of theoretical models that, if successful, might (it is hoped) remove the need to postulate an absolute beginning to the universe.[33]

But none of these models remove the need for an absolute beginning. The nail in the coffin for these theories came in 2003, in what is now known as the Bord-Guth-Vilenkin (BGV) theorem. Now widely accepted by cosmologists, the BGV theorem states that "any universe which has on average over its past history been in a state of cosmic expansion cannot be eternal in the past but must have a spacetime boundary."[34] Since our universe is not only expanding but expanding at greater speeds, it follows that it must have begun a finite time ago. Philosopher William Lane Craig says that the BGV theorem "single-handedly sweeps away the most important attempts to avoid the absolute beginning of the universe."[35] I conclude that the empirical evidence from science—Lady Nature—reveals a temporally finite universe.

And since whatever begins to exist has a cause, it follows that the universe has a First Cause.

What of our immense yet finely tuned universe? Consider this argument: The fine-tuning of the universe for life is not surprising given theism. But it is enormously surprising given naturalism (and atheism). Therefore, it is more likely than not that the universe was fine-tuned by a fine-tuner. Why think the universe is not surprising, given theism? Recall our definition of God as a personal being worthy of worship. What kind of universe might God create? Given God's supreme goodness and rationality (remember, the idea of worship-worthiness does a lot of work in helping us conceive of what God is like, if God exists), we would expect any universe created by God to be beautiful, moral, sustaining of life, and capable of bringing forth conscious beings. But if naturalism and atheism are true, it is enormously surprising that we find ourselves in this universe full of life, consciousness, rationality, and value. How surprising? Recall the odds discussed earlier. There are many ways the universe could have been in which life would not exist; if the cosmic dials on any number of finely tuned parameters (of the initial conditions, laws, or constants of nature) were just a little bit different, life would not arise. The odds of a finely tuned universe arising by chance are highly improbable. Therefore, it is much more likely, as the argument goes, that the universe was finely tuned by a fine-tuner.

But what if our universe is just one universe within the multiverse? While it is highly unlikely, given a single universe, that we find ourselves in a life-permitting one, the more universes there are, the more likely it is that at least one will be life-permitting. Thus, if there are many—perhaps infinitely many—universes, it is no longer surprising, given naturalism (atheism), that one of them is fine-tuned for life. We're the lucky ones who find ourselves in one of those rare (uncaused) universes in which life is possible.

How are we to understand the multiverse hypothesis? There are three basic multiverse proposals.[36] First, there are *serial multiverse theories* in which universes come into being and pass away

28

in an eternal series of expansions (i.e., Big Bangs) and contractions (i.e., Big Crunches). Second, there are *multiple-domain multiverse theories* in which our *observable* universe is just one domain within a larger and more complex space-time structure full of other domains/universes. Theories in this group posit some kind of universe-generating mechanism that generates other domains/universes. Finally, there are *causally isolated multiverse theories* that posit infinities of causally disconnected universes. None of these theories, however, remove the need for a fine-tuner. Each family of multiverse theories either lacks empirical support (*serial* and *causally isolated* multiverse theories) or does not remove the need for a fine-tuner (*multiple-domain* multiverse theories).

Serial theories suffer from at least two problems.[37] First, on the standard model of the Big Bang, the singularity is not a physical portal through which some earlier universe can tunnel but rather the absolute beginning of space, time, matter, and energy. As we saw earlier, attempts to remove the singularity and the need for an absolute beginning are implausible, given the BGV theorem. Second, there is no known mechanism capable of causing an expanding universe to collapse and "reset" the entropy levels such that the next universe can begin with some usable energy. For at least these reasons, serial theories are not popular among multiverse enthusiasts.

The main problem with causally isolated multiverse theories is that there is no empirical evidence to confirm (or disconfirm) them. We can never determine empirically—in principle—whether the multiverse theory is true; by definition, each universe is causally isolated, and thus impossible to detect empirically. As a philosophy professor, I'm pretty comfortable with weird ideas, including ideas that require no scientific evidence in support of them. But a good scientific theory usually has data to justify it; we tend to expect discernible facts that lead to the postulation of a theory. When it comes to postulating these causally isolated universes, to avoid the implication of the fine-tuning argument, the move appears to be *ad hoc* (i.e., done to avoid the theistic implications of the fine-tuning argument). Lady Nature gives us no reason to think these multiverse scenarios are true; there aren't any *scientific* reasons to think they are true.[38]

Regarding the family of multiple-domain theories, the most commonly accepted mechanism for producing a multiverse is *eternal inflation*: our universe is pervaded by an inflation field that expands forever, birthing "bubble" universes along the way, each with their own laws, constants, and initial conditions. The main problem with eternal inflation is that it, too, requires fine-tuning.[39] Fine-tuning is not explained, just relocated at another level.

I conclude that the argument from fine-tuning to a fine-tuner is successful: theism is more probable than naturalism, given fine-tuning. Of course, the argument from fine-tuning doesn't establish once and for all that theism is true. When we join the argument from fine-tuning with the other arguments in this chapter, however, we find good reasons to think that there is more to reality than the physical universe.

It's time to take stock. We've embarked on our journey to discover the true story of the world, joining Lady Nature as our guide. Our first "stop" is to consider the universe as a whole. We've looked at four features—its contingency, finitude, immensity, and finely tuned nature—and considered three questions. The Existence Question led to the discovery, through the argument from contingency, that the universe is explained in virtue of a necessary being. The Beginning Question led us to the discovery, through the *kalām* cosmological argument, that there is a personal cause to the universe. The Indifference Question led to the discovery of a fine-tuner—that is, a Mind that brought this universe into being with embodied, rational moral agents like us in view.

Not bad for us "working thinkers"! We didn't need Deep Thought or seven and a half million years. There is more to reality than physical reality. The world is not flat! The universe is our first clue, our first "stone," to help us discover the true story of the world.

But our journey has just begun. It's time to move on. Lady Nature has more wonders to show us. It's time to narrow our focus from the universe as a whole to the life found on our little speck of a rock called Earth.

2

Life

Is it easy or hard for life to emerge from the chemistry of early planets? In the lab, we try to work out a complete, step by step, plausible pathway all the way from simple chemistry to more complex chemistry to simple biology and if we can actually show that there's a continuous pathway to life with no super hard steps along the way, then we could conclude that it's likely that there's abundant life out there.

—Jack Szostak, molecular biologist, Harvard University

Those who think scientists understand the issues of prebiotic chemistry are wholly misinformed. Nobody understands them. Maybe one day we will. But that day is far from today. . . . The basis upon which we as scientists are relying is so shaky that we must openly state the situation for what it is: it is a mystery.

—James Tour, "Animadversions of a Synthetic Chemist"

You exist. We noted that truth in chapter 1. If you didn't exist, you wouldn't be reading this. But you are reading this; ergo, you exist.

We can say more. Some things—diamonds, carbon atoms, gravitational force, the giant star Betelgeuse, this sentence—*exist* but are not *alive*. You are a living being. If you weren't a living being, you wouldn't be reading this (or so it seems to me). But maybe I've moved too quickly.

My son's dog exists and is alive, but she can't read this book. So, the ability to think can't be the thing that makes you and me living beings. (In "philosophy speak," thinking is *sufficient* for being alive, but not *necessary*.) Plants are alive, too, but they can do even less than my son's dog. (In philosophy speak, sensing is *sufficient* for being alive, but not *necessary*.)

The question of life's essence has become more complicated in our technological age, or at least a near-future technological age. Consider Philip K. Dick's 1968 novel, *Do Androids Dream of Electric Sheep?*, the source for the movie *Blade Runner*. The world has been ravaged by nuclear war. Almost all living creatures have been wiped out. Nonhuman animals are rare, expensive to own, and the kinds of creatures we tend to view in our day as ordinary: goats, rabbits, spiders, squirrels. Only the wealthy can afford a *real* animal. Less affluent people can purchase a *false* animal made of mechanical parts. Even in post-apocalyptic worlds, it seems people want to keep up with the Joneses.

There are also *androids* in Dick's world—manufactured biological creatures that are nearly indistinguishable from humans except for one thing: they can't empathize. In a poignant scene in the book, Rick Deckard, a bounty hunter tasked with the job of "retiring" runaway androids and in the midst of a kind of midlife crisis, has just slept with an android named Rachael. Temporarily awestruck, Rick exclaims, "If you weren't an android, . . . if I could legally marry you, I would." Rachael replies, "Or we could live in sin, except that I'm not alive." Rick's reply is provocative: "Legally you're not. But really you are. Biologically. You're not made out of transistorized circuits like a false animal; you're an organic entity." And then Rick thinks, "And in two years . . . you'll wear out and die. Because we never solved the problem of cell replacement. . . . So I guess it doesn't matter anyhow."[1]

While Dick's story raises many questions about the nature, value, and origin of life, answers are elusive. His story reminds us that life is awe-inspiring and mysterious. It's easy to destroy and difficult to create. It's hard to define or even describe, yet we know it—and in our best moments cherish it—wherever it is found. While we often take life for granted, we shouldn't. We see, upon reflection, that life is something of great value. Life is a gift. But a gift from whom?

In this chapter, with Lady Nature as our guide, we'll consider three pressing questions under the surface in Dick's story that will aid us in our search for the true story of the world: What is life? What kinds of life are there? And how did life begin? To find answers to these questions, we'll need to travel forward in time and space. We'll also need to do some intellectual heavy lifting. We'll need to wade into the details and get our hands (metaphorically) dirty as we dig deep into the bedrock of reality. So if the next few chapters feel a bit heavy on the technical side, hang in there. It's worth it in the end. Let's begin with a working definition of life.

What Is Life?

According to my son's biology notebook, living things have seven features: movement, respiration, sensitivity, growth, reproduction, excretion, and nutrition. Not one to take my son's biology notes as the final word, I cross-checked his list with another venerable authority: *The Complete Idiot's Guide to Life Science*. It tells us that things must meet six criteria to be considered alive: movement, organization, homeostasis, energy, reproduction, and growth.[2] We could add other features: metabolism, information, the ability to adapt to evolutionary development, and more have all been suggested as the "hallmark" or "sign" or "criteria" or "necessary conditions" of life.[3]

The problem with these features, and more like them, is that they only tell us what life *does*, not what life *is*.

Let's begin again. Consider our pet dog Mrs. Painter and a pet rock. When I come home, Mrs. Painter rushes to the door, wagging her tail. The pet rock stays put on the counter. It could move, but the source of its movement would be outside itself. Mrs. Painter is a self-mover; the rock is not. Notice, also, that Mrs. Painter can grow and flourish. She takes in food, converts it to energy, and uses it to maintain an internal, ordered state. The pet rock, on the other hand, requires upkeep to maintain its plastic eyes and painted mouth and nose. Mrs. Painter is a self-maintainer; the pet rock is not. Finally, Mrs. Painter is capable, if we'd let her, of reproducing members of her kind. The only way the pet rock is going to reproduce is if I take a sledge hammer to it. Mrs. Painter is a self-replicator; the pet rock is not. This ability to act as a self-mover, self-maintainer, and self-replicator helps us see more clearly the essential function of living things. What, then, is this essential function of living organisms? The answer is *immanent causation*.

This raises two questions: What is immanent causation? And why did we name our dog Mrs. Painter? The second question is far too complicated (it has to do with our beloved Purdue Boilermakers), so let's talk about immanent causation. According to philosopher David Oderberg, it "is causation that originates with an agent and terminates in that agent for the sake of its self-perfection."[4] This requires some unpacking. To say of some object that it is "self-perfective" means that it acts for *itself* "so as to produce, conserve, and repair its proper functioning as the kind of thing it is." Immanent causal activity is the kind of causation that can be volitional (e.g., thinking, willing, etc.) and nonvolitional (i.e., unconscious processes) and that "begins *with* the agent and terminates *in* the agent for the sake *of* the agent."[5] In other words, "Living creatures do things *to* themselves *for* themselves, whereas non-living things do not."[6]

Arguably, the common criteria for life are descriptions of immanent causation. Consider *homeostasis*, the ability of an organism to regulate and preserve itself in a changing environment, or *metabolism*, the ability of an organism to take in matter/energy, use it, and expel it for growth and flourishing. Consider *adaptation*, the ability of organisms to adapt to evolutionary pressures in order to flourish. These hallmarks of life "presuppose rather than replace" immanent causation.[7] In other words, they are paradigm cases of immanence.

Let's pull back and consider where we are. I've claimed that there is an *essence* to life. Life is immanent causation. Living things are agents of immanent causal activity. While we might not be used to talking about "immanent" causation, we do regularly *experience* it. As you read this, *you* are engaging in immanent causal activity—thinking, reading, sensing—for the sake of your own flourishing or perfection. (And your *living* body is too, as it breathes, pumps blood, and produces energy.)

I now introduce two more sets of distinctions that I hope will bring clarity. First, there are two kinds of ordinary objects: *substances* and *aggregates*. Mrs. Painter is a substance. That pet rock is an aggregate. Substances are deep unities of properties (like *having a tail*), powers (like *being able to wag a tail*), and parts (like *a tail*) organized for the sake of the entity's fulfillment.[8] As a deep unity, the properties, powers, and parts find their identity in virtue of the whole. Aristotle somewhat gruesomely described this feature of substances by arguing that a severed human hand is not really a human hand anymore. Once disconnected from the whole, the former human hand becomes a lump of flesh. Lest you doubt, just wait a week! Aggregates are collections of material parts—like cars, computers, pet rocks, even like piles of trash and heaps of sand. Mrs. Painter and all other living things are substances.[9]

So, we have substances and aggregates. A dog is a substance. A computer is an aggregate. Now, focusing on substances, I distinguish between a substance's nature and a substance's properties. Consider again Mrs. Painter. She is a dog. She is by nature a sensory animal of the doghood kind. Mrs. Painter also has certain properties that "flow from" her nature: essential properties such as *being a dog* and *being a mammal* as well as accidental properties such as *being such and such a weight* or *being a pet*. If we draw a line between the nature of Mrs. Painter and the properties of Mrs. Painter, we can better see why immanent causation is truly the essence of life.

Recall the list of commonly cited features of living things on my son's list from biology class. Notice that sometimes living things do not, or cannot, exhibit some of those features. Consider reproduction. Some living things cannot reproduce due to damaged chromosomes. If we distinguish between a thing's nature and its features or properties that flow from its nature, we can see how certain common features or properties can be blocked due to damage or mutation.[10] Thus, we see that our definition of life has explanatory power. It rules out borderline cases (such as viruses and flames), it explains what is common to the core set of features typically noted (like my son's list from biology class), and it offers a clear line of demarcation between the living and nonliving world.

What Kinds of Life Are There?

Now that we've defined life and introduced the concept of substance, we can better understand what kinds of living things exist. Let's set aside living things that are *wholly* immaterial, such as angels and God, and focus on the only place we know of where there are material living beings, the earth. In other words, we'll focus on embodied living substances, even if (say, for humans) some of these embodied living substances have an immaterial part (i.e., a soul or mind). Remember, Lady Nature is our guide; we're considering the world around us and looking for clues to help discover the true story of everything.

According to the *Idiot's Guide*, the kinds of living things (either extinct or currently alive) are classified into five kingdoms: Monera, Protista, Fungi, Plantae, and Animalia.[11] The two major groups of microscopic organisms—the moneran and protistan groups—are in separate categories because of their cell structure. Monerans don't have a cell nucleus (i.e., they are prokaryotes), whereas the protistans either are (as single-celled organisms) or have (as multicelled organisms) cells with a nucleus (i.e., they are eukaryotic organisms). The five-kingdom classification of terrestrial living organisms was upended in the 1970s by Carl Woese's discovery of Archaea ("ancient ones"), organisms capable of existing in extreme conditions.[12] Today biologists prefer to speak of three domains: Archaea, Bacteria, and Eukaryota. On this newer scheme, the prokaryotes span the first two domains, and all the eukaryotes, from slime molds, mushrooms, oak trees, dogs, and humans, are grouped into the third domain.

Modern attempts to classify and organize life into a taxonomy are generally structured according to *origin* instead of *essence*.[13] At the base of the "tree of life" we have prokaryotes. They, in turn, spin off new kinds of organisms of more complex prokaryotes and eventually eukaryotes, including humans, as history unfolds. This way of classifying things is interesting and helpful, but it is rather tentative, given the lack of information (as we'll see shortly) about what kinds of living organisms first appeared.

I propose a more ancient system, rooted in Aristotle, that classifies things according to *what they are* instead of *where they came from*. On this older scheme, there are four basic kinds of substances found in the universe, organized into a Great Chain of Being. At the top of the chain we find humans, then animals, then plants, and finally, inanimate things (molecules, atoms).[14] As we move from the bottom of the chain to the top, we observe an expansion of the collection of powers that substances possess. For example, atoms and molecules possess causal powers to repel, attract, and fuse (let's say). Moving up the chain, plants (called "vegetative animals" by Aristotle) possess additional powers for nutrition, growth, and reproduction. Moving up the chain again, animals (called "sensory animals" by Aristotle) share the powers of plants and add the ability for sentience, appetition (the capacity to pursue and avoid objects of awareness), and locomotion (to self-move from place to place in pursuit or avoidance of other objects). Finally, moving up the chain again, humans (called "rational animals" by Aristotle) share the powers of plants and animals and possess additional powers for thinking, moralizing, and relating.

We'll return to the question of *kinds* of life in the next chapter when we explore the question of life's diversity. For now, my claim is that our threefold taxonomy—vegetative, sensory, rational—of substances and the metaphor of the Great Chain of Being are, together, a better way to classify living things that exist now or did in the past.[15] This essentialist approach helps us see more clearly the true nature and structure of the universe.[16] It aids us on our journey to discover the true story of the world. It's time to explore the question of life's origin.

How Did Life Begin?

I know how to sneak onto a plane without a valid ticket. All you need to do is make it through security, get past the boarding agent at the gate, and pick an unoccupied seat, if there is one. Easy, right? No, thankfully, not really. Security agents, screening technology, and check-in procedures make sneaking onto planes very difficult.

But it can be done. How do I know this? Meet Marilyn Hartman, the "serial stowaway." From 2014 to 2021, Hartman attempted to sneak onto a plane without a valid ticket at least twenty-two times.[17] She always got caught. Sometimes she made it no farther than the airport premises. At times, she made it through security. On a few occasions, she managed to board a plane. And in at least three instances, she hitched a ride from one city to another. Hartman shows us it's not impossible to hitchhike on a plane. But it's highly unlikely. The odds of successfully stowing away are very low, and success would require a large number of improbable circumstances to conspire at just the right time and the right place.

Many people today see the origin of life like one big serial stowaway. Life sprung into being from inorganic materials through improbable circumstances that conspired at just the right time and at just the right place. Getting life from nonlife—called *abiogenesis*—is difficult, to be sure. It has happened, and we're not sure *how* it happened, but it's not impossible. There's no need, we are told, to invoke God. Just as we can know the general steps for stowing away on a plane, many scientists and philosophers of science today assert that we know the general outline of how life arose from nonlife by natural processes.

Let's consider a couple examples, one by a scientist and one by a philosopher of science, demonstrating the hopeful optimism of many today that a wholly naturalistic explanation for life is forthcoming. Cosmologist Sean Carroll writes, "There is no reason to think that we won't be able to figure out how life started. No serious scientist working on the origin of life, even those who are personally religious, points to some particular process and says, 'Here is the step where we need to invoke the presence of a nonphysical life-force, or some element of supernatural intervention.' There is a strong conviction that understanding abiogenesis is a matter of solving puzzles within the known laws of nature, not calling for help from outside of them."[18]

Or consider Daniel Dennett. He admits "that the first concoction of molecules capable of reliably reproducing itself was—must have been—an 'engineering' marvel, composed of thousands of complex parts working together." On the other hand, Dennett asserts that any invocation of a divine cause represents a "failure of imagination." "Confidence runs high" that we'll eventually discover how life arose from nonlife by "utterly blind and purposeless" processes.[19]

Others are less optimistic. James Tour is a professor at Rice University and one of the world's leading synthetic organic chemists. In an open letter to colleagues, Tour called on scientists to more openly acknowledge some of the challenges to a plausible scientific account of how life arose from nonlife: "We synthetic chemists should state the obvious. The appearance of life on earth is a mystery. We are nowhere near solving this problem. The proposals offered thus far to explain life's origin make no scientific sense. Beyond our planet, all the others that have been probed are lifeless, a result in accord with our chemical expectations. . . . Life should not exist anywhere in our universe. Life should not even exist on the surface of the earth."[20]

How might we answer the question of life's origin? Is life something unique, even sacred, pointing to a divine cause? Or is life something that just happened via blind and purposeless forces? As scientists differ dramatically on this question, we're going to need to do some thinking ourselves. Let's journey in time, moving from the beginning of the universe to the beginning of the earth, to see if we can make any progress ourselves.[21]

Roughly 4.5 billion years ago, the sun and planets of our solar system formed out of a collapsing cloud of gas and dust. The basic story is one of collision, aggregation, and dispersion: "As the cloud contracted toward its center, particle collisions eventually resulted in most of the particles spinning in the same direction. Gravity pulled most of the mass toward the center of the rotating cloud, and the cloud collapsed into a spinning disk. . . . Our Sun formed out of the concentration of mass at the center of the cloud, and the planets aggregated out of the collisions of rock and ice in the spinning disk."[22] For the first 700 million years (or so), the earth was too hot to support life. With the end of the Late Heavy Bombardment period roughly 3.8 billion years ago, the earth was cool enough—and calm enough—to support life.[23]

The oldest widely accepted evidence of life—a strand of fossilized stromatolites found in Australia—dates to 3.48 billion years ago.[24] So, the amount of time for life to develop on earth is roughly 320 million years, the time between 3.8 and 3.48 billion years ago. Geologically speaking, this is a short amount of time for life to arise via natural processes. Interestingly, in a newly exposed outcrop of rocks in Greenland, scientists have discovered an even older set of stromatolites dating to 3.7 billion years ago.[25] If these new discoveries are in fact the earliest traces of life, the time frame shrinks to roughly 100 million years. Either way, in geological time, life, including all the macromolecules necessary for life—DNA, RNA, proteins, metabolic systems, and so on—developed virtually overnight.[26]

Where on earth did life begin? Darwin postulated his "warm pond" as the place where methane, ammonia, hydrogen, water, and free energy mixed together at just the right time and in just the right way to form proteins and other microscopic parts of the cell. Ever since, scientists have proposed various locations for this prelife soup, including deep-sea thermal vents, the edge of the ocean, the atmosphere, the edge of volcanoes, and the surface of clays.[27] Other scientists, including Francis Crick and Stephen Hawking, have maintained that life originated in space and was transported to the earth by asteroids or intelligent beings.[28] This latter option, called *panspermia*, simply pushes the question back: If life didn't originate on earth, how did it originate in space or on some other planet? More to the point: there is no evidence of biological life beyond earth.

So let's assume that life originated on earth. Even if scientists could identify a location suitable for the appearance of life, two problems remain if abiogenesis—life from nonlife—is to claim the mantle of truth. First, the *ingredients problem*: How can the basic building blocks of life arise from natural processes? Second, the *assembly problem*: How can the building blocks necessary for life be assembled in the right sequence for life to arise from natural processes?

First, the ingredients problem. Every living organism has at least three material components: *proteins*, *genetic materials* (DNA and RNA), and *lipids* (i.e., cell membranes).[29] Each of these material components, in turn, are built out of simpler parts: for example, proteins are made out of amino acids, RNA and DNA are made out of nucleotides, and lipids are made out of sugar and phosphate. And all of those midlevel parts are built out of atoms or collections of atoms (i.e., molecules). In theory, if abiogenesis is true, it should be possible to recreate the basic macromolecules of life in the lab. All we need to do is gather the right ingredients, add some energy (a spark of electricity will do), and "poof"—out comes the basic building blocks of life. Right?

Scientists *have* produced some of the midlevel parts that make up our three building blocks of life. In 1953, University of Chicago professor Harold Urey and graduate student Stanley Miller mixed methane, ammonia, hydrogen, and water in a flask and sparked it from time to time to simulate lightning. They were able to produce a variety of sugars, amino acids, and nucleotides. While the experiment was initially heralded as the first breakthrough in origin-of-life studies, most today think it failed, mainly because the experiment doesn't simulate the atmospheric conditions of early earth. When the experiment is rerun with a more accurate simulation of early earth, the results are significantly diminished.

Still, many think Miller and Urey's basic approach was correct. It goes like this: Mix together a small number of reactants under controlled conditions to bring about a desired result. Isolate that result. Then mix the result together with a small number of new reactants under controlled conditions to bring about a further desired result. Isolate that further desired result. Continue this process of isolation and mixture under controlled conditions until the desired components—i.e., proteins, genetic materials, lipids—are obtained.[30]

There are two problems, unfortunately, with this basic approach to origin-of-life studies. First, the highly regulated environment of the lab doesn't fairly represent the early earth. It is difficult to know, let alone re-create, the exact conditions for any prebiotic-soup scenario that might have obtained in the actual world—the world as it is "in the wild" instead of the world as it is "in vitro" (literally "in the glass"). Second, while scientists have had *some* success at synthesizing *some* of the subparts of the building blocks necessary for life, there has been no *real* success in producing the building blocks themselves (the polymers—i.e., the proteins, DNA and RNA, and lipids).[31] There are plenty of "just so" stories about how the polymers might have arisen through natural processes, but the fact that no one has been able to create the necessary building blocks for life in toto in the lab, let alone a living organism, gives us little reason to think that it could be done in nature. To date, the ingredients problem remains unsolved.[32]

Next up is the assembly problem. The simplest living organisms are single-celled animals. They were once thought to be relatively simple, but we now know the cell is a "functionally coherent whole"[33] with many subsystems. Those subsystems are themselves functionally coherent assemblies that work together to perform all the processes of life. As Gerald Rau explains, "The cell is a highly complex integrated system, with molecular machinery as sophisticated as any human factory."[34] Cells are composed of proteins and other microscopic parts. Proteins, in turn, are built out of complex chains of amino acids. If the sequence of amino acids—there are twenty *kinds* of amino acids—along a polypeptide chain has the right properties, the whole chain folds to form a three-dimensional object. The shape is crucial to its function; the shape of proteins is specified by the sequence of amino acids, and the sequence of amino acids is determined by the genetic code.[35]

The magnitude of biological information in a living organism is mind-boggling. The number of base pairs of DNA required to produce the necessary proteins for life in the most basic single-celled organism is between 318,000 and 562,000.[36] More complex life requires millions and millions of base pairs to code all the necessary proteins (e.g., the human genome contains over 3 billion base pairs of DNA). So origin-of-life researchers need to answer this question: How did the first cell acquire the genes—the information content within DNA—necessary for life in the first place?

The biologist Doug Axe argues that it is *physically impossible* to assemble a single functional protein by purely natural processes. That's a big claim. In effect, Axe is claiming that there is no *possible* naturalistic process or mechanism that could produce life from nonlife. Stowaways on a plane are (physically) possible; life from nonlife is not. To see how Axe's argument goes, we've got to take a closer look at the numbers. (If you get déjà vu, yes, we did a similar exercise in the previous chapter.)

According to Axe, the likelihood of functional proteins is extremely rare: for every good protein sequence, there are 10^{74} possible bad ones.[37] Given the fact that no more than 10^{40} possible proteins could have ever existed on earth since its formation, "it becomes increasingly unlikely that any functional proteins could ever have been discovered by chance on earth."[38] Of course, generating a functional protein out of a prebiotic soup would require other steps that make the odds more fantastic. Stephen C. Meyer puts it this way: "This calculation can be made by multiplying the three independent probabilities by one another: the probability of incorporating only peptide bonds (1 in 10^{45}), the probability of incorporating only left-handed amino acids (1 in 10^{45}), and the probability of achieving correct amino-acid sequencing (using Axe's 1 in 10^{74} estimate). Making that calculation (multiplying the separate probabilities by adding their exponents: $10^{45\,+\,45\,+\,74}$) gives a dramatic answer. The odds of getting even one functional protein of modest length (150 amino acids) by chance from a prebiotic soup is no better than 1 chance in 10^{164}."[39]

The problem is even more difficult than Axe and Meyer note, however. A single functional protein is not sufficient to sustain life's processes. Roughly 250 functional proteins are necessary to sustain the processes of the simplest organisms.[40] If this is correct, then we need to multiply 1 in 10^{164} by 250. The result is mind-bogglingly big (again): the probability that the minimal set of functional proteins necessary for life will assemble by chance out of a prebiotic soup is 1 chance in $10^{41,000}$.

How are we to make sense of 1 chance in 10^{164} (the probability of a single functional protein arising by chance) or 1 in $10^{41,000}$ (the probability of the minimal set of functional proteins necessary for life arising by chance)? According to Axe, any number that exceeds 100 digits in length is "beyond physical representation."[41] In other words, fantastically big numbers represent physical impossibilities.[42] Let's assume that Axe overstates his case and that fantastically big numbers are not physically impossible. But then this *very* modest claim is true: it is *extremely unlikely* that one functional protein would arise by purely natural processes from a prebiotic soup, let alone the kind of information and complexity necessary for a single-celled life.[43]

Time to take stock. We've discovered that the time span for life to have arisen by natural processes on earth is relatively short, geologically speaking, and that the location of a postulated prebiotic soup is difficult to determine. We've learned that while organic chemists have had *some* success at producing *some* of the monomers necessary for life, they have had *no* success producing in the lab the basic building blocks (proteins, DNA or RNA, lipids); and even if we could figure out how to produce synthetically the building blocks, the chances of the building blocks coming together in just the right way by purely naturalistic processes to form even a single functional protein are extremely small.

We can't stay neutral forever. As truth seekers we must follow the evidence where it leads. Here it is: the most reasonable explanation for life is that it didn't arise from brute, nonintentional, or blind forces; life is the product of nonnatural processes and/or a nonnatural agent.

Can we move from that last statement to a divine cause? Not directly. But I think we can ultimately argue from the fact that life is the product of nonnatural processes to the conclusion that God is the best explanation for life. Here is one pathway forward. Consider that living things, as agents of immanent causal activity, exhibit intrinsic or "built-in" teleology. (Remember, teleology is the idea that organisms have natures that determine their proper end or fulfillment.) This teleology, in turn, is based on the fact that living organisms are substances—that is, form–matter composites. A substance's form or essence grounds the immanent causal activities (i.e., the intrinsic teleology) of living organisms. We've noted that living things have *ends*. But what explains the *existence* of ends? In other words, what explains the existence of substances with essences or forms?

We might argue that substances, along with their essences and ends, exist without an explanation. But as we saw in the last chapter, given that the world is intelligible, it is reasonable to seek an explanation for features in the world unless we have a good reason to think that there wouldn't be an explanation. And there is a plausible explanation to be found, noted long ago by Thomas Aquinas. In his famous Fifth Way, Aquinas argued from the intrinsic teleology found in the physical universe to an intelligent divine cause.[44] Just as an arrow requires an archer to reach its end, so too do the living things found in nature require an intelligence in order to tend toward their ends. Arguably, this intelligent cause must be "beyond" or "outside" the physical universe, since we're talking about unintelligent, natural objects. Moreover, just as a painter first imagines a painting before he paints it, so too the essence or form of finite creatures (i.e., the source of ends) preexist in the divine mind.

Aquinas's story nicely explains the origin of biological information too. Biological information is grounded in and flows from the essence or form of living creatures. Since, as I've argued, essences or forms preexist in the divine mind and ground or explain why we find biological information within living substances, it follows that biological information (like more familiar kinds of information found, for example, in books) is grounded in an intelligence. We are led, again, to the reality of something beyond this world that is responsible for it, and for us. This, plus the previous chapter, lead us to conclude that an uncaused, *intelligent*, transcendent, personal being is responsible for the universe and for life.

Lady Nature is speaking. Can you hear? She is pointing us beyond herself to something responsible for this life, the universe, and everything. The universe is not all that exists. There is more to reality than the physical universe. Let's continue our journey through cosmic history, with Lady Nature as our guide, to see what else we can learn about the true story of the world. It's time to consider in detail the mystery and majesty of life's diversity on this planet.

3

Species

It is not that the methods and institutions of science somehow compel us to accept a material explanation of the phenomenal world, but, on the contrary, that we are forced by our *a priori* adherence to material causes to create an apparatus of investigation and a set of concepts that produce material explanations, no matter how counter-intuitive, no matter how mystifying to the uninitiated. Moreover, that materialism is absolute, for we cannot allow a Divine Foot in the door.

—Geneticist Richard Lewontin,
"Billions and Billions of Demons"

Natural Selection is "the Law of the higgledy-piggledy."
—Sir John Herschel

At the turn of the twentieth century, the age of exploration was coming to an end. Most land masses had been explored or traversed. The North Pole was conquered in 1909. Two years later, humans reached the South Pole. For those with a thirst for adventure, the window of opportunity would soon close—at least until technology could be developed for humans to explore the heavens above or the ocean below.

One of the last great adventures of exploration and conquest into uncharted territory took place in 1913. After a devastating defeat in the 1912 election, former president Theodore Roosevelt hungered for escape and renewal. He determined to explore an unmapped region of river deep within the Amazon basin.

In her book *The River of Doubt*, Candice Millard gives a riveting account of Roosevelt's quest.[1] Roosevelt's roughly five-month, thousand-mile journey through the unmapped Amazon basin is a vivid parallel to our journey to discover the true story of the world. Just as in Roosevelt's case, so in ours there are dangers lurking around us and within us. Still, we travel hoping that there is treasure to be found both in the journey and at the journey's end. (I don't want to spoil Roosevelt's quest for you. Read Millard's account after you read *this* book. I'll just report my own view that Roosevelt's quest rivals those of, say, Bilbo or Frodo Baggins, with at least two obvious differences: one journey took place on earth and the others on Middle Earth, and one involved Orcs and the other didn't, although there were some scary creatures involved.)

The River of Doubt reminds me of two facts relevant to our next stop: the *fragility* of life and the *diversity* of life. For at least two reasons, both facts are easy to miss. First, we live at a time when 99.9 percent of all the species that have lived on earth are now extinct.[2] There simply aren't as many *kinds* of creatures as there used to be.[3] Second, it's possible today to live almost wholly removed from nature. Many us live in manicured suburbs or urban centers where the only animals we interact with are pets and the occasional mosquito or fly. When it comes to plants, our experience of them is mediated, and often muted, by the work involved to purchase, maintain, and display them. When we add to these considerations the fact that we are largely buffered—through technology and medicine—from the ravages of this planet, including disease, at least for a time it's easy to forget the delicate nature of life too.

A 1913 journey through the Amazon reminds us of a world full of strange and wonderful creatures: insects, poison dart frogs, snakes, jaguars, monkeys, sloths, trees stretching 150 feet into the air as they reach for sunshine, climbing vines that hitch a ride to that same sunshine, air plants that establish themselves along the forest canopy and then send their roots hurtling to the forest floor, neon tetras, manatees, dolphins, sharks, four-eyed fish, electric fish, fish that can jump twice their body length into the air to snatch animals from low-lying trees, human-devouring piranhas, alligators, and tiny blood-sucking catfish known as candiru that can prove deadly if they wiggle their way into a human urethra. This is a sampling of the creatures that greeted Roosevelt and his crew.

In our last chapter, we focused on life itself. We noted key features of living things and explored various explanations for life's origin. In this chapter, with Lady Nature again as our guide, we'll continue to trace our journey in time through cosmic history. I'll repeat that we are in the middle of some pretty technical stuff. Lady Nature wants us to work a bit to discover our treasure. We begin with the first living organisms in place and trace the development of new living forms as time unfolds. We are seeking an explanation for the amazing diversity of life (existing or now extinct) found on this planet.

The History of Life on Earth

The story of life's history on earth is one of expansion and diversification. Creatures abounded, especially once creatures took to land. But for large pockets of time, life on earth was sparse and simplistic—single-celled bacteria, soft-bellied sea creatures, microscopic plants, and so on. We pick up our story roughly 3.5 billion years ago. At that time, the atmosphere was primarily carbon dioxide, methane, sulfur dioxide, and nitrogen.[4] There was little oxygen. As a result, the first living organisms were single-celled, anaerobic bacteria, capable of operating in the absence of oxygen.

Roughly 2.4 billion years ago, about a billion years after the first life forms appeared, the atmosphere began to change. During the period dubbed the Great Oxygenation Event, the level of oxygen found within the atmosphere increased to 1 or 2 percent of modern levels, and continued to increase.[5] With the rise in oxygen, more complex, multicell organisms appeared. The oldest confirmed multicell fossil is an organism aptly named *Bangiomorphia*, dated to be 1.2 billion years old, thought to be one of the earliest organisms capable of sexual reproduction.[6]

The next step was the advent of organisms with skeletons. Skeletons began to appear in the fossil record around 530 million years ago during a period known as the "Cambrian explosion."[7] Thought to have lasted around 50 million years (544–490 million years ago), the Cambrian period witnessed an abrupt infusion of new body types and animal groups, most appearing within a window of roughly 5 or 6 million years (hence "explosion").[8]

Most of the creatures that appeared during this period were water-dwelling—sea worms, arthropods, mollusks, that kind of thing.[9] Around 450 million years ago, the "land began to become green."[10] With the advent of life on land, soil developed, preparing the earth for increased biodiversity. "Land life exploded" during the Carboniferous period (360–300 million years ago) as rich forests developed and insects took to the sky.[11] With oxygen levels around 35 percent (oxygen makes up roughly 21 percent of the earth's atmosphere today), the plants and animals found during the Carboniferous period were very big, the stuff of science fiction and Freudian analysis: dragonflies with two-foot wingspans, cockroaches as big as a human hand, and millipedes extending six feet long.[12]

The Carboniferous period was a kind of "high point" when it comes to the diversity of life on earth. By the Permian period (251 million years ago), 96 percent of all species had died out, probably due to massive volcanic activity.[13] Yet life rebounded and expanded once again during the Mesozoic period (from 251 to 65 million years ago) as the ecosystem reset. The first dinosaurs appeared

230 million years ago. While they would have been the most obvious creatures, given their size, this period witnessed a steady increase in the diversity of plant and animal life, with a "major kick upwards" roughly 100 million years ago.[14] The "age of the dinosaur" ended 65 million years ago when a massive meteorite hit the earth, clearing "some space in terrestrial ecosystems" for the eventual appearance of human life.[15]

Two lessons can be drawn from this brief story. First, it's *dramatic*. It is a story of a world gradually waking up.[16] It is full of starts and stops, tragedy and comedy, wonder, and plot twists. There is music in the story too, as creatures burst forth singing and bleeping and burping and braying.[17] Second, the staggering diversity of life is *evocative*. We quickly move from wonder and awe to curiosity: How did this diversity of life originate? Before we turn to this important question, the question of the origin of species, it will be helpful to first explore what it means to be a species.

The Definition of Species

We are seeking an account of the nature and structure of the physical universe, including its denizens in all their diversity. Recall the Great Chain of Being from the previous chapter. I argued that the physical universe is best thought of in terms of a hierarchy of beings. At each level you find substances of various kinds. At the bottom of the chain you find inanimate substances like atoms and molecules, then plants, animals, and humans as you move "up" the chain.

Today, this general picture of the physical universe is largely thought to be the image of a bygone, prescientific era. There is little place for essences and ordinary-sized substances for the scientifically minded, we are told. Instead, there is a preoccupation with the infinitesimal. The "really real" is found at the micro level, the bottom floor of physical reality. Tables and chairs—as well as aardvarks and humans—are regarded as nothing but assemblies of atoms arranged table-wise, chair-wise, aardvark-wise, and human-wise. No essences, no natures, just the bare laws of nature and atoms in the void, colliding and colluding together.

With his rejection of the idea of immutable species, Darwin's 1859 book *On the Origin of Species by Means of Natural Selection* was considered the death knell to talk of essences, teleology, and the Great Chain of Being.[18] Species language does not refer to natural kinds or groups of substances that share an essence. Rather, for Darwin, the species concept is *historical*: "All true classification is genealogical; that community of descent is the hidden bond which naturalists have been unconsciously seeking, and not some unknown plan of creation, or the enunciation of general propositions, and the mere putting together and separating objects more or less alike."[19]

Most biologists today follow Darwin's lead. As philosopher of biology Elliott Sober summarizes, "With the exception of pheneticists . . . , biologists do not think that species are defined in terms of phenotypic or genetic similarities." Rather, "biologists treat species as *historical entities*."[20]

I think this is a mistake for at least two reasons. First, a historical species concept leads to absurd consequences. To illustrate, consider my iPhone. What kind of thing is it? An obvious answer is that it is a smartphone. But what about the Samsung Galaxy? What kind of thing is it? An obvious answer is that it too is a smartphone. We could say that the iPhone and the Galaxy are members of the same species—the smartphone species, distinct from the computer and tablet species. But not so, if species are historical entities. Since the iPhone line originated at Apple and the Galaxy line at Samsung, they are not both instances of the smartphone kind. But this is obviously wrong.

When it comes to classifying living organisms, things are even *more* absurd. For it is possible that an earth turkey is a molecule-for-molecule match with some living organism on some other planet (let's call it "twin turkey"), yet they would fail to be members of the same species. According to the now dominant view that species should be classified according to evolutionary line of descent, if the earth turkey and twin turkey had different lines of descent, they would not be classified as the same species. But this too is absurd—even more so than the iPhone/Samsung example. The philosopher David Oderberg puts his finger on the problem when he notes that the absurdity of the above scenarios involves "the replacement of metaphysics and good science by sheer dogma."[21] Oderberg grants, as do I, that "we can tell a lot about a thing's form and properties by knowing where it came from." Yet "where it came from is not the same as what it is."[22]

Second, essences or natures do work. There are three features of living organisms—that is, substances—that are best explained by postulating essences: *unity*, *recurrence*, and *resemblance*.[23] Consider again Mrs. Painter. Notice that our dog is a deep unity of parts, properties, and powers. This unity is deeper than the unity found in, for example, my computer or a heap of sand. This deep unity, arguably, is best explained by postulating an essence from which properties, powers, and parts flow. Next, notice that Mrs. Painter, if we would let her, could produce offspring that possess the same suite of traits and powers. If Mrs. Painter were pregnant, her offspring would be dogs, not pigs or birds. This recurrence of character traits and powers between offspring and parents is best explained by positing essences. Finally, note that Mrs. Painter, as a dog, resembles other living organisms. Moreover, living things seem to fall into natural resemblance classes that are fairly easy to discern (at a certain level of generality). This too is best explained by positing essences.[24] Essences do explanatory work. They explain things, including "the distinctive and characteristic behaviors of organisms in a way that marks them off one from another according to their repeatable natures."[25] I propose, then, a biologically informed metaphysical classification of species in terms of essences or natures. Living organisms that have natures and species are classes of substances whose natures are functionally equivalent.[26] It's time to now consider the question of life's diversity. What best explains the origin of species?

The Origin of Species

Since Darwin's 1859 release of *On the Origin of Species by Means of Natural Selection*, evolution has been the dominant explanation for the diversity of life on earth.[27] The basic idea is that there is an unbroken chain of living organisms from simple to complex, all of which share a common ancestor in the first single-celled organism that emerged out of Darwin's prebiotic soup over three billion years ago. Sean Carroll, representing the dominant view among scholars, effectively marginalizes all who would challenge the Darwinian story, with the claim that "essentially every working professional biologist accepts the basic explanation provided by Darwin for the existence of complex structures in biological organisms."[28] "Evolution," writes Carroll, "is the idea that provides the bridge from abiogenesis to the grand pageant of life."[29] The evidence during Darwin's day came primarily from paleontology. Today, given the advent of genetics, biological evolutionists focus on the genome and the idea that evolution works by selecting advantageous mutations (i.e., mutations that are conducive to survival) in genes of organisms.[30] It's time to take a fresh look at the evidence to see if evolution is in fact the best explanation for biological diversity.[31] To keep things relatively simple, we'll focus on the evidence from genetics.

With the advent of genetic theory in the twentieth century, Darwin's theory underwent a major upgrade. A problem with Darwin's theory, as originally proposed, was its explanation of how organisms preserve and pass on structural changes. A key insight from classical genetics is that the characteristics of organisms are grounded in the genetic information found in the cell. This information is passed on from generation to generation. Applied to evolutionary theory, small-scale variations among the genetic codes of individuals in a population take place through genetic drift, gene flow, and mutations. Then natural selection determines whether or not the genetic code for these variations will ultimately survive. In this way, "microevolutionary" variations can accumulate and eventually result in "macroevolutionary" innovation.[32] This picture, often called the *modern evolutionary* or *neo-Darwinian synthesis*, adds a theory of discrete (gradual) inheritance to Darwin's thesis: the evolution of new species descending from a common ancestor happens via natural selection by means of random mutations.[33]

But advances in molecular biology have cast doubts on whether selection and mutation are powerful enough to account for the diversity of life, especially given the functional information present within all forms of life. The fundamental problem for the neo-Darwinist, as Stephen C. Meyer puts it, "is the problem of the origin of new biological information."[34] In other words, the mechanism of natural selection acting on random mutations cannot produce the kind of information necessary to build new animal forms.

Consider in more detail the neo-Darwinian story of how new species evolve.[35] Radically new species require new body plans (the term "body plan," referring to a grouping of basic body structures, functions as a loose analog to the idea of form or essence without commitment to form or essence). New body plans require new cell types. New cell types require new kinds of (functional) proteins. New kinds of (functional) proteins require new genetic information. New genetic information is generated by random, unguided mutations in existing organisms. Mutations that contribute to the survival of an organism are passed on via natural selection to the next generation. Over time, as beneficial changes accumulate, a population changes and new species evolve.

There are two problems with this story. First, natural selection can only act on already existing organisms; it can't invent new species. In other words, selection can only preserve innovations within existing species. Doug Axe calls this the "gaping hole" in evolutionary theory.[36] Natural selection is an "aimless wanderer, incapable of inventing,"[37] and the "editor, rather than the composer, of the genetic message."[38] As the botanist Hugo De Vries colorfully described in his 1904 book, "Natural selection may explain the *survival* of the fittest, but it cannot explain the *arrival* of the fittest."[39]

The power of inventing must lie elsewhere. This leads to the second problem: the accidental invention of new functional proteins by random mutation is highly unlikely.[40] Recent studies in protein science have shown the extreme rarity of arrangements of DNA bases capable of generating new functional proteins. Meyer writes, "For every DNA sequence that generates a short *functional* protein fold of just 150 amino acids in length, there are ten to the seventy-seventh power *non*functional combinations—ten to the seventy-seventh amino acid arrangements—that will not fold into a stable three-dimensional protein structure capable of performing a biological function."[41]

It is highly unlikely, then, that random genetic mutations would accidentally stumble upon a new DNA sequence that codes for a single new functional protein, let alone the *many* new functional proteins needed to generate new body plans and new species. How unlikely? Consider that during the entire 3.5-billion-year history of life on earth, "only ten to the fortieth individual organisms have ever lived—meaning that at most [there are] ten to the fortieth power [of opportunities to generate and pass on new gene sequences]. Yet ten to the fortieth power represents only a small fraction of ten to the seventy-seventh power—only one ten trillion, trillion, trillionth, or $1/10^{37}$ to be exact."[42] Thus, "it is overwhelmingly *more likely than not* that a random mutational search would have *failed* to produce even one new functional (information-rich) DNA sequence and protein in the entire history of life on Earth."[43]

Many biologists today admit that natural selection can't be the whole story. Natural selection doesn't have creative power to generate novel biological information needed for new body plans. According to biologists Gerd Müller and Stuart Newman, while "the neo-Darwinian paradigm still represents the central explanatory framework of evolution," it "completely avoids the origination of phenotypic traits and of organismal forms." It "has no theory of the generative."[44]

While there are significant challenges to the Darwinian paradigm, it is important to note that the consensus is largely united around common descent by means of some naturalistic mechanism or mechanisms. But can any of these new mechanisms—individually or together—account for the origin of novel genetic information and new body plans?

There are good reasons to think they cannot. For example, horizontal gene transfer, whole-genome duplication, and symbiogenesis do not provide "any novel *functional* (or *specified*) genetic information," according to Meyer.[45] Rather, they "merely transfer preexisting sequences from one organismal context where those sequences may have performed a function, to another where they likely will not."[46] Epigenetic inheritance mechanisms involve structures that either do not change or, if they do change, do not persist over more than several generations. Importantly, "neither case generates significant evolutionary innovation in animal form."[47] Self-organizational processes can produce order, but they cannot produce the "kind of non-repetitive 'order' on display in DNA and RNA" and thus cannot generate novel information or body plans.[48]

A more general problem is that these mechanisms do not "aim" at any functional outcome. They represent undirected, natural processes wandering aimlessly through the "vast sequence space of neutral, functionless possibilities with nothing to direct them, or preserve them in any forward progress they happen to make, toward the rare and isolated islands of function represented by complex adaptions."[49] None of these newly proposed mechanisms provide much hope of generating large amounts of novel biological information, and thus none of them—individually or taken together—provides the best explanation for the origin of radically new species.

What is the best explanation for the origin of species? In other words, what accounts for the explosion of novel body plans and novel information throughout the history of life on earth? I've argued that there is no known purely naturalistic, unguided mechanism capable of explaining the origin of species. There is a cause, however, that *is* capable of generating new information: intelligence. It seems once again that we are led, through our investigation of science, to an intelligent cause beyond nature.

Suppose I'm wrong about the empirical evidence. Suppose that one or more of the mechanisms I've noted can in fact explain the generation of novel body plans and novel information. Does this undercut the design hypothesis? I don't think so. We can argue, as I've done, directly from the existence of novel biological information to an intelligent cause responsible for that information. But there is another route. We can also argue, as we saw in the previous chapter, from the reality of essences or natures to an intelligent cause.

Since I've already argued that there are biological essences, why bother with a long, drawn-out discussion about evolution and the origin of species? The answer is this: we want to discover the true story of the world. We are journeying with Lady Nature, looking carefully at the evidence from science to see what we can learn. There is a widespread belief that evolution is the best explanation for the amazing diversity of life on earth. It is important that we leave no stone unturned on our quest. Granted, the debate over the origin of species has become quite toxic. Add to this the fact that it is difficult for the non-specialist to keep up with or understand all of the technical literature. But that need not detain us, for I've made a discovery that might startle you.

My claim: evolution only works if there are biological essences. And of course, as I've already argued, if there are biological essences, then there is a Mind—that is, *God*—responsible for their existence. Why think evolution requires essences? If a population is going to evolve, individual organisms must adapt to their environment, and this requires that organisms be both stable and mutable.[50] As it turns out, this is exactly what we find, as evidenced by *phenotypic plasticity*. Individual organisms can and do remain stable within well-defined limits that allow for some change. If those limits are passed, then a new species would result, but this is possible only if essentialism is true. The philosopher Denis Walsh summarizes: "In order to understand how changes in populations of genes explained by the modern synthesis theory of evolution are realised as adaptive changes in populations of *organisms*, we must understand the role that the natures [i.e., essences] of individual organisms play in influencing the trajectory of evolutionary change."[51] In other words, the evolutionary process requires a deep kind of stability and order, including stable reproductive and developmental mechanisms to guide the many complex means-to-ends adaptations found in nature. This deep orderliness is best explained by positing essences. To sum up: if evolution is true, then there are biological essences.[52] And if there are essences, as I've argued, there is a Mind responsible for them.[53]

Either way—whether the neo-Darwinian grand evolutionary story is true or not—the evidence from science points to an intelligence beyond the physical universe as the best explanation for life's diversity. This *is* a startling claim! Darwin did not explain away design. But Lady Nature is not done. She has more surprises in store for us. Our next stop on the journey holds the mirror up to the one creature found within the physical universe that stands out as utterly unique: humans.

4

Humans

Dust in the wind
All we are is dust in the wind.

—Kansas, "Dust in the Wind"

It is not natural to see man as a natural product.

—G. K. Chesterton, *The Everlasting Man*

In the opening scene of *Little Women*, we see at once the mystery and majesty of humans.[1] In this novel set in New England during the Civil War, four young sisters sit at home on Christmas Eve talking about their loves and longings, struggles and strivings, obligations and opportunities. We learn of Meg, responsible, motherly, on the eve of womanhood yet not too old at sixteen to play-act. Then there is Jo, the impulsive, creative, iconoclastic dreamer and storyteller who lives as if she is part of a great story. Next is Beth, a humble servant of all who rarely draws attention to herself and yet, when playing the piano, stirs others to delight. Finally, there is the youngest, Amy, who at twelve is a typical teenager: prone to selfishness yet loyal, regal yet impulsive. The girls do clash, but in the end, they love each other fiercely. They are known and they know; they are loved and they love; they find comfort in each other's presence. With their father at war and little money, life is full of sacrifice, to be sure, but also faith, hope, and love.

As the night draws to an end, Marmee, their mother, returns home with a letter from Father. He implores the girls to "do their duty faithfully, fight their bosom enemies bravely, and conquer themselves so beautifully" so that upon return he would be "fonder and prouder than ever of [his] little women."[2] Warmed and challenged by the letter, each girl determines to play the part. Marmee reminds them of a time when they play-acted *Pilgrim's Progress*. Traveling from the bottom of the house to the top, releasing their burdens along the way, they journeyed together toward the Celestial City. Amy half-heartedly renounces such childish play-acting: "If I wasn't too old for such things, I'd rather like to play it over again."[3] Marmee replies, "We never are too old for this, my dear, because it is a play we are playing all the time in one way or another. Our burdens are here, our road is before us, and the longing for goodness and happiness is the guide that leads us through many troubles and mistakes to the peace which is a true Celestial City. Now, my little pilgrims, suppose you begin again, not in play, but in earnest, and see how far on you can get before Father comes home."[4] The children are comforted by Marmee's words. After knitting by the fire together and a bedtime song, they drift to sleep, warmed by each other's love.

From chapter 1 on, *Little Women* displays the panoply of the human experience: intelligence, creativity, imagination, emotion, will, relationship, duty, desire, struggle, frailty, community, and pilgrimage. We laugh and play, love and long, strive and fail. What kind of creatures are we? Why is it, as many philosophers, theologians, and writers have noted, that we are *homo viators*: pilgrims, creatures "on the way" toward fulfillment?[5] What story best explains human origin, journey, and destiny? Are humans truly unique among all living creatures, or just creatures with bigger brains? Are we majestic beings created in God's image, as the religious story holds, or organized mud, as the nonreligious story tells us? Are we just dust in the wind or kings and queens of a world made by God?

Lady Nature has saved the best for last. It's time to get personal.

Human History

In the previous chapter, our tour of the history of life on earth ended around 65 million years ago. The age of the dinosaur had come to an end. The earth's environment was once again changing, becoming suitable for the eventual appearance of humans. It's time to reenter that history. I offer two words of caution. First, there is no *scientific* consensus of what it means to be human. Some—perhaps the majority—of scientists think that all creatures belonging to the genus *Homo* are humans. Others think that it is only *Homo sapiens* that are humans.[6] Eventually, we'll need the help of philosophy—even theology—to discover what it means to be human.

Second, questions of human destiny show the limits of science. Science can't provide us with a final definition of what it means to be human. Moreover, our interpretation of the evidence is shaped by our prior philosophical commitments. The story we find ourselves in—the nonreligious or religious story—shapes how we assess the data. Humility is needed as we continue on our journey. But so too is courage. We are seeking a great reward—the discovery of our true name. Let's press on in hope and openness to reality.

The Hitchhiker's Guide to the Galaxy is a helpful starting point as we fast-forward in time. According to *The Hitchhiker's Guide*, "The History of every major Galactic Civilization tends to pass through three distinct and recognizable phases, those of Survival, Inquiry, and Sophistication, otherwise known as the How, Why, and Where phases. For instance, the first phase is characterized by the question How can we eat? the second by the question Why do we eat? and the third by the question Where shall we have lunch?"[7]

The Hitchhiker's Guide points us in the right direction. Three distinct, recognizable phases of human history roughly correspond to *The Hitchhiker's Guide*'s Survival, Inquiry, and Sophistication phases: the Cognitive, Agricultural, and Scientific Revolutions.[8] Tracing this history will help us understand what it means to be human. It also raises important questions, not only about how, why, and where we eat, all important questions, but also about identity, meaning, and purpose. In what follows, I begin by sharing the story of human history, including human origins, as delivered to us by evolutionary science. I then consider three possible ways that the evidence from evolutionary science regarding human origins can be understood from within the religious, and specifically theistic, framework. The moral of the story, as will become clear, is that however the evidence from science is understood, it is compatible with both the nonreligious and the religious stories. Our question will then shift, in the final sections, to which story is the most plausible.

Between 4 and 6 million years ago, as the historian Yuval Noah Harari colorfully describes, "A single female ape has two daughters. One became the ancestor of all chimpanzees, the other is our own grandmother."[9] The next great transition on the journey occurred roughly 2 and a half million years ago as the first creatures of the *Homo* genus split from an earlier genus of apes called *Australopithecus*. Over the last 2 million years, distinct species within the *Homo* lineage have existed, often together, including *Homo habilis* (the earliest *Homo* fossils discovered to date), *Homo erectus* (the longest surviving *Homo* line, existing from roughly 1.8 million to 200,000 years ago), Neanderthals, and Denisovans.[10] Supporting the thesis that modern humans evolved out of Africa, the earliest *Homo sapiens* fossils date to about 315,000 years ago, found in Jebel Irhoud, Morocco.[11] No species from the *Homo* lineage exist today except *Homo sapiens*.[12]

A significant step in the development of human culture was the domestication of fire. "By about 300,000 years ago, *Homo erectus*, Neanderthals and the forefathers of *Homo sapiens* were using fire on a daily basis. . . . The best thing fire did was cook."[13] The advent of controlled fire changed the way humans ate, furthering the divide between humans and non-human animals. Humans could eat new foods not easily digestible in their natural forms such as wheat, rice, and potatoes. They could also defend themselves from the cold and predators. Humans began to master their environment. "The domestication of fire," according to Harari, "was a sign of things to come."[14]

Homo sapiens began to migrate and eventually colonize the planet. The first great revolution of human history that shapes our story occurred about seventy thousand years ago. "*Homo sapiens* started doing very special things. . . . They drove the Neanderthals and all other human species not only from the Middle East, but from the face of the earth. . . . The period from about 70,000 years ago to about 30,000 years ago witnessed the invention of boats, oil lamps, bows and arrows and needles (essential for sewing warm clothing). The first objects that can reliably be called art date from this era . . . , as does the first clear evidence for religion, commerce and social stratification."[15]

Something special happened—perhaps the result of a fortuitous genetic mutation in the inner wirings of the brain: The Cognitive Revolution opened a "fast lane of cultural evolution bypassing the traffic jams of genetic evolution."[16] Humans' capacity for advanced thought, creativity, language, and cooperation exploded as "history declared its independence from biology."[17] Art, religion, technology, and group cooperation began to inform human life and culture.

Up until twelve thousand years ago, humans were hunter-gatherers. Beginning with the Agricultural Revolution, *Homo sapiens* "began to devote almost all of their time and effort to manipulating the lives of a few animal and plant species."[18] The hope was that increased food production and permanent settlements would increase human leisure. The opposite was the case: "The average farmer worked harder than the average forager, and got a worse diet in return. The Agricultural Revolution was history's biggest fraud."[19] Humans hoped permanent settlement and a stable food supply would bring greater luxury and happiness. In fact, it increased human—and animal—misery. The domestication of certain plants and animals did result in one significant benefit: as a species, the *Homo sapiens* populations exploded. As history unfolded, human life and culture became increasingly more familiar to us: settlements became cities, cities kingdoms, kingdoms empires. Society stratified into elites—kings and priests—and commoners. Written language developed, law codes were codified, economies were established, technology advanced, philosophies were birthed, and human populations rose. So too did human misery through slavery, disease, and religious and political wars.

The next great revolution occurred roughly five hundred years ago. "Around AD 1500, history made its most momentous choice, changing not only the fate of humankind, but arguably the fate of all life on earth. We call it the Scientific Revolution."[20] With increasing confidence in the power of reason and of progress, philosophers advanced new theories of knowledge and scientists began to crack many of nature's mysteries. As a result, today we are surrounded by gadgets and technology that a person living in 1500 couldn't dream of: smartphones, computers, cars, planes, dishwashers, vacuum cleaners, televisions, air conditioners, and lightbulbs. We regularly circumnavigate the globe, and since 1969 we've had the power and insight to send humans to other planets. Our medicine and technology cure diseases, extend life, and buffer us from many of the ravages of nature. In our leisure, we inhabit virtual worlds or lose ourselves in novels, movies, or sports. We dine in restaurants, exercise in gyms, and cultivate community gardens. Our future, of course, is uncertain. We now have the power to end human life or, according to some, to extend it indefinitely. Which way things will go, we do not know. One thing is clear: human beings have indelibly placed their mark on the earth and taken history into their own hands.

Our tour of cosmic history, which began in chapter 1, has covered a lot of ground—13.8 billion years! With Lady Nature as our guide, our journey through time has arrived at the present moment. Where history goes from here is anyone's guess.

It's time to pay a promissory note. So far in this section, I've summarized the history of humans, including human origins, according to evolutionary science. Often, evolutionary science is wedded to the nonreligious story, as it is by the historian I am primarily pulling from, Yuval Noah Harari, the author of *Sapiens*. But it need not be. The theist is free to either accept evolutionary science or reject one or more aspects of it. In fact, there are three basic positions among believing theists with respect to evolutionary science and human origins. The first option is to accept evolutionary science and incorporate it into a broader story of a world created and designed by God: that in creating the world, God "front load[ed]" it with all the necessary ingredients so that life, species, and humans would arise via natural processes.[21] Or, as suggested by Joshua Swamidass, perhaps God created humans according to evolutionary processes and then later created an individual couple—Adam and Eve—out of the dust six thousand years ago in a garden in the Middle East.[22] Adam and Eve are our *genealogical* ancestors, even if they are not our *genetic* ancestors.

The second option is to accept the standard understanding of the universe as ancient, but deny that evolutionary science can explain the origin of humans. On this account, the theist might point to limitations in the ability of currently known scientific processes or mechanisms to generate novel information or novel body plans, including the origin of human bodies.[23] Alternatively, the theist might sidestep the debate about the evolution of human *bodies* (as I'll do below) and argue that certain features of humans, such as a soul or mind, cannot arise via evolution. If so, then evolutionary science doesn't fully explain human origins, even if it can explain the evolution of human bodies. (Of course, this option is consistent with the view that evolution doesn't explain the origin of human bodies either.)[24]

Finally, the theist can deny both evolutionary science and an ancient universe and argue instead that God created the universe, life, species, and humans recently—somewhere between six thousand and ten thousand years ago.[25] This third option posits that the universe appears old but is in fact young.

All of these options have benefits. All of them have costs. For our purposes, we can simply note that the religious story is compatible with science regardless of how the science is interpreted. Compatibility is important. But we are chasing a different quarry: the true story of the world. We are interested in discovering whether that account includes something beyond this world as an explanation for certain features of this world. The question of human origins presses us to consider, of all the competing explanations regarding ultimate reality, which one best explains the fact that there are creatures like us. In the final two sections of this chapter, we turn to this question of *rational preferability*. Which story—the nonreligious or religious—provides the best explanation of the origin of humans? We begin by considering the question of human uniqueness.

Human Uniqueness

Evolutionary theory has powerfully shaped our understanding of human significance. On the traditional view of nature and the natural, the Great Chain of Being connects earth to heaven. Humanity is the pinnacle of God's creation, endowed with great dignity and value. On at least one version of the religious story, humanity is *like* God, created in the divine image. As a divine image bearer, humanity is literally priceless. Humans are unique *kinds* of beings. The goal of God's good creation was beings like us endowed with an intellect and a will.

Darwinism called into question human beings' uniqueness and significance. While acknowledging humans' higher powers, Darwin characterized human distinctiveness as a difference in degree, not kind.[26] Others, such as the evolutionist George Gaylord Simpson, have argued that humans are unique *kinds* of things, yet cosmically insignificant: "Man is the result of a purposeless and natural process that did not have him in mind. He was not planned."[27] The nonreligious story speaks of a *genetic* chain of being that links the present to the past, but it does not speak of a Great Chain of Being linking earth to heaven.[28] The universe, or natural selection, or whatever materialistic processes are responsible for producing humans have not bestowed any special significance on humans. It's up to us to find our way in the universe now that evolution, through chance or some combination of chance and necessity, has produced minds.

Others, myself included, see a tighter connection between human uniqueness and human significance. We intuit that we do matter, that our lives mean something. At least this is my intuition; I invite you to examine your own. We sense that we are beings of great value. Yes, trees, ants, and works of art are of great value. But it does seem—again reporting my own intuition—that, relative to other living beings and artifacts on earth, we are of supreme value. We are the kind of being that shouldn't be bought and sold.

As G. K. Chesterton writes, "The simplest truth about man is that he is a very strange being; almost in the sense of being a stranger on earth."[29] Humans alone create art. Humans alone are free, self-determiners of their own action, character, and life story. Humans alone love and relate. Humans alone communicate with a language and humor infinitely more complex than any animal.[30] As Chesterton continues, "Alone among the animals, [man] is shaken with the beautiful madness called laughter; as if he had caught sight of some secret in the very shape of the universe hidden from the universe itself." Thus, it is "not natural to see man as a natural product."[31] Human uniqueness suggests human significance, and that suggests we were made by an intelligence. Human uniqueness cries out for explanation.

In the previous chapter, we considered the evidence for evolution as the best explanation for the origin of species. Perhaps surprisingly, I raised scientific challenges to the theory of evolution as a global and sufficient explanation for life's diversity. This is surprising because many practicing biologists (including many believers in God) often tell us that the evolutionary explanation for life's diversity is an established fact. That is an important sociological claim about many (but not all) scientists. But we want to balance this sociological truth with another principle: just because a group of people believes something is the case, it does not follow that it is the case.

I'm not suggesting we should distrust scientists. In most cases, we have good reason to accept the consensus view when it comes to the scientific literature. I do think, however, that when it comes to the various origin debates and what we might call historical science, philosophical presuppositions or worldview considerations play a bigger role in how the evidence is presented and interpreted than they often do in more familiar empirical science. For that reason, we have reason to tread more carefully as we consider the expert testimony of scientists. Let's listen to all parties with intellectual humility and hospitality. But let's engage critically.

Granted, it is difficult for nonexperts to know what to do when two experts disagree about something, but as we seek truth we can do our best to examine the evidence, as well as the philosophical underpinnings that color how we interpret the evidence. Our job as truth seekers is to courageously examine the evidence to the best of our ability. (Remember, at this point in our journey, Lady Nature is our primary guide. In other words, we are looking chiefly at the empirical evidence regarding the universe, life, species, and humans to see what we can discover about the true story of the world. We'll be joined by other guides shortly.) Recall that earlier, I argued that even if evolution is true, it couldn't be a wholly material and naturalistic process. Intelligence is needed. Evolution requires essences, and essences require a (divine) mind.

In considering human uniqueness, I claim we are led once again to the idea that there must be a divine cause or intelligence behind it all. We are unique. And our intuition, when we are not being talked out of it, is that we are significant. We are beings with great value and dignity. This uniqueness and significance are often traced to the fact that humans, and humans alone, have an intellect and a will. We are human *persons*. This fact explains the way in which we are unique, and it opens up another line of inquiry: What best explains the origin of human minds? As Chesterton observes (a judgment that still applies today), there is a "broken trail of stones and bones faintly suggesting the development of the human body. There is nothing even faintly suggesting such a development of the human mind."[32] A person is, as Aristotle noted, a rational animal; only a human being has—or is—a mind. Our main question to be explored in this chapter has come into focus: Since human beings alone are rational animals, minds, did they come into being by evolution or by revolution?[33] Is there a naturalistic, evolutionary explanation for minds, or have we been led, yet again, to a clue that points beyond the physical universe to a transcendent reality? What is the best explanation for the origin of minds?

The Origin of Human Minds

In the opening line to *From Bacteria to Bach and Back*, the philosopher Daniel Dennett asks, "How come there are minds?" Dennett's short answer, representative of many in the grips of the nonreligious story, is that "minds evolved and created thinking tools that eventually enabled minds to know how minds evolved."[34] On the traditional—religious—way of understanding human beings' place in the cosmos, mind is prior to matter. God—the divine mind—brings into being creatures, including finite embodied minds (i.e., humans). Comprehension precedes competence; the idea of humans precedes humans, just as the idea of a painting precedes the painting. According to Dennett, Darwin inverted this picture. Instead of a "trickle-down theory of creation," Darwin offered a "bubble-up theory of creation."[35] Evolution explains how there can be design without a designer. Uncomprehending matter and blind processes are prior to minds. Minds emerge from mindless matter, but not merely through evolution. Once brains of a certain size and function arrived on the scene, as time progressed a new kind of evolution—cultural evolution—and a new kind of subpersonal mechanism—memes—radically changed the content and structure of human brains.

The journey from great apes with brains to *Homo sapiens* with minds was gradual, according to Dennett. The primary driver of change was not genetics, however. Rather, brains evolved into minds through culturally transmitted adaptations that in turn fueled a loop of further genetic adaptations and increasingly sophisticated cultural memes that eventually resulted in minds. Dennett summarizes his main argument as follows: "The claim that I defend is that human culture started out profoundly Darwinian, with uncomprehending competences yielding various valuable structures in roughly the way termites build their castles, and then gradually de-Darwinized, becoming ever more comprehending, ever more capable of top-down organization, ever more efficient in its ways of searching Design Space. In short, as human culture evolved, it fed on the fruits of its own evolution, increasing its design powers by utilizing information in ever more powerful ways."[36] Apes with brains became apes with meme-infected brains, which became, due to selective pressures resulting in genetic changes, meme-infected brains with increased abilities for thinking, which became, eventually and gradually, brains that comprehend—that is, human minds.

A key difference between animals and humans is that animals act for reasons, whereas humans have reasons for acting. Thus, a challenge for any evolutionary account of minds is explaining how reasons "get installed in the brain."[37] The answer, according to Dennett, is "via cultural evolution, a whole new process . . . —less than a million years old—that designs, disseminates, and installs thinking tools by the thousands in our brains (and only our brains), turning them into minds."[38] Memes "spread among human beings more or less the way germs or viruses do."[39] Importantly, "human comprehension—and approval—is neither necessary nor sufficient for the fixation of a meme in a culture."[40] Meme-infected brains can act without comprehension in the same way that a computer program can "do" arithmetic without understanding it. Comprehension or understanding, according to Dennett, arise out of competence, not the other way around.

Once language arrived on the scene, however, there ensued a "runaway process of ever swifter and more effective amassing of novel designs and discoveries" that bear the marks of understanding.[41] We now live in the age of intelligent design and soon, as artificial intelligence advances, we will live in an age of post-intelligent design when computers do much of the thinking for us. Consciousness, free will, and the notion of an enduring rational self are illusions, part of our "manifest image" or way of conceiving of the world of everyday objects. The real work is done by the entities that inhabit our "scientific image" of the world: atoms, forces, neurons, natural selection, and everyday physical processes.

According to Dennett, computers show us that there can be competence *without* comprehension. He also asserts that natural selection explains how there can be competence *prior* to comprehension. Both of these claims can be challenged, however.

First, Dennett has not established that there can be competence without comprehension. Computers do perform certain functions without comprehending the nature of those functions, but it does not follow that competence is severed from comprehension. Comprehension is still needed. Switching to the language used in earlier chapters, computers and other human artifacts exhibit *extrinsic* teleology—which is the product of intelligence. Computers function toward a goal because they are the product of a human mind. Computers and the like do not establish, as a global thesis about nature and the natural, the possibility of "competence without comprehension." What Dennett needs to sever competence from comprehension is a clear case of mental comprehension that arose from natural and uncomprehending processes. It is not controversial to note, as Dennett does, that "competence *without* comprehension is the way of life for the vast majority of living things on the planet."[42] This is surely correct. I'm simply questioning the inference from nonconscious, uncomprehending living things with competencies to the claim that those nonconscious, uncomprehending things arose without any appeal to a mind or intelligence. It is the latter inference that is crucial to Dennett's argument.

This leads to the second problem with Dennett's argument: he asserts, but doesn't demonstrate, how natural selection wields the creative power necessary to generate minds. It could be, as I argued in the previous chapter, that natural selection doesn't possess the necessary creative power to generate the requisite novelty required for the emergence of minds. Or it could be that natural selection requires essences, as I've also argued, and essences require a divine intelligence. Or finally, it could be, as I'll argue below, that even if natural selection were sufficient to generate human bodies, it cannot plausibly account for the origin of minds. This latter claim will require a brief exploration into the nature of minds.

What are minds? I will consider my own mental life and invite you to consider yours. I begin with a basic fact of our experience: *we are the kind of beings capable of thinking, understanding, feeling, desiring, and sensing.* I can think about various things—my wife, that tree, this proposition, differential equations. I can reflect on Dennett's argument and consider whether it is true or false. I can understand the meaning of the sentence "All humans are mortal" as I reflect on my own finitude. As I write, I'm also aware of a pain in my back. While the pain might be in my back, the *experience* of the pain is not. It is found as part of my mental life. There is a certain feeling, a "what it is like to be in pain" that I experience, and this experience of pain is uniquely mine. I also have certain desires directed toward distinct objects: the desire to finish this paragraph, to eat that chocolate chip cookie, to love my family, and so on. Moreover, I am aware of the world around me: I see that book of Plato's *Republic*, I hear that noise over there as my wife works in the kitchen, I taste my coffee as I drink, I feel this keyboard as I type, and I smell my dog sitting beside me.

Minds are mysterious things. The mystery has to do with the nature of these mental events (i.e., thinking, understanding, feeling, desiring, and sensing). Time for another claim: *mental events are not the same as physical events.* Physical events are things like electrons orbiting the nucleus of an atom or a baseball being hit over the fence. They are, according to the philosopher J. P. Moreland, events "such that no one person has a special way of knowing something about it."[43] Physical events are publicly available events that can be known from a third-person perspective. By constrast, mental events are those "in which the subject who is having it has privileged access, that is, a way of knowing it (through introspectively experiencing it in the first person) that is not available to anyone else (someone else cannot know directly by introspection what my mental states are)."[44] In other words, mental events are *conscious events*, "an experience of which the individual who has it is aware of having."[45] Minds are *conscious minds*.

Dennett denies all this. Consciousness, our subjective first-personal experience, is an illusion. Conscious events are part of our "manifest image" but not part of reality as it truly is according to the "scientific image." The world and everything in it, according to Dennett, is purely physical or reducible to physical things. The rest—consciousness, morality, religion, beauty, love, meaning, art—is useful fiction.

Unfortunately for Dennett, it is self-contradictory to claim that consciousness is an illusion. Illusions are experiences that seem to be the case but aren't. But seeming to be so-and-so is a subjective experience, and so the illusion of being conscious is itself a conscious experience. As Thomas Nagel points out, "It cannot appear to me that I am conscious though I am not: as Descartes famously observed, the reality of my own consciousness is the one thing I cannot be deluded about."[46] Moreover, arguably our introspective awareness of what are called phenomenal properties—that is, the "raw feel" of a pain, the "what it is like" to taste a chocolate chip cookie or to think of my wife—gives us access to those properties as they really are. And these experiences reveal that mental properties, states, and events are *ontologically distinct* from physical properties, states, and events. Mental properties, states, and events are correlated with brain properties, states, and events, but they are not the same as brain properties, states, and events. The physical properties of brains and brain states are structural and complex, whereas mental properties and states are nonstructural and simple. Importantly, our intimate, genuine acquaintance with the "feel" of our mental lives, according to Kevin Kimble and Timothy O'Connor, "rules out widespread illusion with respect to the way things seem phenomenally to the subject."[47] Dennett is wrong. Consciousness is not an illusion. There are genuine conscious events and thus *conscious* minds.

In fact, as David Bentley Hart argues, "If Dennett's book encourages one to adopt any position at all, reason dictates that it be something like the exact reverse of the one he defends."[48] I think Hart is right. Dennett's overall argument can be boiled down to the following:

[**Dennett**] If naturalism is true, then there are no *conscious* minds. Naturalism is true. Therefore, there are no conscious minds.

But, as I've argued, there are conscious minds. Consciousness is not an illusion. But then the exact opposite of Dennett's central argument follows:

[**Reverse-Dennett**] If naturalism is true, then there are no *conscious* minds. There are conscious minds. Therefore, it is not the case that naturalism is true.

In sum, consciousness is not "at home" in a purely physical world. Philosophers have dubbed the difficulty of fitting the first-person perspective into a wholly material world the *Hard Problem*.[49] There is "an absolute qualitative difference . . . between third-person physical events and first-person consciousness," according to Hart, and it's unlikely there ever will be, or can be, a purely naturalistic narrative uniting these two "phenomenologically discontinuous regions."[50] There are attempts to fit one into the other. But many of those attempts—like Dennett's—either are wildly implausible or end up smuggling in the very thing they seek to explain away.[51]

On the theistic story, however, consciousness is already part of reality prior to the existence of humans. Mind is primary. Mind is fundamental. The right kinds of building materials, and the right kind of builder, are already part of reality before humans appear. The Hard Problem dissolves. Human minds exist because God— the divine mind—brings the universe into being and eventually brings minds into being. Conscious minds are best explained by the existence and creative activity of a divine mind.[52] Exactly how God brought about minds is a question we need not settle here.[53] With God in the picture, minds in a physical world are possible. Theism naturally predicts the appearance of minds, for a good God would want to spread joy and delight to creatures who could experience joy and delight. We are led, once again, to another feature of our world that points beyond this world.

It's time to take stock. In the first four chapters we've been traveling with Lady Nature as we look at fundamental features of our world: the universe, life, species, and humans. In each case, we've considered the empirical evidence regarding the history and origin of the phenomena in question, and we've seen that the best explanation for each is God. We've traveled through time, from the origin of the universe to the present moment. But our journey has just begun. There are other features of reality that we must explore as we seek the true story of the world. There are other guides for us to meet along the way. We begin, in the next chapter, to look at morality. Our next stop is prison.

5

Morality

Wander without reason

—Bumper sticker on car,
central Illinois

These, then, are the two points I want to make. First, that
human beings, all over the earth, have this curious idea that
they ought to behave in a certain way, and cannot really get
rid of it. Secondly, that they do not in fact behave that way. . . .
These two facts are the foundation of all clear thinking about
ourselves and the universe we live in.

—C. S. Lewis, *Mere Christianity*

I've been in prison three times. I should say, "in *a* prison." The first
was a childhood visit to the maximum-security penitentiary on
Alcatraz Island, located in San Francisco Bay. While it was functioning as a prison from 1934 to 1963, thirty-six men attempted
to escape.[1] All attempts ended in recapture or death. Walking the
empty cell blocks and listening to the tour guide drone on about
the prisoners once held within its walls, I wondered, What kinds
of crimes earn a one-way ticket to this island fortress?

Fast-forward to my early twenties. My wife Ethel and I found ourselves in the famous Mamertime Prison in Rome. This ancient dungeon may have been the prison that held the apostles Peter and Paul. As we stood in what is basically a hole in the ground, we imagined Paul writing letters to the young churches throughout the region. I gazed at a single ledge in the hole, imagining Paul writing by candlelight. I wondered if Paul, imprisoned for his faith in Christ, knew how his story would end (execution). His prison letters reveal a man of deep moral conviction and joy. Why was Paul willing to die for his belief in a dead-now-raised-to-life King? What is this good news of which he speaks? How could he possess joy in the midst of difficult circumstances?

My final experience is not really an experience of being in a prison. Rather, it is an experience of a different sort of prison. I refer to the spring 2020 COVID-19 lockdown. Life as we knew it changed overnight. Austin came home from college to finish out the semester online, studying in his upstairs room. Mattie, Travis, and Josh's high school and middle school were shuttered. Eventually they too finished the school year online. My travel ceased. There were no more visits with friends for coffee or book club. Entering a grocery store felt like a scene from a postapocalyptic world: empty shelves, panicked patrons, frazzled workers. Thank goodness we had Netflix. Watching *Tiger King* was eerily comforting; at least we weren't as crazy as Joe Exotic! Each night, we'd tune into *NBC Nightly News* with Lester Holt—bad news, all of it. No vaccine. No cure. No certain way forward. Tales of economic collapse. Images of overrun hospitals. The death toll climbing. Each night, watching the news, my heart would grow anxious. But then we stumbled on a web series by *The Office* star John Krasinski called *Some Good News*.[2] We watched and my heart soared. Finally—some *good* news. As I watched with tears, I wondered, What kind of creatures are we that long for good news to calm our hearts and allay our fears? What kind of world do we live in, a world full of horror and suffering as well as love and joy?

My prison encounters reveal certain features of the human heart that cry out for explanation. We seem to be creatures that can do wrong and suffer pain, yet long for goodness, meaning, and happiness, among other things. What explains this sense of right and wrong that we find deep within the human heart? What does our deep longing for goodness teach us about the true story of the world? It's time to explore the realm of human affairs to see what clues we can uncover as we continue on our journey. In this chapter, we'll begin by exploring the idea of morality. We'll focus on three key questions to help us discover the true story of the world: Is there a moral order? Is this moral order objective? What best explains the reality of the (objective) moral order?

In subsequent chapters, we'll pick up the question of meaning and meaningful happiness. In order to better explore these topics, we'll be joined by another guide. She's actually been with us for quite some time but hasn't been properly introduced. We'll do that by traveling back in history once more to another place and another prison.

The Consolation of Philosophy

A perfect world wouldn't need prisons. No one would hurt another. Everyone would work for societal flourishing. And we'd all be free: not only free from constraint but free to do what we ought to do. But we don't live in a perfect world. People do bad things. Prisons exist to punish bad behavior and to protect others from bad people. Ideally, a perpetrator's penalty fits the crime. But of course, we don't always get that right either. History, including recent history, is riddled with unjust imprisonments: Socrates, Henry David Thoreau, Dietrich Bonhoeffer, Martin Luther King Jr., the Central Park Five, and Nelson Mandela, to name a few.[3]

It is a difficult thing to be stripped of your freedom. It is even more difficult to be stripped of your freedom *unjustly*. Such was the case for Anicius Manlius Severinus Boethius. Boethius once had it all: money, rank, power, and a loving family. Born a Roman aristocrat living in Italy after the fall of the Roman Empire, he had risen to the highest position of service to the Ostrogothic king Theodoric. But Theodoric was a paranoid leader, and one day in AD 524, he falsely accused Boethius of conspiracy and unjustly threw him into prison.

Far from home, alone, shamed, and awaiting execution, Boethius despaired. He began writing—not to instruct others as the apostle Paul did, but to comfort his own wounded heart:

> To pleasant songs my work was erstwhile given, and bright were all my labours then; but now in tears to sad refrains am I compelled to turn. . . . White hairs are scattered untimely on my head, and the skin hangs loosely from my worn-out limbs.
> . . . "Why, O my friends, did ye so often puff me up, telling me that I was fortunate? For he that is fallen low did never firmly stand."[4]

With his confidence in a rational and congenial universe shattered, Boethius was exposed. No longer, it seemed, could reason and virtue buffer him from the wheel of (mis)fortune. The die had been cast. His luck had run out.

But even in our darkest moments, an ember of hope remains. "While I was quietly thinking these thoughts over to myself and giving vent to my sorrow with the help of my pen," Boethius writes, "I became aware of a woman standing over me. She was of awe-inspiring appearance, her eyes burning and keen beyond the usual power of men."[5] At first, the identity of this majestic lady was uncertain to Boethius. But then, "I turned my eyes and fixed my gaze upon her, and I saw that it was my nurse in whose house I had been cared for since youth—Philosophy."[6] Boethius had not been abandoned. He had simply fallen off the path of truth. For, as Lady Philosophy reminded him, "It is not simply a case of your having been banished far from your home; you have wandered away yourself."[7] Boethius had lost his faith in the rationality of the universe, and so he fell into a prison of his own making. The cure, according to Lady Philosophy, was to walk the path of reason in search of truth.

We've considered the beginning of all things, with Lady Nature as our guide, and have surmised, looking at all the evidence, that all things come from God. The universe is rational, orderly, designed— but for what or whom? Lady Philosophy can help. As she put it to Boethius, "How can it be then, that you know the beginning of things but don't know their end?"[8] In other words, if God is the *source* of all things—Life, the Universe, and Everything—then perhaps God *governs* all things too. And if so, then perhaps we might find additional clues within the realm of human affairs that will help us discover the true story of the world.

We continue on the road and into the realm of the human heart to explore our longings and loves, our hopes and desires, to see what they might reveal. But we don't want to "wander without reason" as this chapter's first epigraph implores. While the path is marked—the stones are starting to stack up—there are still many opportunities to lose our way.

Consider Chicken John. In *A Walk in the Woods*, Bill Bryson recounts a summer spent hiking the Appalachian Trail. One day, months into his journey, Bryson runs into Chicken John, who's famous among hikers for his ability to wander off the trail, turn himself around, or walk in a circle. After Chicken John recounts a particularly costly error—a three-day hike in the wrong direction— Bryson asks how it happened:

> "Well, if I knew that, I wouldn't do it, I suppose," he said with a kind of chuckle. "All I know is that from time to time I end up a long way from where I want to be. But it makes life interesting, you know. I've met a lot of nice people, had a *lot* of free meals. Excuse me," he said abruptly, "you sure we're going the right way?"
>
> "Positive."
>
> He nodded. "I'd hate to get lost today. There's a restaurant in Dalton." I understood this perfectly. If you're going to get lost, you don't want to do it on a restaurant day.[9]

Chicken John was hungry. A successful journey that day would be rewarded with a warm meal. While wandering without reason might be fun for a time, it's not a good strategy if we want to eat real food. We want to satisfy our hunger—for truth, for authenticity, for a story that is alive and alluring. But the "terrain of our interior life," according to James K. A. Smith, "is a wilderness of wants." It's easy to get lost. We need help mapping "the geography of desire."[10] And so we walk, but *not* without reason. Lady Philosophy will lead us, especially through this chapter and the next two, as we search for meaningful happiness.

Is There a Moral Order?

When I was young, maybe seven or eight, I went with my dad to an office supply store. As I walked the aisles marveling at the stacks of pens, paper, calculators, protractors, and erasers, for reasons that still remain elusive to me, I started grabbing things off the shelf and stuffing them in my pockets. Before I knew it, my dad and I were out of the store and on our way out of the mall. My first—and only—heist was a success! As I walked, boxes of pens and pencils drummed to the beat of my gait and the box of paper clips boisterously shuffled back and forth, arousing my dad's attention. I was caught. As I emptied my contraband out of shirt and pants pockets and onto the mall floor, dread filled my heart. I knew I was in trouble. And I was. I was lectured on the wrongness of stealing and was grounded indefinitely. My dad returned my loot to the store. But my heist wasn't a complete failure. Hidden deep in one pocket of my pants was a protractor. The next morning, racked with guilt, I snuck out of my room and buried my guilt, and the protractor, in my backyard.

Was it wrong for me to steal those office supplies? Or was my only fault that I got caught? Was my guilt a clue revealing a deep truth about the universe or just a culturally imposed feeling foisted on me by those in power? Some would say there are no moral facts or moral values; there are social contracts, the legislation of morality, and rules to follow, to be sure, they would say, but at rock bottom, there is no way the world *ought* to be, and there are no rules one *must* follow. According to the moral nihilist, there is no moral order, no true moral facts, no moral landscape to be found in the human heart or anywhere else.

The moral-nihilist vision of the world is expressed in a pivotal scene in William Golding's *Lord of the Flies*. Things turn deadly as a group of school boys stranded on an island, unshackled from the conventions of the adult world, explore their newfound freedom. The once-united group has splintered in two. The smaller group, led by Ralph and Piggy, argues that their main task is to keep a fire going so that passing ships might rescue them. The larger group, led by Jack Merridew, wants to hunt and eat. In the pivotal scene, Jack and his band of "savages" have stolen Piggy's glasses. Ralph and Piggy confront Jack: "You pinched Piggy's specs. . . . You've got to give them back." Jack's reply: "Got to? Who says?"[11] Jack and his band of schoolboys-turned-savages are arguing from a position of power. No one can force them to do anything. If they want to hunt and to steal Piggy's glasses, who's to stop them? Might makes right. This is moral nihilism. The argument between the two groups doesn't end well. As the argument escalates, Piggy shouts, "Which is better—to have rules and agree, or to hunt and kill?"[12] The answer is given in the form of a boulder pushed from on high that smashes into Piggy, killing him and sending his mutilated body careening over a rocky ledge and into the ocean—a vivid image of a universe devoid of any moral landscape.

Is the idea of morality a superstition, a fiction? What does reason tell us? Let's make some distinctions so that, with Lady Philosophy's direction, we can find our way. First, there is a distinction between obligation and value. Obligations have to do with what is right and wrong, whereas value has to do with the worthiness or unworthiness of some thing or person. Second, there is a distinction between the subjective and objective. A belief, statement, or fact is subjective if it is true or false relative to some speaker or mind. It is objective if it is true or false independent of a speaker or mind. With these distinctions in hand, let's consider: Did I do anything wrong when I stole those office supplies? Did Jack and his band of savages do anything wrong when they killed Piggy? What do you think?

I'll report my intuition. I did wrong when I stole those supplies, and Jack and his group did wrong when they killed Piggy. I ought not to have stolen, and Jack and his band ought not to have killed. It wasn't hard for me to arrive at these conclusions. I simply *see* the wrongness of those actions. I submit that you can too (but that's for you to decide).

These observations lead to an important discovery: *moral nihilism is false*. There are moral obligations (and moral values). Notice that to this point, I've not argued that there are any *objective* moral obligations (and values); I've simply ruled out moral nihilism, the view that there are no moral facts whatsoever in the universe. There is a moral landscape—a moral order—found in the hearts and minds of humans. With our distinction between subjective and objective obligations and values in hand, it is time to explore our next question: Is this moral order part of the fabric of the universe or just something based on personal preference? In other words, are there some moral obligations and values that are objective, or are they all subjective?

Is There an Objective Moral Order?

I recently binge-watched *Cobra Kai*. I'm slightly embarrassed to admit that, for this is a show that seems to be written for teenagers. I suspect that it's not written only for teenagers, however, given its throwbacks to the 1980s. *Cobra Kai* picks up the story of Johnny Lawrence and Daniel LaRusso, who fought decades ago in the final match of a karate tournament. I refer, of course, to the original 1984 *Karate Kid* movie, in which LaRusso defeated Lawrence with the now-famous crane kick. That kick and the resultant second-place finish shaped the trajectory of Lawrence's life. As *Cobra Kai* begins, he now is in his 50s and basically a failure. LaRusso, on the other hand, has it all: a beautiful wife and family, wealth, and his face plastered all over Los Angeles promoting his successful car business. Things change for Lawrence as he reopens the Cobra Kai dojo. He begins to find success, and redemption, in training a new crop of students. The founder of Cobra Kai, John Kreese, was a ruthless man who instilled in his students a ruthless ethic: Strike first. Strike hard. No mercy. Even with Kreese gone, his influence persists in Lawrence's life and, with the reopening of Cobra Kai, in the lives of a new generation of students.

The show, along with the ethical stance of Cobra Kai, raises interesting questions about morality. Let's consider the question of objective morality, with Lady Philosophy as our guide and *Cobra Kai* as our foil.

We've established that there is a moral landscape. Minimally, there are moral facts about obligations and values indexed to individuals. *Subjectivism* is the view that *all* moral values and obligations are grounded in individual beliefs or preferences. *Objectivism* is the view that at least some moral values and obligations are independent of minds or speakers. I now argue that subjectivism is false. The upshot: there is an objective moral order to the world.[13]

Subjectivism is false for at least three reasons.[14] First, if subjectivism is true, then *moral error* is not possible. But moral error is possible. Therefore, it's not the case that subjectivism is true. In a pivotal scene from season 1 of *Cobra Kai*, Lawrence's student Hawk performs an illegal kick to the back of his opponent Robby, dislocating Robby's shoulder. In the final match, Lawrence's star student Miguel faces Robby, showing no mercy as he beats Robby by punishing his hurt shoulder. The season ends (spoiler alert) with a sinister figure returning to Cobra Kai: John Kreese. Students' actions, it seems, have called back from the dead their mythic (evil) founder. Here is the problem: Watching this scene, it is obvious that what Hawk and Miguel did was objectively wrong. But if subjectivism is true, then what they did was not wrong, since they thought it was the right thing to do. They were following the Cobra Kai ethic: Strike first. Strike hard. No mercy. This problem generalizes. If moral facts are made true simply by believing them

91

to be true, then we become infallible—but none of us are infallible. I'll just focus on myself. I'm often wrong about moral obligations and values. Just ask my wife and kids. The possibility, indeed the reality, of moral error reveals a deep truth about the world: some moral facts are independent of minds or speakers.

Second, if subjectivism is true, then all *moral claims* are equivalent. But it is not the case that all moral claims are equivalent. Therefore, it is not the case that subjectivism is true. The *Cobra Kai* series pits two dojos, with two different moralities, against each other. As already noted, there is the merciless ethic of the Cobra Kai dojo. As the story develops, LaRusso opens up his own dojo, following in the footsteps of his beloved sensei Mr. Miyagi (yes, the "wax on, wax off" Mr. Miyagi). The Miyagi-Do ethic is one of honor and respect. The problem is this: If subjectivism is true, then the competing moralities of both dojos are equivalent. Neither is better or closer to the truth than the other. But it is obvious that a ruthless disregard for others (as embodied in the Cobra Kai ethic) is morally inferior to the ethic of the Miyagi-Do. Generalized, if subjectivism is true, we cannot say that the morality of Mother Teresa is any better than that of Adolf Hitler or that the morality of John Kreese is any better than that of Mr. Miyagi. This is a difficult pill to swallow. Better to reject subjectivism and argue that some moral values and obligations are closer to the truth than others.

Finally, if subjectivism is true, then there can be no moral progress. But there is moral progress. Therefore, it is not the case that subjectivism is true. One of the things I love about *Cobra Kai* is the moral development of John Lawrence. He is on a quest to find himself, and this quest involves rising above a ruthless ethic. Lawrence wants to be better than his master. He sees the injustice of Hawk's illegal kick and the coldness of Miguel's merciless attack in the season 1 finale. He longs for a better way. But none of this is possible if all moral facts are subjective, indexed to minds or speakers. The fact that we can and do make moral progress—in our own lives, in our society—reveals a deep truth about the world:

there is an objective moral order, and we do well when we conform our lives to that order.

We've briefly looked at three reasons, three arguments, that show subjectivism is false. But we didn't really need them. For if we pay attention to our own moral experience, we can "see" that there are objective moral values and obligations. Philosopher Joshua Rasmussen suggests a "self-test" as a way to help us see objective value in the world.[15]

Consider yourself. Look in the mirror. What do you see? You see something, a person, of genuine value. No matter how you feel about yourself, you are valuable. No matter what anyone else might think or say or do, you have value. You see it, don't you? This is an instance of being directly aware of something in this world with objective value, value independent of minds or speakers.

We can do other sorts of tests. Consider the "wallet test." Steal someone's wallet. Notice that person's reaction. They will charge you with a crime. You did something wrong, really wrong. The wrongness isn't just their own belief. It's something that you too see as wrong—really wrong. That's because you can see, rationally, that "stealing is wrong" is true. You can see a bunch of other objective moral truths too: "Racism is wrong," "Murder is wrong," "Truth-telling is right," and so on. C. S. Lewis expresses well the idea that we can see objective moral values and obligations: "I believe that the primary moral principles on which all others depend are rationally perceived. We 'just see' that there is no reason why my neighbour's happiness should be sacrificed to my own, as we 'just see' that things which are equal to the same thing are equal to one another. . . . Their intrinsic reasonableness shines by its own light."[16]

Consider the people around you. Notice their value. Then consider various moral obligations and see if "their intrinsic reasonableness shines by [their] own light." What do you find? I submit that what you will find is a collection of objective values and obligations, moral facts, that hold independent of minds or speakers. In other words, there is an objective moral order.

What Grounds the Objective Moral Order?

This leads naturally to our final question. If there is a moral land-scape, and if at least some objective values and obligations hold independent of minds and speakers, then what best explains the reality of objective morality? What grounds it or makes it true? There are a few options: nothing, the universe, or God. Let's consider each in turn.

If nothing grounds objective morality, then the objective moral order is just a brute fact. There is no explanation. Moral values and moral obligations just exist. Period. End of story. On a prominent version of this approach described in Erik Wielenberg's *Robust Ethics*, moral values and obligations are abstract objects.[17] Abstract objects are funny sorts of things. They exist just like more familiar concrete objects such as tables, chairs, and the like, but they do so outside space and time. To endorse belief in these abstract things is to endorse Platonism, in honor of Plato and his theory of Eternal Forms. Wielenberg defends what we might call a kind of Platonic Atheism. We could also call Wielenberg's view a kind of Brute Fact Atheism since moral facts are brute or unexplained. According to Brute Fact or Platonic Atheism, then, there is the physical universe and an abstract realm of moral facts. This view is a philosophically viable option. As Wielenberg points out, explanations must stop somewhere, so why not with brute moral facts?[18]

For at least four reasons, I don't think that Brute Fact Atheism is the best explanation for objective morality. First, it seems utterly mysterious how properties in the abstract realm—for example, being good, being evil, being right, being wrong—hook up to various things and actions in the physical world.[19] Why is it that my childhood act of stealing office supplies hooks up with the abstract property *being wrong* instead of *being right*? The answer, at the end of the day, is that it just does. Period. But this makes Brute Fact Atheism less attractive than the alternatives, for now the amount of brute facts needed to make the theory work has multiplied. Not only does it offer no explanation for the objective moral order; it also offers no explanation for how the moral and natural orders connect.

Second, Brute Fact Atheism can't explain the authority or obligatoriness of moral duties. Why is it that we have an obligation to be honest? What explains this "oughtness"? Obligations and duties attach, it seems, to persons, not things. I'm not obligated to the chair I'm currently sitting on. I don't owe it anything. Suppose I'm thinking about jumping off a roof for fun and, in my infinite wisdom, consider landing on a chair to soften the impact. Suppose too that if I jump, I'll likely break the chair (and suppose I see this likelihood). As I consider this (foolish) action, an action I regularly contemplated as a kid, we might ask: Would I owe it to the chair to refrain from jumping? No. I'm not obligated to things. I am, on the other hand, obligated to people. I'm obligated to myself to not do stupid and unsafe things like jumping off roofs. And I'm obligated—in this case to my wife and kids—to not put them in a position of needing to care for me when that leg breaks. Obligations naturally attach to persons, not things. In this way, theism—belief in a personal being worthy of worship—better accommodates the obligatoriness of moral duties by locating a proper ultimate source of moral authority.

Third, Brute Fact Atheism cannot account for the guilt we feel when we do wrong.[20] Suppose I had a magical ring that made me invisible. Why be moral? (Plato famously presses this question in the *Republic*, and Tolkien playfully presses this idea in his Middle Earth novels.) If I cheated, lied, even raped and murdered, no one would know it was me. Yet I'd still feel guilty. I'll bet you would too. (Don't take my word for it; imagine yourself in this scenario. What do you find?) If there is a moral law but no moral lawgiver, then why do I have this sense of guilt when I do wrong—even if no one can see what I do? This need to rectify our moral failures is best explained if there are both a moral law and a moral lawgiver.

Finally, Brute Fact Atheism cannot account for why we have mental capacities that track moral truths.[21] If the grand, naturalistic, evolutionary story explains why we have the cognitive capacities that we have, then we have no good reason to trust what our mental lives tell us. After all, evolution selects traits for survival, not truth. Thus, we have no reason to think that our cognitive capacities are aimed at truth, and we have no reason to think that our moral beliefs track truth. In other words, the fact that we do have moral knowledge is hard to explain given Brute Fact Atheism. On the other hand, if God exists, we have good reasons to think that our cognitive faculties are in fact reliable for tracking moral truths; arguably, God wants us to know moral truths, and thus he ensured (through either natural or supernatural processes) that our cognitive faculties develop such that they are capable of tracking moral truths.

I conclude that Brute Fact Atheism doesn't best explain objective morality. But what about the universe itself? Perhaps the universe best explains the emergence of values and obligations. How might this go? There are two options. Morality arose either via mechanistic laws of physics, chemistry, and biology or through nonpurposive teleological laws. If the first option is correct, naturalism plus evolution explains the emergence of morality. The problem, however, is that naturalism plus evolution cannot explain an objective moral landscape. At best, evolutionary naturalism explains why we do, in fact, behave in moral ways. But an account of *why* we behave morally (e.g., that it is conducive to survival) does not explain why we *ought* to behave in certain ways.[22] Evolutionary naturalism cannot ground objective moral obligations. (Nor, as we saw earlier, can evolutionary naturalism ground our confidence in the reliability of our cognitive faculties for tracking moral truths.)

Perhaps, then, in addition to mechanical laws of nature there are nonpurposive teleological laws of nature. As Thomas Nagel suggests, "The universe is rationally governed in more than one way—not only through the universal quantitative laws of physics that underlie efficient causation but also through principles which imply that things happen because they are on a path that leads toward certain outcomes—notably, the existence of living, and ultimately conscious [moral], organisms. . . . Teleology means that in addition to physical law of the familiar kind, there are other laws of nature that are 'biased toward the marvelous.'"[23]

Why, we might ask, is the universe "biased toward the marvelous"? It just is. But that seems wrong: arguably, biases attach to persons, not principles. Moreover, according to Nagel these "biases" or teleological laws possess causal powers to bring about valuable features in the universe. But, as Angus Ritchie points out, this is a category mistake.[24] Normative laws are not the kind of things that have creative powers. Norms can and do impose obligations on us, but they can't bring into being embodied, conscious, moral agents. Ends, as we discussed in an earlier chapter, imply agency. Teleology cannot be so easily disentangled from agency. As Ritchie argues, "The only things that can act purposively [i.e., act creatively] are *agents*. It is only through such agents' cognition of norms, and the powers those agents have to act in the world, that we have any reason to think objective value can have a causal impact on the universe."[25]

But on theism, the connection between ends and agents finds a proper ground. Objective moral goodness exists because God exists as a perfectly good and self-existent being that wills to bring into being various valuable states of affairs. Objective moral obligations exist because God has created humans to flourish in various ways, and when we live as we *ought* to live, we flourish in light of that nature.[26] Thus, theism provides the best explanation for objective moral values and obligations.

If God doesn't exist, then we do live in a prison of sorts. The world is an iron cage, a dungeon, and there is no actual goodness—in this life or the next. But as we've seen, there are good reasons to think there is an objective moral order, and God is the best explanation for this fact. The world is not a prison and we are not, as the atheist Bertrand Russell describes, "the product of causes that had no prevision of the end they were achieving." Our lives need not be built on that "firm foundation of unyielding despair."[27] Rather, because God exists, there is goodness. And since there is goodness, there is the genuine possibility for some good news—some way out of the prisons of this world and of our own failures. We now turn to the question of meaning, as we continue on our journey of discovery.

6

Meaning

I just hope my death makes more cents than my life.

—Joker, *The Joker*

There are problems in this universe for which there are no answers.

—Paul Atreides, *Dune Messiah*

Arthur Fleck has no name. I know, it seems like I've already refuted myself. What I mean is that Arthur Fleck lacks an identity, a story, a place to stand. Raised without a father by a mother who was mentally unstable, he was abused and beaten as a child. Now an adult, Arthur suffers from a laughing disorder. When in pain, he laughs. When he laughs, he's in pain. Tragedy is comedy. Comedy is tragedy. Life is absurd.

Arthur wants to be a comedian. His jokes, however, are too dark, too forced, too tragic. He finds work, at least for a time, as a clown. He finds comfort behind the mask. As a nameless clown, Arthur can take on any persona he wants when in costume. He can hide his pain, his angst, his emptiness, as he walks the thin line between being and nothingness.

99

But then, tragedy strikes again. While on the subway and still dressed as a clown, Arthur is assaulted by three successful men. They represent everything wrong with the universe. They are the privileged, lucky ones, the cosmic lottery winners. And now they are rubbing it in Arthur's face. As the men begin to beat Arthur, something snaps. Arthur pulls out a gun and kills them all. This is the defining moment of Arthur's life. This is his naming event. Over the next few days, as the newspapers report on a clown murdering three wealthy businessmen, the working-class citizens of the city find their champion: The clown who murders the rich. The clown who stands up for the underprivileged. The hero of Gotham City.

All that remains is the naming ceremony. Arthur is invited to go on the Murray Franklin show. Franklin's producers had received a clip of Arthur's failed comedy routine. They thought his awkward laughter was funny enough that it merited an invitation to the show. Everyone needs to see this "Joker." Arthur appears on the show dressed as a clown. As the interview between Arthur and Franklin unfolds, Arthur confesses to the train murders. As the interviewer moves from confusion to shock to horror to anger, Arthur pulls out his gun, killing Franklin on live TV. The scene ends with Arthur saying into the camera, "Good night! And always remember, that's life." Arthur is no more. He has discovered his true name. He is the Joker.

The movie I speak of, of course, is the 2019 blockbuster of the same name. One of the most pressing questions the movie invites is the question of meaning. Is there any meaning in the universe or our lives? Is life tragedy all the way down? Or comedy? Who gets to name us? How can we find our place in this world? In this chapter, we'll continue our journey to discover the true story of the world by considering the question of meaning.

Finding Our Place in the Universe

The meaning of *meaning* is hotly debated among philosophers and suffers from being somewhat vague. There are a number of ways we might define the quest for meaning, but I think the most fundamental is *the quest to find our place in the universe*; all other meaning or purpose, I think, derives from this.[1] Find your place in the universe, and you've discovered the meaning of it all.

There are four things to notice about this understanding of meaning. First, the question of meaning is partly a question about the universe. In order to understand if there is any meaning, we must first understand what kind of universe we live in. Thus, the question is cosmological, even metaphysical. Second, there is the distinction between defining and discovering meaning. Notice that I've only defined a meaningful life: a life that has found its place in the universe. It is one thing to define meaning and another to discover that there *is* meaning. Third, there is the distinction between meaning and happiness. It is possible to live a life that is meaningful but not (subjectively) happy. Likewise, one can live a (subjectively) happy life without meaning. (We'll explore the question of happiness, or meaningful happiness, in the next chapter.) Fourth and finally, notice that above I said "finding our place in the universe," not "space in the universe." *Space* and *place* are two different things. The concept of space is descriptive whereas the concept of place is normative. All physical beings exist in space. But merely existing at certain spatial locations doesn't, at least directly, help us determine the meaning of life (although the fact that we live in a fine-tuned universe on a planet that is positioned just right for life does give us a clue, as we explored in chap. 1). Place is a richer concept than space. Place is where we belong, where we are known and know, where we make a difference, where we are valued and value. Thus, while *place* includes the concept of physical space, it is a much richer concept that also includes value, significance, and purpose.

When we find our place in the universe, we discover our true name. We discover the true story of the world. We discover how all things, including our lives, hang together. The question of meaning comes up again and again in the history of philosophy. It distills down to six deep human longings: the longing for purpose, value, significance, intelligibility, identity, and transcendence. Let's call this set of deep and natural longings the *Existential Set*. What we are seeking, then, is a proper fit between world and desire. We embark on a quest in the hope of finding a true story that satisfies.

The question of meaning is a really hard problem. To start with, we have dueling intuitions. One intuition is that our lives matter only if they have "staying power," only if they *last*. Another intuition is that our lives matter precisely because death is imminent. Life is precious, and scarce; it is meaningful because it is so limited and fragile.[2] The question of meaning is also hard because it is tied up with the question of the universe itself, and whether or not there is a God. Philosopher Owen Flanagan thinks the question of meaning is one of the hardest problems for those who view the world as merely molecules and matter to answer: "Consciousness exists, and if we accept Darwin's theory it probably serves a biological function. But whether meaning exists is controversial. We tell stories about what it is to live a meaningful life. But it is not clear that any of these stories give us insight, let alone an answer, to the question of what a truly meaningful life is or might be."[3] Flanagan, a materialist, believes it's possible to find meaning in a material universe. Others think that there is meaning in the universe only if God exists.

To sort through these competing intuitions and questions, we'll need the help of Lady Philosophy. As Wilfrid Sellars famously says, "The aim of philosophy . . . is to understand how things in the broadest possible sense of the term hang together in the broadest possible sense of the term."[4] We hope there is a story that is both true and satisfying. We seek a fit between world and desire, between map and Existential Set.

So far, we've journeyed together without a map. We've considered the question of origin in detail. And in the previous chapter, we began to explore the cartography of the human heart and the idea of quest and destiny, beginning with morality. It's time to think more deeply about the human side of the world-desire ledger to discover if there is a story that can satisfy. It would be nice if the true story of the world were also a satisfying story, one that satisfied longings for purpose, value, significance, intelligibility, identity, and transcendence.

To assist us in our "contextualizing pursuits," I've invited four travel companions to join us: two French philosophers from the near and distant past and two Duke University philosophers from contemporary America.[5] They'll help us explore four possible pictures of the world that frame the human quest for meaning: Absurdism, Nice Nihilism, Enchanted Naturalism, and Enchanted Supernaturalism. We'll test each of these possible stories in terms of fit and see what clues they might offer us, if any, about the true story of the world. We begin with Absurdism, as we take a brief stop in a French café in the late 1930s.

Absurdism

Originally published in 1938, Jean-Paul Sartre's "experimental metaphysical novel" *Nausea* explores the question of meaning in a godless world.[6] The hero, Antoine Roquentin, is a French writer struggling with the emptiness, contingency, and horror of existence. Written as diary entries, the novel chronicles Roquentin's impressions of everyday life in the port town of Bouville. He takes walks, studies at the library, eats at the café, writes a book, and occasionally interacts with those around him: the self-taught man who is reading all the books in the library in alphabetical order, a waitress, a former love interest named Annie, and others.

Roquentin thinks of himself as an adventurer. Early in the book, he writes, "I have had real adventures. I can recapture no detail but I perceive the rigorous succession of circumstances. I have crossed seas, left cities behind me, followed the course of rivers or plunged into forests, always making my way towards other cities. I have had women, I have fought with men; and never was I able to turn back, any more than a record can be reversed." As he sits in a café watching a group of old men playing cards, a question surfaces: "And all that led me—where?"[7]

A week later, an answer presents itself as an "unnameable" idea.[8] This "great white mass . . . [that] has rolled itself into a ball . . . explains nothing, it does not move, and it contents itself with saying no. No, I haven't had any adventures."[9] Rather, Roquentin realizes, his life is a series of disconnected events: "I have never had adventures. Things have happened to me, events, incidents, anything you like. But no adventures. It isn't a question of words; I am beginning to understand. There is something to which I clung more than all the rest—without completely realizing it. It wasn't love. Heaven forbid, not glory, not money. It was . . . I had imagined that at certain times my life could take on a rare and precious quality. There was no need for extraordinary circumstances: all I asked for was a little precision."[10]

Roquentin longed for life to "take on a rare and precious quality." What is the object of this longing? What is this "precision" he seeks? He seeks real adventure. He longs to be part of a story that is alive and inviting and exhilarating. He seeks a story with a real beginning, a real quest, and a satisfying ending. He feels that life *ought* to mean something, and so he wanders, seeking "that rare and precious quality" that we might call joy or purpose or meaning. He longs to discover his true name. "Yes, it's what I wanted—what I still want," writes Roquentin. "I am so happy when a [woman] sings: what summit would I not reach if *my own life* made the subject of the melody."[11]

But the horror of existence, according to Absurdism, is that there is no song from a far-off country. There is no God-orchestrated drama. The universe cares not for man, nor beast, nor pebble. There is just existence, and that's all. And this realization leaves us cold, empty, alone, and afraid. Life is tragedy all the way down. We don't belong anywhere. Roquentin realizes while leaving a café one night, "I want to leave, go to some place where I will be really in my own niche, where I will fit in. . . . But my place is nowhere; I am unwanted, *de trop*."[12] Nothing—and no one—has a name; everything is "*in the way*."[13] Things just exist. The universe, life, everything . . . is absurd. Period.

According to Absurdism, there is no meaning to be found anywhere. There is no place for you to fit in, no story to locate your life, and no true name that picks out your authentic self. None of the longings within the Existential Set will ever be satisfied. There is no fit between world and desire. If true, then all we can do is bravely build our lives on Bertrand Russell's "firm foundation of unyielding despair."[14] But is it true?

There are at least three reasons for thinking it's not. First, *the fact that the universe is intelligible suggests there is cosmic meaning.* We know a great deal about the universe. The world is intelligible to us, and as we discovered in earlier chapters, this intelligibility is partly explained by the fact that the universe is ordered, hierarchical, and rational. Things don't just exist; they exist as certain *kinds* of things, things with natures or essences. This is why the universe is intelligible to us. Existence does not precede essence, as Sartre would have us believe. Rather, things come into being as certain kinds of things: carbon atoms, oak trees, honey bees, horses, humans. And this intelligibility suggests cosmic meaning.

Second, *the fact that we naturally engage in contextualizing activities suggests by analogy that there is cosmic meaning.* My kids are arguing in the other room. I hear yelling and banging. Someone is mad. I intervene. "What happened?" "Why are you yelling at each other?" "How did this begin?" I seek the meaning, the context for their actions. Notice three things about this scenario: my kids' actions are meaningful, that meaning is revealed by a narrative, and this narrative is discovered by me asking them questions. By analogy, the quest for the meaning of life is like my quest to understand my children's actions.[15] But then, we have at least some reason to think our lives are meaningful, that meaning is revealed by a narrative, and that this narrative is discovered by asking questions of deep importance.

Third, *the intelligibility of the universe and the contextualizing activities of humans suggest cosmic meaning.* We have reason to be suspicious of Absurdism. I take this last reason as decisive,

however. Recall that according to Absurdism, there is no meaning in the universe. It is tragedy "all the way down." This is false.
Even if there is no cosmic meaning, there is subjective meaning, at
least in the sphere of human life. There is a "meaning landscape"
found within the belief states and attitudes of humans. So, meaning nihilism, like moral nihilism, is false.

Nice Nihilism

But there is another posture many today are taking. Is there a
meaning to life? "No." Does God exist? "No." Does the fact that
there is no meaning and no God lead to despair? "Nah. Let's
party." We can call this posture, following the Duke University philosopher of science Alex Rosenberg, "Nice Nihilism."[16] "Farewell
to the purpose driven life," Rosenberg proclaims.[17] Science tells us
our longing for a true story of the world is an illusion. There is no
place for us. There is no "I" or "self" that longs, either. There are
just the physical facts. So, what do the physical facts tell us about
how to live life? Nothing, really. Still, "the really scientistic person
will cultivate an Epicurean detachment. . . . Epicureanism encourages a good time."[18] If the truth of atheism and meaning nihilism
cause you angst, Rosenberg writes, science has a solution for that
too: "If you still can't sleep at night, even after accepting science's
answer to the persistent questions, you probably just need one or
more little things besides Epicurean detachment. Take a Prozac or
your favorite serotonin reuptake inhibitor, and keep taking them
till they kick in."[19] There's no God, no meaning to life, no way
things ought to be. So let's have a good time. And let's call the
doctor when we feel down. Actually, forget the doctor; let's find
the really good stuff. Let's party.

According to Nice Nihilism, life is not a tragedy. Life is a comedy. It is comedy "all the way down." As the Australian writer
Wendy Syfret explains in an essay titled "Sunny Nihilism," the
realization that her life has no meaning was "one of the most
comforting revelations" of her life:

I was chronically stressed at work, overwhelmed by expectations, grasping for a sense of achievement or greater purpose and tiptoeing towards full-on exhaustion. Then it hit me: "Who cares? One day I'll be dead and no one will remember me anyway."

I can't explain the crashing sense of relief. It was as if my body bumped its cortisol stores allowing my lungs to fully inflate for the first time in months. Standing on the side of the road I looked at the sky and thought: "I'm just a chunk of meat hurtling through space on a rock. Pointless, futile, meaningless." It was one of the most comforting revelations of my life. I'd discovered nihilism.[20]

According to Syfret, Generation Y and Z are taking a more enthusiastic posture toward nihilism. Nothing in life matters? Well then, let's do a bunch of crazy stuff—eat Tide pods; ask celebrities to punch us, step on our necks, or run us over.[21] "Turns out the descent into nothingness can be pretty fun."[22]

I like Nice Nihilism a lot more than Absurdism. If life is in fact meaningless, I'd at least want to enjoy it. The problem is that pleasure and meaning are tightly related. Get rid of meaning, and pleasures lose their luster. Comedy becomes tragedy. And comfort becomes an illusion too.

While it would be nice if Nice Nihilism were a viable option, it turns out to be self-refuting. We are told that there are no stories. Our longing for a true story in which to find meaning, purpose, significance, and an identity is an illusion. But then, we are told that naturalism is the true story of the world. On this story, the physical facts are all the facts; the scientific person will seek to enjoy life, and if that is not possible, they will take comfort through Prozac. This is a meta-narrative that orders our life and helps us make sense of it all. It's just a really bad story.

In the end, then, Nice Nihilism isn't any better than Absurdism. Without meaning, even the pleasures this life offers are too fleeting to sustain us. Like Absurdism, Nice Nihilism is false anyhow, since there is at least a subjective meaning landscape. It's time to explore this meaning landscape as we continue our quest to discover the true story of the world.

Enchanted Naturalism

Like Rosenberg, Owen Flanagan is a Duke University professor, and he shares Rosenberg's view that we live in a godless universe. But Flanagan is more optimistic. He does not think the universe entails nihilism (nice or otherwise). He thinks that there is space in a material world for selves, persons, minds, phenomenal consciousness (the "what it is like" or the feel of conscious experience), and meaning: "If one adopts the perspective of the philosophical naturalist and engages in realistic empirical appraisals of our natures and prospects, we have chances for learning what methods might reliably contribute to human flourishing."[23] Flanagan offers a picture of the universe we can dub *Enchanted Naturalism*.

Enchanted Naturalism is a version of naturalism, so the overarching story doesn't change: in the end, we die, and ultimately the universe dies too. There is no cosmic significance, purpose, or meaning. But from the perspective of the human species—*sub specie humanitatis*—it is possible to live meaningfully, and this is good news. There is adventure. Our lives can be a work of art. *Enchantment* is possible: "The reason [the naturalistic picture of persons] isn't disenchanting . . . is that our remarkable powers as persons remain. We are creatures who can and sometimes do make sense of things and find meaning."[24] There is no single meaningful life; rather, as "psycho-poetic" creatures, we find meaning as we embed our stories into the larger matrix of culturally embedded spaces of meaning found in art, science, technology, ethics, politics, and spirituality.[25] Death is the end of our story. But our lives still matter. If we lived a happy and moral life, we will have left "good karmic effects."[26] Then we can be proud when we die. That is good enough.

Is it, though? Does Enchanted Naturalism satisfy our deep human longing to find our place in the universe? Does it provide the possibility, individually or as a species, for meaning, purpose, value, significance, and identity? Does it help us discover our name and guide us on our quest to discover the true story of the world?

There are at least three reasons to think it does not. First, there is *the problem of fit*. It is not obvious that selves, persons, minds, phenomenal consciousness, objective values, spirituality, and natural teleology cohere well with a naturalistic universe. If matter is all there is, then, as we saw in chapter 4, it is hard to make sense of nonphysical minds, mental causation, and the like. In chapter 5, we saw that objective duties and values make the most sense in a supernatural world. Finally, the reality of living organisms with natures or essences that guide these organisms toward their fulfillment or flourishing, as we noted in chapters 2 and 3, makes the most sense within a theistic view. I'm not saying that Enchanted Naturalists can't help themselves to all of these features. My claim is more modest: these features seem out of place in a naturalistic universe. They don't fit well. Even if Enchanted Naturalism does well in terms of the Existential Set, I'm focused here on the *world* side of the world-desire nexus.

Second, there is *the problem of depth*. Enchanted Naturalism gets a lot right. We *are* story-making animals. We *do* long for goodness, truth, and beauty. But a "choose your own adventure" is not good enough. We long for a story bigger than ourselves—a story that understands and transcends us. At best, our freedom to choose an adventure can secure for us a subjectively meaningful life and a modicum of transcendence as we live for our family, or community, or even the human species. But we long for something deeper, more enduring, and more meaningful. When it comes to our quest for goodness, truth, and beauty, we don't merely long for the goodness, truth, and beauty found within some "Space of Meaning[Early 21st century]."[27] Rather, we want a source of goodness, truth, and beauty beyond a specific cultural context. Moreover, we long for our lives to matter and make sense from the widest possible frame of reference; we long for cosmic significance and meaning. For many—most?—there is a deep-seated desire for transcendence, for God, and for eternity. Enchanted Naturalism cannot account for this deep-seated desire. Enchanted Naturalism, at best, offers significance and meaning only for our brief time on earth.

Finally, there is *the problem of the end*. From a human perspective —*sub specie humanitatis*—the Enchanted Naturalist will argue that our lives can be meaningful in the sense that they matter and are valuable to humankind or human history. The problem is this: given the narrative ending to Enchanted Naturalism, it is difficult to maintain this belief in meaning. The cosmic end of our lives, of humankind, of the universe, infects the rest of the story and empties it of any significance or meaning.

Recall that our search for meaning can be understood as a search to find our place in the universe. It is a search to discover the true story of the world. This story has a beginning, a middle, and an end. But, as philosopher Joshua Seachris argues, how a story *ends* shapes how we evaluate the story as a whole.[28] If, for example, Ken was dating Barbie but knew that the relationship would not end in marriage, this knowledge would arguably taint the dating experience. In the same way, if we know that the naturalistic metanarrative (enchanted or disenchanted) ends in death, this knowledge infects our lives now with a kind of futility or meaninglessness.

If Enchanted Naturalism is true, in the end it will be as if we never existed at all. This ending, given the power of narrative endings to affect the rest of a story, renders our search for meaning futile. Good karmic effects are not good enough. "Choose your own adventure" is not good enough. Enchanted Naturalism can't fully satisfy the deep longings of the Existential Set. Again, there is no fit between world and desire.

Enchanted Supernaturalism

This leaves us with one final possibility: Enchanted Supernaturalism. Like Flanagan, a defender of *Enchanted* Supernaturalism thinks the world is full of deep beauty, mystery, order, purpose, and love. Unlike Flanagan, a defender of Enchanted *Supernaturalism* does not think the world is godless. God exists and is responsible for the universe. As humans, we come into this world as part of an ongoing drama and take our places. There is an Author. We are part of a Play. And as we enter the Stage of Life, meaning is possible. There is a God's-eye point of view and thus a wider perspective to it all. We live *sub specie aeternitatis*. Because there is a meaning of life, we can find *fulfilling* meaning in life.

As the seventeenth-century French philosopher Blaise Pascal puts it in the *Pensées*, writing about the cravings found within the Existential Set: "What else does this craving [i.e., the craving for satisfaction of the desires within the Existential Set], and this helplessness, proclaim but that there was once in man a true happiness, of which all that now remains is the empty print and trace? This he tries in vain to fill with everything around him, seeking in things that are not there the help he cannot find in those that are, though none can help, since this infinite abyss can be filled only with an infinite and immutable object; in other words by God himself."[29]

C. S. Lewis describes these cravings more succinctly in *The Problem of Pain*: "Your soul has a curious shape because it is a hollow made to fit a particular swelling in the infinite contours of the divine substances."[30] There is, as Pascal and Lewis suggest, a God-shaped void in the human heart that nothing else can fill. If God exists, then there is a genuine possibility of a satisfying story. According to Enchanted Supernaturalism, the possibility of a world-desire fit is real. There is a tight fit between the world and the deep longings of the human heart, just as a key fits into a lock or a hand into a glove.

Pascal and Lewis didn't have a generic Enchanted Supernaturalism in mind. They both were Christian theists. The God responsible for the origin and existence of the universe, life, species, and humans is also the God that satisfies the deep longings of the human heart. Consider again the Existential Set. According to Christian theism, we were created by God for perfect happiness, which means there is a *purpose* to life. (We'll discuss this idea in the next chapter.) There is *value* in life because God creates us with great dignity and worth, and there are genuine goodness, truth, and beauty in the world because God is the source of goodness, truth, and beauty. There is *significance* to our lives; your life matters—to God, to you, to others. You will leave a trace, and since life never ends, you'll leave this trace forever. The world *makes sense* from the widest possible frame: there is an overarching story to the world, and it is one of love. God creates in love, spreading his joy and delight and inviting us as creatures to take our place in this divine drama and share in his goodness in creaturely delight. It is possible to discover our *true name* within the Christian story too. We don't need to name ourselves. We are named by Another, and our name is Beloved. Finally, the longing for *transcendence* can be satisfied too. There is more than just the mundane; the universe turns out to be enchanted, haunted by Spirit, and porous enough that God is ever present and active in human history and individual lives.

To conclude, among our four possible stories canvassed in this chapter, there is a story, a picture of the universe, that fits with our deep and natural desires. This *is* good news! It *is* possible to satisfy the deep longings of the human heart—if, that is, Enchanted Supernaturalism is true. We've already seen good reasons coming from science and philosophy (thanks to Lady Nature and Lady Philosophy) for thinking that God exists. Thus, we have good reasons for thinking that some version of Enchanted Supernaturalism is true. I've claimed in this chapter that at least one version of Enchanted Supernaturalism—Christianity—can satisfy the deep longings of the human heart found within the Existential Set. The fact that there is a story that makes sense of our own loves and longings gives us reason to think that Christianity, unlike its competitors (Absurdism, Nice Nihilism, and Enchanted Naturalism), also makes sense of everything else. Let's continue to explore the human heart and its deep longings for happiness, love, justice, beauty, and more to see whether they all point to the Christian story as the true and satisfying story of the world. We turn next to the question of happiness. Back to Lady Philosophy, Boethius, and that prison.

7

Happiness

There is no such thing as not worshipping. Everybody worships.
The only choice we get is *what* to worship.

—David Foster Wallace, *This Is Water*

Give it away, give it away, give it away now.

—Red Hot Chili Peppers, "Give It Away"

What is left when everything you have is taken away from you? At age thirteen, Odie O'Banion might not have put the question that way, but his life and his heart longed for an answer. He'd lost his parents, home, and possessions. He found himself, along with his brother Albert, as a boarder at the Lincoln Indian Training School along the banks of Minnesota's Gilead River. Behind closed doors, the headmistress, dubbed "the Black Witch" by students, was evil personified. Life for Odie was full of adversity. During the day, he worked long hours under the oppressive gaze of the Black Witch. At night, he was often banished to the "quiet room" for some perceived (or actual) slight against the Black Witch.

There was hope too: Odie had his brother and his friends Mose and Emmy. Even better, Emmy's mom, Mrs. Frost, planned on adopting Odie. He would soon have a family again. But a tornado changed all that. Mrs. Frost perished, and with her, Odie's hope. When Odie got in a tussle with the Witch's henchman, Mr. DiMarco, things went from bad to worse. A life-and-death struggle ended with Mr. DiMarco plunging to his death, careening headlong into a quarry. Odie fled with his brother and friends. They embarked by canoe down the Gilead River in search of a long-lost aunt in St. Louis.

This is the beginning of their journey as told in William Kent Krueger's novel *This Tender Land*, a tale of quest and conquest that's part *Odyssey* and part *Adventures of Huckleberry Finn*.[1] Odie's journey and the characters he meets along the way help us answer the question that began this chapter. When everything you have is taken away, what remains? *The longing for home.* This deep longing is powerfully illustrated in a scene that takes place one night after Albert has been miraculously healed from a snake bite. Odie sits on a porch swing talking with Sister Eve, a tent revivalist and healer who can look into a person's past, and their heart, by touching their hands. As they gently swing back and forth on the porch, Odie asks with fear, "What about me? What do I want?" Sister Eve's reply: "You're the easiest of all, Odie. The only thing you've ever wanted is home."[2]

Odie is not alone. Home is the place where we experience life as it *ought* to be. Home is a metaphor to help us picture the deep human longing for perfect, meaningful happiness. It's the one thing we all seek, even when we've lost everything else. It's the one thing that can make us whole. In this chapter, we'll explore the quest for meaningful happiness with Lady Philosophy and Boethius as our guides. We'll return to Boethius's prison cell, which was introduced in chapter 5, as he wrestles with our questions: What remains when everything else you once possessed is stripped away? Is happiness still possible? If so, where can it be found?

Boethius's (and Our) Lament

Like Odie, Boethius lost almost everything. All that remained was for him to die. Sitting in that lonely prison cell, lamenting his misfortune, Boethius seemed beyond consolation. Adding to the pain, the wicked seemed to prosper. Why were the cheats, the criminals, and the unjust happy? It didn't make sense. Boethius's lament is ours too. We long for happiness, yet it remains elusive. And if our social media feeds are accurate, it seems everyone else has found what we lack: a picture-perfect, happy life.

At the risk of personal embarrassment, I'll share a bit of my life story. I grew up in middle-class suburbia. As a child, I had everything I needed, and most everything I wanted. Still, I longed for more. In high school, I noticed social strata developing, and I didn't like the layer in which I found myself. The jocks, the lookers, and the rich—and the smart kids who happened to also be jocks, lookers, or rich—were part of the "in" crowd, the upper crust who basked in the warmth of notoriety and the crisp air of privilege; this was our high school version of fame and fortune. The rest of us were left to eke out an existence in the lower strata: the clay pits of the Future Business Leaders of America, student council, or the yearbook committee; the coal swamps of drama, chess, or art club; and the sand dunes of study groups, church youth groups, band, or choir.

In my mind, I wasn't as bad off as I might have been. I wasn't a total loser, or even a loser. Occasionally, I was admitted into the circle of cool people. I was a decent athlete with average intelligence, a pleasing personality, and not abhorrent looks. I tasted glory. But at the end of the day, I remained on the outside.

I became obsessed with getting in. (And now the embarrassing part.) I wrote out lists of popular people whom I wanted to befriend. I lifted weights to gain strength and all the right body angles. I dressed to impress. I associated with the cool people and cooled to my friends who weren't. I worked to become a straight-A student instead of a bland B student. At the top of my lists and plans, I wrote "#1." This was my goal: not just to get into the inner circle but to be *the best*. *Then* I would make it. *Then* I would be happy.

My plan worked, sort of. For the last two years of high school, I got straight As. I had a string of girlfriends and consistently spent more time with the cool crowd. But I was never fully accepted. Happiness remained elusive. I could see it, but like a perpetually receding end zone, it was always ten yards away.

The pursuit continued into college. As a freshman, my three priorities were grades, girls, and galas.[3] I thought if I could do well in school, I'd one day land that big job. In turn, I'd one day have that big house and nice car. My obsession with girls was connected to my desire for sensual pleasure and (eventually) personal satisfaction through marriage. My love of parties was fueled by my desire to be known. I bought into the aphorism that life is all about who you know and who knows you. I wanted it all—fame and fortune—and I was willing to work hard to get it. Then, finally, I'd find happiness. Right?

My life as a young man was characterized by this pursuit of happiness. I could have told this story with fewer embarrassing details, but I wanted you to see it for what it was, because I don't think I'm alone in this frantic pursuit. The details of your life and the lists you keep will be different, but the longing is the same. As Lady Philosophy put it to Boethius, "In all the care with which they toil at countless enterprises, moral men travel by different paths, through all striving to reach one and the same goal, namely happiness, beatitude, which is a good which once obtained leaves nothing more to be desired."[4]

This seems right to me. We all long for meaningful happiness. We long for our true home. Like my younger self, we seek it with a sense of desperation; we think, *If only I get that job or that raise, or meet that person, or purchase that house or that boat or* . . . Most of us have so much, yet we want more. Boethius once had it all, and he thought he had happiness. But he didn't. He was about to find out why. Boethius was heartsick, not because he'd been stripped of all his earthly possessions but because he thought happiness was found in them. Lady Philosophy diagnosed Boethius's main problem: "You have forgotten your true nature."[5] And worse, he'd forgotten his true name. The real tragedy of Boethius's circumstance, according to Lady Philosophy, is that he'd forgotten where true happiness lay. Most of us, like him, have no clue. Let's listen in as Lady Philosophy applies the balm of reason to soothe Boethius's lamenting heart—and ours too.[6] Maybe, just maybe, genuine happiness is possible. But first, we've got to rule out some counterfeits. We begin with the idea that money can buy happiness.

Wealth

I felt a bit sheepish as our minivan packed with three generations of Goulds pulled up to the front gate at the Breakers Hotel on Palm Beach Island. Leaning out my window, I asked the guard where I could park. The guard saw through my charade. I clearly didn't belong. More meekly, I added, "We want to walk the grounds and get a drink." In that moment, I determined to purchase the family some drinks. Calculating how much money I'd have to drop to buy six Cokes, I thought, *What the heck? A small price to taste the good life.* The guard reluctantly let us in, directing me to a side lot. We walked the 105-acre resort for about an hour, taking in the beauty, opulence, and sense of privilege that comes with money. Walking back to our car, passing Ferraris, Bentleys, Teslas, and Aston Martins, we laughed, exclaiming as we piled into our ride, "Wow, look at this car—a minivan!" We triumphantly drove away without spending a dime. I couldn't bring myself to spend $10 on a Coke, so instead we settled for ice cream on the way home.

Reflecting on this little adventure across to "the Island," I found myself wondering if money really could bring happiness. Everyone *seemed* happy sipping lattes and reading the Sunday paper on $300 rented pool chairs. Not only did wealth buffer them from the ravages of life; it also allowed them to enjoy the many good things life has to offer. They were self-sufficient, independent, happy creatures, or so it seemed to me.

Boethius would have fit in at the Breakers. I like imagining him as a proud owner of a row of Lamborghinis and Ferraris. But as he sat in that lonely cell, stripped of wealth and possessions, he imagined Lady Philosophy beginning to press him on the connection between money and happiness:

> "So first I will ask you a few questions, since you yourself were a wealthy man not long ago. In the midst of all that great store of wealth, was your mind never troubled by worry arising from a feeling that something was wrong?"
>
> "Yes it was," I replied; "in fact I can't remember when my mind was ever free from some sort of worry.". . .
>
> "And so you felt this insufficiency even though you were supplied with wealth?"
>
> "Yes, I did."
>
> "So that wealth cannot make a man free of want and self-sufficient, though this was the very promise we saw it offering."[7]

In the end, money failed Boethius. When he had it, it didn't fully satisfy. Moreover, being wealthy can create new needs and worries, including dependency on others to maintain and protect the wealth (as witnessed by the many wealth-management companies on Palm Beach Island) and, at least in our day, the guilt that comes with being one of the "haves" in a "have-not" world.[8] Money can—and often does—make us more anxious, depressed, and self-centered. According to empirical evidence, the "dark side of the American Dream" is that those who prioritize the pursuit of "'extrinsic goals' such as fame, fortune, or glamour . . . tend to experience more anxiety and depression and lower overall well-being than people oriented towards 'intrinsic goals' of close relationships, self-acceptance and contributing to the community."[9] Money is necessary to meet basic needs and to help us enjoy many good things. But if we make the pursuit and accumulation of wealth our goal, we'll be left unsatisfied. Lady

Philosophy concludes, "If you say that rich people do have the means of satisfying hunger and driving away thirst and cold, I will reply that although want can be checked in this way by riches, it can't be entirely removed."[10]

Self-sufficiency is a valuable good; it is a constituent of happiness. But since money and things can't make us self-sufficient, and since having too much money and things can decrease our well-being, they can't be what makes us happy. In his 2005 commencement address at Kenyon College, David Foster Wallace warned of the high cost of placing our faith in money and things: "If you worship money and things—if they are where you tap real meaning in life—then you will never have enough."[11] Money can't lead us home.

Success

I didn't grow up wanting to be a philosopher. Granted, I didn't know there were paying jobs for thinking really hard about life's deepest questions. My interests were more concrete. I grew up watching my dad run a factory. I liked the idea of being in charge of a place that made widgets and whatnots. I followed in my dad's footsteps, majoring in business as an undergraduate and then landing a job in a public accounting firm. As a young CPA, my job was to audit the financial books of manufacturing companies. I'd secured my dream job. And I looked the part too: each day, wearing an Armani look-alike suit and carrying a leather briefcase full of pens, a stapler, a calculator, and financial ledgers, I'd strut into a client's office with a deep sense of importance. I was climbing the ladder of success and loving the climb. In fact, I was so wrapped up in my work that I read Eli Goldratt's novel *The Goal* to Ethel on our honeymoon. I know what you are thinking: *How romantic. He reads to his wife.* Manufacturing theory is in fact not very seductive. Thankfully, Ethel loved the fictional story Goldratt weaves throughout the how-to-build-widgets-and-whatnots-efficiently book. At least that's what she said at the time.

Upon reflection, she probably was being gracious and kind. (And love-struck. Newlyweds can do little wrong, I suspect.) The point is that my work defined me. It gave me an identity. I was a Certified Public Accountant. I wore power suits. It was only a matter of time, I reasoned, before I'd be running a company. Success was on the horizon, and with it, happiness.

In our hyperindividualistic culture, people often explicitly or implicitly regard achievement, status, and success as life's highest goals. Consider a recent study by the Harvard Graduate School of Education. When asked if their parents cared more about being kind to others or about personal success, eighty percent of ten thousand middle and high school students said their parents cared more about success.[12]

Let's return to Boethius and his discussion with Lady Philosophy. She considers whether the attainment of high office or power—in modern parlance, *success*—brings happiness. Lady Philosophy asks Boethius, "Can being a king or being the friend of a king give a man power? If the answer is 'Yes, because their happiness endures uninterrupted,' I shall reply that history, and our own times too, is full of examples of kings who exchanged happiness for ruin. What a splendid thing power is, when we find it insufficient even for its own preservation!"[13] The point is that power and rank are fleeting. If success is happiness, happiness is fleeting too.

Worse, when we achieve personal success of some kind, we soon discover it was not the thing we longed for after all. As Lady Philosophy queried, "What is this power, then, which cannot banish the nagging of worry or avoid the pin-prick of fear?"[14] The question is rhetorical. Power and personal success can't make us whole. If we worship at the altar of success, we'll become an empty, flat self. David Brooks explains the soul-flattening effect of frenetic workaholism:

> Suddenly your conversation consists mostly of descriptions of how busy you are. Suddenly you're a chilly mortal, going into hyper-

people-pleasing mode anytime you're around your boss. You spend much of your time mentor shopping, trying to find some successful older person who will answer all your questions and solve all your problems. It turns out that the people in your workplace don't want you to have a deep, fulfilling life. They give you gold stars of affirmation every time you mold yourself into the shrewd animal the workplace wants you to be. . . . You begin to view yourself not as a soul to be uplifted but as a set of skills to be maximized.[15]

If we aim at success, we'll become an "insecure overachiever."[16] Our constant striving "encourages [us] to drift into a life that society loves but which [we] don't." As Brooks concludes, "It's impossible to feel wholehearted" if we think that personal success will satisfy our hearts' deepest longings for meaningful happiness.[17] It may be, as we'll see below, an ingredient of meaningful happiness, but it is not the thing that will make us happy.

Fame

As a teenager, I didn't want others to know I carefully crafted my public image. In high school, I formed a band aptly named Who Cares? Obviously, I did. A lot. I wanted to be known. Unfortunately, our band wasn't very good. My quest for musical godhood was short-lived, ending after a couple failed gigs at high school dances. But my longing to make a name for myself didn't go away; it was just redirected. Eventually, I found my way into academics. My first full-time job as a philosophy professor was at a seminary in Texas. In some circles, this is a big deal. Whenever I went to speak at another university, the red carpet was rolled out. I was somebody important. I had a platform. People wanted to hear from me. I had finally achieved a modicum of that elusive fame I longed for as a teenager.

Then I lost my job. Everything changed. The invitations ceased. Instead of red carpets, I walked the desert of obscurity and irrelevance. My two years in academic purgatory (i.e., my two years languishing on the job market) were challenging times for me and my family. I had learned by then that fame, however it's defined, doesn't bring happiness. Crowds are fickle. One moment they'll adore you; the next, they'll ignore or abhor you. Our platforms aren't firm-enough foundations on which to build our lives and rest our hopes. Fame cannot make us whole.

I'm a philosophy professor again, but I'm more aware of the subtle allure of fame. "You're Paul Gould. You're an author. You're a professor. Look at your social media following." All of these claims subtly feed the ego. They whisper, "Fame is happiness." I now see this idea for what it is: an empty yet alluring falsehood.

The pursuit of fame for fame's sake, or for happiness's sake, is "a shameful thing," according to Lady Philosophy.[18] The idea that fame brings happiness is another dead end, barely "worth mentioning" except for the fact that many think it worth pursuing.[19] From the widest perspective, *sub specie aeternitatis*, we might ask: What does fame offer? Lady Philosophy begins, "But just think how puny and insubstantial such fame really is." The earth is a tiny speck of rock in a remote outpost of a mediocre galaxy in the midst of a vast, expanding universe. Consider the earth: even here, humans inhabit "scarcely the smallest of regions," a "tiny point within a point."[20] Moreover, our lives on earth are a mere moment: "When compared with unending eternity it is shown to be not just little, but nothing at all."[21] So whatever degree of fame we might attain in this life, from the perspective of eternity it is insignificant. This is why Lady Philosophy thinks the idea that fame is a means to happiness is barely worth mentioning. It doesn't make us happy. "Its acquisition is fortuitous and its retention continuously uncertain."[22]

The problem is that fame is "so often deceptive."[23] It offers us glory but in the end consumes us. In actor Jim Carrey's semiautobiographical novel *Memoirs and Misinformation*, Jim Carrey (the fictional character) is talking with the director Lonnie Lonstein about unfettered capitalism and celebrity culture. Lonstein remarks that celebrity, like capitalism, "yearns for its own destruction. . . . I think that's why you all eat, at the end. . . . Elvis. Liz Taylor. Bardot. Brando. All the real greats gorge toward the end." With "a long cheese strand hanging from his chin," Carrey weakly replies, "Thanks?"[24] The fictional Carrey realizes something the real Carrey already knows: fame doesn't satisfy the heart's deepest longing for meaningful happiness. In a 2014 commencement speech, Carrey observed, "I wish people could realize all their dreams and wealth and fame so that they could see that it's not where you're going to find your sense of completion."[25] Fame, like wealth and success, will never be enough; it will never make us whole; it won't lead us home.

Pleasure

Suppose you could plug into a machine that would simulate any experience you want: the rapture of sex, the thrill of a drug-induced high, the multilayered fullness of an 1896 Château Chalon, the grandeur of reading—or writing—a novel, the sublimity of a Beethoven symphony *and* the riot of a punk-rock concert, the exhilaration of summiting Everest, the satisfaction of winning the Boston Marathon, the sacredness of becoming a parent, and so on. The philosopher Robert Nozick famously asks, "Should you plug into this machine for life, preprogramming your life's experiences?"[26] Should you? Would you? Nozick thinks we shouldn't plug ourselves into the machine, for three reasons:

> First, we want to *do* certain things, and not just have the experience of doing them. . . . A second reason for not plugging in is that we want to *be* a certain way, to be a certain sort of person. Someone floating in a tank is an indeterminate blob. . . . Thirdly, plugging into an experience machine limits us to a man-made reality, to a world no deeper or more important than that which people can construct. There is no *actual* contact with any deeper reality, though the experience of it can be simulated. Many persons desire to leave themselves open to such contact and to a plumbing of deeper significance.[27]

I agree with Nozick. I want to summit a mountain, not merely *experience* summiting a mountain. I want to write this book, not merely have the *experience* of writing this book. (The experience of writing a book, for me, isn't all that pleasurable anyhow. I take joy in the finished product.) Regarding Nozick's third point, I want to be rightly related to reality, not a simulacrum of reality. What about you? Would you plug into the experience machine? If you wouldn't, then you've made an important discovery. Many today think that happiness is chiefly found through the *experience* of pleasure. Happiness is the maximization of pleasure and the minimization of pain, according to the nineteeth-century philosopher John Stuart Mill.[28] But this idea is false. Pleasure might be an ingredient in meaningful happiness, but it is not equivalent to happiness. Otherwise, why not plug in to the experience machine and enjoy?

Lady Philosophy has little patience for the idea that happiness is found in pleasure. The fact that pleasure doesn't bring happiness is "known to everyone who cares to recall his own excesses."[29] It's time to be blunt: if your goal in life is to go from one experience of pleasure to another—that is, to live a hedonistic lifestyle— you'll never find rest. At best, as Lady Philosophy indicates, you'll become anxious. At worst, your life will be full of remorse. Philosopher Blaise Pascal puts it this way: "Present pleasures are false, . . . absent pleasures are vain."[30] The pursuit of pleasure *as the end* will leave you dissatisfied.

Yet hedonism seems attractive. After all, we are bodily creatures, wired for pleasure. Why not turn the pleasure dial to maximum? The lives, and often early deaths, of those who have done so tell a different story.[31] Consider the lead singer of the Red Hot Chili Peppers, Anthony Kiedis. Aptly described as a modern-day hedonist, Kiedis has experienced the pleasures of life in spades: drugs, alcohol, sex, fame, beauty, wealth, and more, pursued with a reckless fervor and abandon. If pleasure brings happiness, then Kiedis should be among the happiest people on earth. But a sober-minded reading of his autobiography, *Scar Tissue*, reveals a more complex picture. In one poignant passage, Kiedis describes both the thrill and the high cost, in the end, of addiction: "Once you put that first drug or drink in your body, you don't have to worry about the girlfriend or the career or the family or the bills. All those mundane aspects of life disappear. Now you have one job, and that's to keep chucking the coal in the engine, because you don't want this train to stop. If it stops, then you're going to have to feel all that other s[—]. "Pleasure can buffer us, for a time, from the pains and anxieties of life. But the relentless pursuit of pleasure enslaves us. For Kiedis, the demon was drugs: "You immediately give up your love and your light and your beauty, and you become a dark black hole in the universe, sucking up bad energy and not walking around putting a smile on someone's face or helping someone out or teaching someone something that's going to help his or her life. You're not creating the ripple of love; you're creating the vacuum of s[—]. . . . In the end all the romantic glorification of dope fiendery amounts to nothing but a hole of s[—]."[32]

Pleasure, like wealth, fame, and success, might be an ingredient in happiness, but it is not the thing our hearts long for most deeply. Pleasure cannot lead us home. Hedonism doesn't usher us into an Elysian field, only a "dark black hole in the universe."

Home

Lady Philosophy continues, "There is no doubt, then, that these roads to happiness are side-tracks and cannot bring us to the destination they promise."[33] Having cleared away the dead ends, "the next thing is to show what true happiness is like."[34] Where can true happiness be found? The answer Lady Philosophy arrives at can be summarized like this: Human happiness is found by being united to perfect happiness, and perfect happiness is one and the same with God.[35] The discussion has led us to another important discovery: the happiness we seek cannot be found in this world—or better phrased, *merely* in this world. Our restlessness, our constant striving, and our "road-hunger" should tip us off.[36] We were made for a distant land, another shore. Our sense of "not-at-homeness" has propelled us on this journey, and we travel in *hope*.[37] We travel in search of our true home. Our deliberations suggest that finite things can't satisfy the human heart. As Wallace put it: "Everybody worships. The only choice we get is *what* to worship. And an outstanding reason for choosing some sort of god or spiritual-type thing to worship—be it J. C. or Allah, be it Yahweh or the Wiccan mother-goddess or the Four Noble Truths or some infrangible set of ethical principles—is that pretty much anything else you worship will eat you alive."[38]

Let me state the idea in my own words. Perfect happiness has four basic components. First and most fundamentally, happiness is found in being rightly related to God (Boethius's perfect happiness). This is our highest good and our deepest desire. Why? Because happiness is being fully known and fully loved, and only God has the capacity to provide both. Second, happiness consists in right relations with others and the world around us. Why? Because happiness obtains when harmonious and just relations with others obtain. Third, happiness is found in a right relationship with self. Why? Because happiness is found in being whole, being a certain kind of person, a virtuous person whose thinking, willing, and actions are all pointed in the same (good) direction. And finally, happiness is found by being rightly related to our end, our telos, our purpose. Why? Because God created us to flourish in light of our nature. We were made to find rest in God; we journey to God, and this is where we find our home. On this view, happiness is a *relational* good: being rightly related to God, others, self, and our end. This is what human flourishing looks like.

What of wealth, success, fame, and pleasure? These are all good things, both ingredients in and the results or overflow of perfect happiness. But each is transformed in Boethius's vision. On the Christian version of theism, we all, as image bearers, are rich beyond our wildest dreams: everything is gift, everything is ours to steward and enjoy in creaturely response. The success we aim at is to complete our journey and find our way home. The fame we attain, as C. S. Lewis describes in his essay "The Weight of Glory," is the fame or weight given to us by God in heaven such that we become an ingredient in God's happiness.[39] Finally, the happy life is a pleasurable life, because in the Christian vision of things we are able to connect pleasure with meaning, which results in joy.

While the Red Hot Chili Peppers didn't mean it in quite this way, there is a deep truth lurking within their song "Give It Away": we find meaningful happiness, true life, when we cease striving and find our life not in self and the things of this world but in Another—when we "give it away, give it away, give it away now." As Jesus put it, "Whoever wants to save their life will lose it, but whoever loses their life for me will find it" (Matt. 16:25). It is right and good that we seek happiness. It is also important, however, to be clear about what happiness is and what it isn't. In the Christian story, the home we've always wanted is with God.

8

Pain

Nature shows us no particular favors: we get parasites and
diseases and we die, and we are not all that nice to each other.
True, we are moderately clever, but our efforts to use our
intelligence . . . quite often backfire. . . . That, more or less, is
the scientific picture of the world.

—Simon Blackburn, "An Unbeautiful Mind"

Why, God?

—Every human heart

Let's rest for a moment and consider our journey so far. I've
argued that God is the best explanation for the origin of Life,
the Universe, and Everything. We've explored the contours of the
human heart, noting that morality and meaningful happiness are
possible. We've listened to Lady Nature and Lady Philosophy and
interacted with a number of fellow travelers on the way. We seem
to be making good progress. We've journeyed through time and
space and into the human heart. Thus far, the clues point to the
religious story, perhaps even the Christian story, as the true story of

the world. The stones are stacking up, leading us toward a happy end. But we're not home yet. We're still on the road.

As we rest, let's survey the landscape. What do you see? Have we missed anything? Off in the distance I see dust. Just down the road, over there. It's coming toward us. Do you see it? Closer now, human shapes come into focus. It's a group of weary travelers. They seem to be yelling. Maybe the road is closed ahead. Have we traveled this far only to be turned around? Is the way unpassable? Closer still, among the formidable group I spy Voltaire and maybe David Hume (being rather big, he's hard to miss, after all). Let's see what they have to say.

Voltaire is the first to greet us. "Turn around. This road cannot be the way home. It is too painful, too difficult, too full of misery and unspeakable horror." I've heard this before. But looking at Voltaire, along with the impressive band by his side, I can't ignore the question of pain and suffering. We have to give these travelers a say if we are to discover the true story of the world. There are many, such as Voltaire, who think that pain and suffering make it highly unlikely there is a God. Voltaire hands me his book *Candide*, which he wrote after witnessing the horror of the Great Earthquake of 1755 in Lisbon, Portugal. He finds it inconceivable that this world is lovingly created and sustained by a good and powerful God. Voltaire's story takes us on a satirical journey with Candide, the young ward of the Baron of Thunder-ten-tronckh, a fictional Westphalian town. Candide's tutor, the philosopher and theologian Pangloss, argues that this is the best of all possible worlds:

> Since everything was designed for a purpose, everything is necessarily meant to serve the best of all purposes. Observe how noses are designed to hold up eyeglasses, and therefore we have eyeglasses. Legs are obviously meant for wearing shoes, and so we have shoes. Rocks having been designed to be quarried and used for building purposes, the Baron has a singularly beautiful mansion. The greatest Baron in Westphalia requires the greatest dwelling—and

because pigs were made to be eaten, we dine on pork all year long. Accordingly, those who have suggested that everything is good have spoken obtusely: what they should have said is that everything is for the best.[1]

Voltaire is making a serious, if humorous, point as he explores Pangloss's view. Just as it is absurd to think the nose is made for glasses, legs for stockings, and pigs for pork, it is absurd to think that everything in this world is made by God for some good and noble purpose. If God exists and designed things as they are for some end or purpose (as I've argued), then it seems this is the best possible world (as Leibniz argued). But Voltaire and many others have argued that this *doesn't* seem like the best possible world. In fact, it seems like a pretty cruel world. Voltaire puts the Panglossian creed to the test, and as the story's hero is thrown out of the frying pan of one horror into the fire of another time and time again, the idea that this is the best possible world begins to ring hollow. No one is actually happy. Life is full of pain and suffering, and so Candide concedes by the story's end that the best we can do is to "work our fields" without thinking in order to tolerate this life.[2]

In this chapter, we'll consider the arguments of some fellow travelers like Voltaire and Hume, whom I respect, although I think that in the end they are wrong. Do pain and suffering give us reason to think God doesn't exist? In order to keep this question as concrete as possible, I'll venture back into my own story and my own experience of pain and suffering to see what we might discover about the true story of the world.

Facing Pain

I've lectured for years on the problem of evil. In class after class, I've set up the argument from evil to God's nonexistence and happily shown my students where each version of the argument goes wrong. I've pointed to free will, the idea of the greater good, the

133

concept of soul building (i.e., that suffering produces moral character), and more to show that there is no logical contradiction to the reality of God and evil. I've argued that there is no good reason to think that the amount, distribution, or intensity of pain and suffering make it unlikely that God exists. I've upheld the premises of what are now called the *logical* and *evidential* arguments from evil at arm's length and dispassionately argued that evil doesn't render belief in God irrational. To the contrary, I usually conclude that if there is no God, then there is no *objective* evil. Evil is only a problem for the atheist!

I still believe all of that—but I'd never experienced much pain or suffering myself. The question of pain and suffering was something I approached abstractly, in the way I might approach a math problem. It was a puzzle to be solved, a brain-teaser to untie. I'd never really experienced deep pain or loss until I lost that job as a philosophy professor a few years ago. My identity was bound up with my role as a philosophy professor. When I lost that job, I felt like I lost myself. And it hurt. Deeply. Existentially. Painfully. I couldn't eat or sleep. I lost about fifteen pounds in a week. I had lost a deep desire of the heart—the desire to be a professor—and all my other desires seemed to drain away with it.

During that time, I was reading a book on pain and suffering by the philosopher Eleonore Stump. *Wandering in Darkness* is a rigorous, deeply nourishing discussion of the question of God and suffering. I found Stump's work illuminating and comforting. She points to and names something I had missed in my years of teaching on the problem of pain: when you lose a deep desire of the heart, many of your other desires fade away too. And then Stump names the new experience I was in the midst of: heartbreak. I realized in that moment, reading this work in philosophy, that I was heartbroken.[3] I had never experienced heartbreak. I didn't know, experientially or cognitively, that heartbreak was a real thing. I certainly didn't know its feel, its phenomenology, until that moment. I was learning a deep truth about the human condition. And yes, I'm embarrassed that my experience of heartbreak barely registers on the scale of human misery—but pain is still pain, and loss is still loss to the person experiencing it.

I noticed something more startling. I began to look at people with a different set of eyes as I walked around the grocery store or surveyed faces at a coffee shop. I saw heartbreak on other people's faces. The problem of evil—which is the problem of pain and suffering—took on new meaning. It was now also an existential reality for me, and I realized with greater appreciation that this is true for many, many others. Voltaire, that great "destroyer of optimism," is not wrong to press the theist.[4]

The pain, suffering, and loss we experience in life hurt. Your pain, suffering, and loss hurt. I want to approach the question not simply as an objection to be answered or a problem to be solved (although we'll consider the problems raised by pain and suffering) but as a clue to the meaning of our story. What do pain and suffering tell us, or teach us, about the true story of the world? Do they give us reason to think God doesn't exist? Let's tread carefully, bearing the weight of our pain together, as we consider the evidential implications of suffering. Serious-minded atheists have a genuine complaint. Let's have a listen. Hume, what say you?

The Consistency Problem

Pain and suffering—what is often called "evil"—are an "ought-not-to-be, an 'Oh, no!'"[5] Evil is an alien intruder, or so it seems. It doesn't belong in this world, especially if God exists. Yet there is evil. So, we have a problem. The problem is how to consistently hold together the horror of evil and the belief in a good and powerful God. The great Scottish skeptic David Hume crystalizes the problem in his *Dialogues concerning Natural Religion* (published posthumously in 1779).[6] Through the character Philo, Hume raises two worries. The first concerns the *consistency* of theism given the reality of evil; the second concerns what we can *infer* about the true story of the world from the reality of evil.

135

We'll consider the second worry when we explore the evidential problem of evil in the next section.

In Philo's words, the consistency worry is as follows: "*Epicurus'* old questions are yet unanswered. Is he willing to prevent evil, but not able? Then is he impotent. Is he able, but not willing? Then is he malevolent. Is he both able and willing? Whence then is evil?"[7] Hume is advancing the logical problem of evil. The idea is that the propositions "God exists" and "Evil exists" are inconsistent. They can't both be true. But obviously evil exists, so the other proposition, "God exists," must go. The apparent contradiction isn't immediately obvious, however. But it doesn't take much to make the contradictory nature of God and evil explicit.

Remember our definition of God, which we discussed in the introduction: "God" is *an immaterial personal being that is worthy of worship*. Hume asserts that beings considered worthy of worship share two common attributes: omnipotence (they are regarded as all-powerful) and omnibenevolence (they are regarded as wholly good). A less than maximally powerful deity, or a less than perfectly good deity, is not worthy of worship. Hence, if God exists, God is all-powerful and perfectly good.

Fair enough. Now we are in a position to see the inconsistency more clearly. "God exists" entails that "God is omnipotent" and "God is omnibenevolent." But as Hume suggests, "God is omnipotent" entails that "God is able to prevent evil," and "God is omnibenevolent" entails that "God is willing to prevent evil." So if God is *willing* to prevent evil and God is *able* to prevent evil, there would be no evil. But evil exists. Hence, there is a contradiction between "God exists" and "Evil exists."

In reply, I do not think the logical problem of evil succeeds. The reason is that the argument's more fine-grained propositions about God are not necessarily true. I'll focus on one proposition within our set, the proposition that God is able to prevent evil. This proposition is thought to flow from the idea that God is all-powerful. But omnipotence doesn't entail that God can do anything whatsoever. There are many things an omnipotent God can't do; remember, our idea of God includes being worthy of worship, so all the attributes of God need to hang together in the right way. Here are two kinds of things an omnipotent God, a personal being worthy of our worship, cannot do. First, God cannot do the logically impossible because that goes against his perfect rationality. (Familiar examples include creating square circles, creating married bachelors, and making it the case that both "God exists" and "God does not exist," a logical contradiction, are true.). Second, God cannot do anything that goes against his perfect goodness. (Familiar examples include lying, breaking a promise, and murder.)

Let's return to our proposition that God is able to prevent evil. Here is one way that this might be false: Suppose God creates free beings, beings with morally significant freedom over their actions, characters, and life stories. If God creates such beings, could God also prevent them from misusing their freedom? There are good reasons to think the answer is no. If God were to prevent free beings from misusing their freedom, then they are not actually free in a morally significant way. This imagined state of affairs, in other words, is logically impossible. God cannot cause *free* creatures to do only what is morally good.[8] The claim that omnipotence entails that "God is able to prevent evil" is not an absolute or strict entailment. There is a suppressed "unless" in the claim: "God is able to prevent evil *unless he creates significantly free creatures.*" If God creates significantly free creatures, then it is not the case that "God is able to prevent evil." Since it is possible that God creates such creatures, then there is no logical contradiction between the propositions "God exists" and "Evil exists."[9]

To show that it is logically possible for God and evil to coexist isn't that hard to do. Even Hume was willing to accept the bare logical possibility of God and evil: "I will allow that pain or misery in man is *compatible* with infinite power and goodness in the Deity, even in your sense of these attributes." Still, Hume presses: "What are you advanced by all these concessions? A mere possible compatibility is not sufficient."[10] I agree with Hume. Our work is not done. It is not enough to show the mere possibility of logical consistency between the propositions "God exists" and "Evil exists." We want to know if it is possible to hold together with real integrity and plausibility the horrendous, corrosive reality of evil and the goodness of a world created by God. If God exists, what actual reason or reasons does he have for allowing pain and suffering? Or as Hume frames the question, From the fact that there is pain and suffering—and lots of them—in this world, what should we infer about the cause of this world?

The Inference Problem

Hume's argument is empirical. It begins by considering actual cases of pain and suffering in the world: "Look round this universe. What an immense profusion of beings, animated and organized, sensible and active! You admire this prodigious variety and fecundity. But inspect a little more narrowly these living existences, the only beings worth regarding. How hostile and destructive to each other! How insufficient all of them for their own happiness! How contemptible or odious to the spectator! The whole presents nothing but the idea of blind nature, impregnated by a great vivifying principle, and pouring forth from her lap, without discernment or parental care, her maimed and abortive children!"[11]

What should we infer about the nature of the world and the cause behind the world from the observed reality of pain and suffering? Does evil give us reason to infer a good and powerful God? Or does evil give us reason to infer that nature is indifferent to living creatures? The inference problem is not about logical consistency. Rather, the question has to do with *probability*: What ought we to reasonably (but not inescapably) infer, given evil? Hume continues: "There may *four* hypotheses be framed concerning the first causes of the universe: *that* they are endowed with perfect goodness; *that* they have perfect malice; *that* they are opposite and have both goodness and malice; *that* they have neither goodness nor malice. Mixed phenomena can never prove the two former unmixed principles; and the uniformity and steadiness of general laws seem opposed to the third. The fourth, therefore, seems by far the most probable."[12] The world is a mixed bag of good and evil, joy and despair, peace and discord. But when we consider the condition of living creatures, the universe appears cold, cruel, and hostile. Given the amount, distribution, intensity, and horror of pain and suffering, Hume thinks it's most likely that the universe is indifferent to living creatures, including humans.

In more recent times, the philosopher Paul Draper has advanced a powerful challenge to belief in God given the reality of pain and suffering. I'm very interested in what Draper has to say. He joined the philosophy faculty at Purdue University while I was a graduate student there. During his interview he spoke to a group of faculty and graduate students on the topic "Why I am not a theist." Draper struck me as someone following the evidence wherever it might lead. As he said to me and a group of fellow graduate students on the way to lunch after that talk (here I'm paraphrasing from memory), "I hope there is a God. I don't understand those who wish there wasn't a God. I just don't think the evidence points to the reality of God." That made sense to me. I could follow this man. I wanted to hear what he had to say. So, let's consider Draper's argument (inspired by Hume) from pain and pleasure to God's probable nonexistence, as discussed in Draper's famous 1989 essay, "Pain and Pleasure: An Evidential Problem for Theists."[13]

Recall Hume's fourth hypothesis regarding the first causes of the universe: "*that* they have neither goodness nor malice." Draper formalizes this hypothesis as the "hypothesis of indifference" (HI): "Neither the nature nor the condition of sentient beings on earth is the result of benevolent or malevolent actions performed by non-human persons."[14]

HI is consistent with the nonreligious story, including the naturalistic story. It is also consistent with some versions of supernaturalism, including those versions that allow for an all-powerful and all-knowing (but not wholly good) Creator. HI is incompatible, however, with theism, the idea that an all-powerful, all-knowing, and wholly good being is responsible for the universe. We have two logically incompatible hypotheses then, HI and theism. If it turns out that HI explains the amount, distribution, and intensity of pain and pleasure better than theism does, then there are good reasons to reject theism in favor of a story consistent with HI. Draper argues that the probability of the observed pleasures and pains of sentient creatures on HI is much greater than the probability of the observed pleasures and pains on theism.[15] But then it is more rational, according to Draper, to believe HI instead of theism.

Why think the probability of the observed pleasures and pains of sentient creatures is much greater on HI than on theism? I'll summarize Draper's argument in two steps.[16] Consider first *biologically useful* pains and pleasures. Examples are fairly easy to see. The nerve endings that signal pain when my finger is held over a fire are biologically useful, alerting me to the threat of burning flesh. The pleasure of sex is biologically useful too, producing (subjective) happiness for the individual and continued survival for the species. A biological explanation of pain and pleasure, in terms of survival and reproduction, is just what we'd expect on HI, according to Draper. But not on theism. If God exists, he would have a morally sufficient reason for allowing any particular pain or pleasure. But for all we know, continues Draper, those reasons might be inconsistent with biological utility—after all, an all-powerful God could have created sentient creatures with goal-directed biological systems but without biologically useful pain and pleasure. According to Draper, then, on HI we expect pleasure and pain to be biologically useful, and on theism we don't. Since we're here considering the observed pleasures and pains that are biologically useful, it follows that the probability of these observations on HI is much greater than on theism.

Second, consider the pleasures and pains that are *not* biologically useful, or that are not known to be. Given what we already have observed about biologically useful pleasure and pain, and given that many sentient creatures are (overall) not happy and that much pleasure and pain seems to be "a biological accident resulting from nature's or an indifferent creator's failure to 'fine tune' organic systems,"[17] it follows, again, that HI is much more probable than theism. In sum, the rational thing to do, given the observed pain and pleasure in the world, is to infer the hypothesis of indifference; as Hume colorfully put it, "The whole presents nothing but the idea of blind nature."[18]

But there are at least three arguments against Draper's HI. First, when we consider the full scope of human experience, it is not obvious that the observed *biologically useful* pleasures and pains are more probable on HI than on theism. As the philosopher Alvin Plantinga has noted, many human activities do not contribute—at least, not obviously or directly—to survival and reproduction, yet are central to human life; he lists "literature, poetry, music, art, mathematics, logic, philosophy, nuclear physics, evolutionary biology, play, humor, exploration, and adventure." But then, Plantinga comments: "It would not be particularly surprising, so it seems to me, if the distribution of human pleasure and pain did not contribute in [a systematic] way to the biological goals of survival and reproduction."[19] In other words, when we consider the full scope of observed pleasure and pain, the probability of the observed, biologically useful pleasure and pain doesn't seem any greater on the assumption of HI than on the assumption of theism.

Second, it is not obvious that the *biologically gratuitous* pleasure and pain are more probable on HI than on theism. Recall that HI is consistent with either naturalism or the theory that an indifferent power created the universe. On naturalism it is reasonable to think, given the observed biologically useful pleasure and pain of sentient creatures, that all pleasure and pain play a biological role. (For Draper, gratuitous pleasure and pain are either pathological, as in the case of terminal cancer, or biologically appropriate even if useless, such as being burned to death by a fire.) But it is not clear how we ought to adjudicate between the naturalistic thesis and the indifferent creationist thesis with respect to HI. Thus, it is not clear, from my epistemic situation, whether I should judge the probability of biologically gratuitous pleasure and pain on the assumption of HI as greater than, equal to, or lesser than the probability of biologically gratuitous pleasure on the assumption of theism (since we don't know whether HI implies naturalism or indifferent creationism).[20] And as we've already seen, many, perhaps most, of the pleasures and pains of human life are not clearly connected with the biological goals of survival and reproduction. Contrary to Draper's claim, that gives us good reason to doubt that these biologically gratuitious pleasures and pain are more probable on HI than on theism. For all we know, God has nonbiological purposes for pleasure and pain that contribute to human flourishing, character formation, and the like.

Consider also Draper's claims that (1) sentient creatures ought to be happy on theism but not on HI, and (2) generally, creatures are not happy. Both of these claims can be challenged, but for now I'll focus on the second one. We do not know much, if anything, about the internal life of sentient nonhuman creatures, which makes it hard to judge their relative happiness or unhappiness. When it comes to humans, it seems that there is a spectrum: some are mostly happy, some mostly unhappy, and some a mixture throughout their lives.[21] So, it is not clear that creatures aren't at least somewhat happy, subjectively. Further, it is not clear that specific versions of theism entail that creatures ought to be happy. (We'll discuss that below).

Suppose I'm wrong and Draper is right that the observed pleasures and pains of the world are much more probable on the assumption of HI than on theism. There's a final problem: it doesn't follow that HI is the only relevant hypothesis, or the most reasonable hypothesis, to consider. Pleasure and pain are a reality. Most theists are not *mere* theists; they are *Christian, Muslim,* or *Jewish* theists. And this more fine-grained theism matters. For it could be true that the observed pleasure and pain of sentient creatures on HI is much greater than on theism (as Draper argues) *and* false that the probability of the observed pleasure and pain of sentient creatures on HI is much greater than on *Christian* theism. As

Richard Otte observes, "Just because the hypothesis of indifference is a better alternative to mere theism does not mean that the hypothesis of indifference is a better alternative to Christianity, Islam, or Judaism." Otte thinks that any of these fine-grained theisms are a better alternative than the hypothesis of indifference, for they "logically imply that there is evil in this world, and even imply much about the specific evils that occur." Thus, "we can easily argue that Christianity, Islam, or Judaism is a better alternative to the hypothesis of indifference."[22] Consider a core belief of Christianity: that humans have sinned, and as a result the world is broken or fallen. Given this belief, we ought to expect that creatures will suffer and that complete (subjective) happiness will remain elusive in this life. But then, the probability of the observed pleasure and pain in this world on the assumption that Christian theism is true is much greater than the probability of the observed pleasure and pain in this world on the assumption that HI is true.

Observations and testimonies related to pleasure and pain in the world do not justify the inference, as Hume and Draper claim they do, to a kind of *naturalism* or *indifferent creationism*. When we add specific beliefs to theism, such as belief in the fallenness or brokenness of the world, the reality of eternal life (a time when all pain and suffering will be wiped away), and the understanding of creaturely happiness in terms of union with God or heaven, the most rational inference from (pleasure and) pain, I submit, is to one of these more fine-grained versions of theism. Hume and Draper are right to consider alternate explanations for evil. But they were wrong to consider pain (and pleasure) in isolation. We ought to look at the "total hypothesis in question" instead of a subset such as mere theism, and we should look at "the total evidence available" when considering the true story of the world.[23] We should not neglect pain and suffering; they have to figure into any story that aims for truth, given its reality. But we need not look at pain and suffering in isolation. We want to discover the true story of the world, and that story should help make sense of all features of human life, including pain and suffering.

In sum, there is no logical inconsistency between "God exists" and "Evil exists," and it is not the case that we should infer the hypothesis of indifference from the reality of evil. Voltaire, Hume, and Draper were right to wave us down. We need to consider their complaint. But they have not given us a good reason to turn back. We still seem to be heading in the right direction. Before we move on and consider a few other clues or "stones," let's linger a bit longer on the question of pain. Let's focus on one version of theism, Christian theism, and ask, Does it offer any resources to help explain *why* God allows pain and suffering?

The Reason

It's time for a bold claim: I think that there is no pointless evil. All pain and suffering is permitted (not caused) by God for some morally sufficient reason. It's easy to make bold claims but harder to make such claims plausible. How might I back up this claim?

I'm of two minds. One option I find attractive is called *skeptical theism*. The skeptical theist is not skeptical of God's existence; rather, the skeptical theist is doubtful that we are able to discern God's reason for every instance of evil. Remember, the skeptical theist thinks God exists. God is omniscient, which means God knows the beginning of all things, the end of all things, and everything in between. By his wisdom, goodness, and power he governs all things, achieving his ends even while taking into account human free agents and their actions. Humans, on the other hand, are finite and limited creatures. We aren't privy to the whole story. To be blunt, and speaking for myself, we're not even always privy to our own hearts and reasons for acting! It is not unreasonable to think that God's morally sufficient reasons for permitting evil are not currently accessible to us.

But I said I was of *two* minds. I also think that we can discern many of the reasons why God allows evil. I also think that it is possible to discern the reason for evil. My reason is not that I think we're smart enough or creative enough to discern it. Rather,

I think it's possible that God has told us, or at least told us in outline form, why he allows pain and suffering. To give a reason, or *the* reason, for evil, is to provide a *theodicy* (a "God-justifying" reason for evil). I used to be firmly on the skeptical-theist side of the aisle when it came to the question of discerning God's morally sufficient reason for all evil. I've been persuaded by Stump and others, however, that the Bible *may* provide a theodicy, or at least strongly suggest one. Let's consider a possible reason for God's permission of pain and suffering by exploring a way—to me, a compelling way—to hold together with integrity the ideas that all things are created by a good God and that evil is an alien invader. The reasoning that follows is rooted in Stump's work, which is rooted in Aquinas's work, which is rooted in much of the Christian tradition, which is rooted ultimately in the Bible.

The biblical narrative suggests the following two conditions for any successful theodicy.[24] First, for any particular person who suffers, that suffering must produce an outweighing good *for that person*. This is a high bar to set for any successful theodicy. It makes it harder to find a viable reason, or set of reasons, for evil. Second, any successful theodicy must extend beyond this present life. Consider the end of J. R. R. Tolkien's *Lord of the Rings* trilogy. Having defeated the Dark Lord, the ruler of the accursed Rings of Power, Frodo and Sam prepare to return to their beloved Shire, presumably to live happily ever after. But Frodo's journey is not done. In bewilderment, Sam asks: "Where are you going, Master?" "To the Havens, Sam," says Frodo. Tears well up in Sam's eyes. "But, I thought you were going to enjoy the Shire, too, for years and years, after all you have done," he says. Frodo's reply has the feel of a deep truth: "So I thought too, once. But I have been too deeply hurt, Sam. I tried to save the Shire, and it has been saved, but not for me. It must often be so, Sam, when things are in danger: some one has to give them up, lose them, so that others may keep them."[25] Tolkien is riffing on biblical themes relevant to theodicy: There are wounds this world cannot heal. Sometimes our healing requires another's loss. Yet we journey in hope. If evil and suffering are to be defeated, we'll need help from another world.

With these two conditions in place, let's give a thumbnail sketch of a possible reason for pain—a theodicy—informed by the biblical narrative. God wants us to flourish, to be happy in the richest sense of that word, as we discussed at the end of the previous chapter.[26] Moreover, God cares about the deep desires of our heart.[27] He cares about what we care about. So why does God allow suffering? Very simply stated, God allows suffering so that we would flourish. This sounds odd. But recall what happiness looks like on the Christian story: relationship with God, chiefly, and right relationship to everything else secondarily. That means our suffering either brings us closer to God (and to being rightly related to everything else) or prevents us from slipping further away from God (and further into discord with everything else).[28] Free will, of course, is a part of this story, although not the whole story. Freedom allows us to determine our actions, our characters, and our lives. It also can be misused, resulting in much (but not all) of the pain and suffering in the world. Free will helps us see how God permits evil, even as it is an alien intruder. God doesn't want us to do wrong or to suffer, but he allows it, even as he makes provisions to overcome it on our behalf. We are genuine agents who act based on desires. Since our deepest desire is for God, it is possible to weave together all the things we subjectively care about into our objective flourishing too. Even a loss of a deep heart desire—such as my own experience of heartbreak when I lost my job—can be enfolded and reconfigured, without losing its identity, in such a way that evil can be defeated and God can be trusted as perfectly good and loving.[29] We find, then, an attractive theodicy—or at least a thumbnail sketch of an attractive theodicy. It's one that satisfies our two conditions for theodicies in general: our suffering benefits us, and our highest good extends beyond this world.[30]

While I've barely sketched a possible reason for pain (i.e., to contribute to our flourishing), it's a start. It helps us see how a good God might work all things for *my* good, and for *yours* too.

It speaks to the brokenness of this world, the alien nature of evil, and the hope of healing. But since we can't heal ourselves, it also points to what I take to be God's answer to the problem of pain and suffering: *Jesus on a cross*. We'll consider Jesus in more detail in chapter 11. For now, what's important to observe, if I'm right, is that the problem of pain has an intimate connection to the suffering of God, the compassion of God, and the goodness of God. Jesus defeats every "Oh, no!" and "ought-not-to-be" of sin: suffering, pain, and evil. God is not indifferent. God cares. Pain and suffering and evil point us, if we listen, beyond this world to Another.[31]

9

Love

It's an old, old story: I had a friend and we shared everything,
and then she died and so we shared that, too.

—Gail Caldwell, *Let's Take the Long Way Home*

I walk a lonely road . . .
But it's home to me, and I walk alone.

—Green Day,
"Boulevard of Broken Dreams"

I understand fantasy football, sort of. It's fun to imagine your favorite NFL players on the same team. The mix of real life with the imaginary tantalizes, even intoxicates. But fantasy *Bachelor* and *Bachelorette*? I don't understand that. Where's the fun? How do we predict a "winning" couple? Yet, for a few years, my son and a group of his friends would congregate every Monday to watch the latest episode of *The Bachelor* or *The Bachelorette*, rooting for their favorite girl and guy match as predicted within their fantasy league.

Upon further reflection, I do get a bit of the appeal: these shows offer hope. We've always suspected that the premise of the shows is faulty. Twenty-five men or women competing for the love and attention of one woman or man? A recipe for disaster. We know it doesn't

149

work. Yet millions of viewers keep coming back. Why? Because we hope to witness true love. If those beautiful people can find it, maybe we can too. So we select our hoped-for couples, get out the popcorn, and eagerly watch—year after year, season after season, spin-off after spin-off—the Hunger Games of romance. Even if true love remains elusive, we enjoy the chase: drama, lust, quest, beauty, intrigue, plot twist, villainy, heroism, romance, posturing, machismo, and more. We are, it seems, obsessed with love. And sex.

It's time to be honest. Let's peel back the surface of our lives a bit. What else do we find? We find something disturbing—depressing, even, coupled with the obsession with love and sex. There is loneliness, along with brokenness and alienation. "We walk a lonely road," according to Green Day. "But it's home to me, and I walk alone."[1] Some would say this hope for love is irrational. I think it is revealing. Consider the words of Amy Kaufman, author of *Bachelor Nation*: "I get a lot of: 'How can you watch that? It's so bad for women.' But I can't lie—when I watch two people connect, it makes me feel like I can have this someday. It might not be in a helicopter or on a mountain, but I can certainly have a guy make me feel like I'm worthy of love."[2]

Why do we walk this boulevard of broken dreams? Because we hope there is true love "out there" waiting to be found. We long to connect, to be found worthy of love. And we watch. We search. We walk. Yet, for many of us, passionate, romantic, absorbing love remains elusive.

Part of the problem is that we're confused about love's connection to sex, in no small part thanks to technology. In his book *Cheap Sex*, sociologist Mark Regnerus chronicles the technological advances that have made sex more widely available and less valuable. In the 1960s, the advent of the birth control pill decoupled sex from procreation, freeing us to explore sex as a form of artistic expression. In the 1990s and 2000s, the internet made online dating possible and easy and made immediate access to pornography a reality. As a result, "sexual acts themselves can be said to have become comparatively 'cheaper' or less expensive, economically and socially speaking." Regnerus explains: "Coupled sexual activity has become more widely accessible, at lower 'cost' to everyone than ever before in human history. Pregnancy, childbearing, and childrearing are, after all, extremely expensive in terms of time, investment, lost (paid) labor and income. . . . Men have to do less wooing (fewer dates, less costly indicators of commitment, etc.) in order to access real sex. Hence, sex is cheaper."[3]

But cheap sex rarely produces enduring love. We are offered "orgasms with a side of loneliness."[4] In the end, we're more addicted to sex than ever before *and* still miserable and lonely. We're confused too, more than ever, about the nature of love. We watch *The Bachelor* or *The Bachelorette* hoping to find romantic, enduring love. In reality—ours and the shows'—what we most often find is what Regnerus calls "confluent love."[5] This is a contingent, emotionally sustained, "you satisfy me and I'll satisfy you" kind of love. We have more sex, or at least greater access to it, but less of the kind of love our hearts long for most deeply.

It's time to consider what love reveals about the true story of the world. Our first task will be to discern the nature of love. As we'll see, there is a rich diversity of thought on this question. For some, love is a "solution to a strategic interaction problem."[6] For others, love is something heavenly; it is that which "moves the sun and the other stars."[7] Is it animal pleasure, or is it poetry? Once we discover what love is, we'll consider which of our competing stories—theism or atheism—best explains enduring love. We'll end by considering the possibility of God's pursuing love. Let's begin by exploring the nature of love.

Love's Fundamental Affirmation

Traditions shape my family's sense of identity. We have a family chant: "Who are we? Ahhh . . . the Goulds!" ending with fingers pointing at each other and "You're the culprit!" (It's a long story.) We have elaborate birthday, anniversary, and Mother's and Father's Day rituals that include a special "You Are Loved" plate. We have the "what I appreciate about you" dinner conversation and love letters that, in my case, consist of each of my boys telling me how fat, ugly, old, and stupid I am (trust me: it's funnier than it sounds). These and other rituals express love and care—even the humorous put-down letters. (Boys, if you are reading this, I love you too.)

But on a recent Mother's Day, I failed. I was busy cooking breakfast (breakfast tacos, another tradition) when I realized that I had forgotten to get Ethel a card. I grabbed a piece of computer paper and wrote a one-sentence love letter: "Ethel, I'm glad you exist. Love, Paul." I was impressed with myself: I had captured, in one sentence, the essence of love. I was sharing a deep truth. For as the philosopher Josef Pieper notes, the fundamental affirmation of love is "It's good that you exist; it's good that you are in this world!"[8] I believe Pieper is correct. The essence of love is the affirmation that it is good that *you are*. But my pithy sentence to Ethel on white computer paper didn't convey this deep and abiding truth. She glanced at my "card" and, well, let's just say she wasn't impressed.

I share this unflattering anecdote for a few reasons. First, to assure you that I'm not an expert on love. Even if I've discovered the essence of love, I love imperfectly. That's okay. You love imperfectly too. Second, my failure points to the complex nature of love: we love in both word and deed, head and heart. I believe my one-sentence letter communicated the depth of my love, but my actions didn't back up my words that day. Ethel deserved more. Love demands more. Third, my failure reminds us that love is long-suffering. Love covers over a multitude of sins. Ethel continues to love me, blemishes included. And I strive to love her—and others—even as I often stumble.

Think about the people and things you love. What do you notice? I think we've already established that my "love language" is to distill massive data into pithy sentences, so let me note five things I see. First, love is *multiply directed*. We love many kinds of objects. We love people, animals, nature, artifacts (paintings, boats, homes, etc.), ideals, countries, projects, and more. Love is *of* someone or something; it denotes a relation between me and someone or something else. (Even self-love is a relation: love *of* self.) Second, love is *complex*. Philosophers have historically used Greek words to distinguish between four kinds of love: *storge* (affection), *philia* (friendship), *eros* (typically understood as sexual love), and *agape* (unconditional love, usually understood as the kind of love God has for humans).[9] Third, love is *deep* and *enduring*. I *like* lots of things: Twinkies, tennis balls, tables, tacos. But I don't *love* everything I like. The people and things we love seem to have a kind of depth and stability: we are moved by them; we identify with them in some sense; we seek the good of the beloved; and we enjoy them—delight in them. The things we like, we often simply use: I use the table to hold my Twinkie; I use the tennis ball to play fetch with the dog. Fourth, love is *active* and *passive*. Here we have dueling intuitions. On one hand, we tend to think love is an activity, something we can do or neglect to do. My Mother's Day card to Ethel was a failure of love because I failed to act lovingly toward her. When I clean the kitchen or help a child with a math problem, these are acts of love. Conversely, when I treat someone harshly, fail to go on date nights with my wife, or never help out around the house, I act unlovingly toward others. So, love is active. On the other hand, love doesn't seem to be something under my direct control. I love my kids. I just do. From the moment they were born, I loved them. I didn't reason toward this love. I didn't force myself to love them. I just found myself in a state of loving them. So, love is passive too. Finally, love is *valuable*. Imagine a world like ours, yet bereft of loving relationships. Would there be anything of value lost in such a world? Intuitively, and obviously, the answer is yes. Love is a great value. It is something of great worth, a fitting object to consider in our quest to discover the true story of the world.

Gazing at love, we have noticed five features: love is multiply directed, complex, deep and enduring, active and passive, and valuable. To better appreciate the phenomenon of love, we'll want to explore its nature. In the end, we'll want to discover which story of the world best explains love's existence. Is there an account of the nature of love that accommodates these five features of love? Let's begin with four contemporary theories of love.

Reasons for Love

Why do you love me? This is a question countless friends, children, parents, boyfriends, and girlfriends have asked over the centuries. Four possible answers to this question help us explore four contemporary theories on the nature of love.[10] (I hope you're not feeling boxed in by all these lists and numbers—*five* features, *four* theories, and so on—I'll try to have some fun as we explore, but I've always found a quick tour of the conceptual landscape to be a helpful aid for finding our way.)

According to the *volitional view*, the answer to the question "Why do you love me?" is "For no reason; I just do." Harry Frankfurt describes this non-rational nature of love: "We come to love because we cannot help loving. Love is a non-rational condition. It requires no reasons, and it can have anything as its cause."[11] So when Adele sings, "Your love drives me crazy, it's hard to understand just why," the volitional view says that it's hard to understand why because you can't: there is no reason.[12] Something's right about the volitional view. Consider the phenomenon of love at first sight. There is a kind of rawness, beauty, spontaneity, and freedom to such love. When someone is asked to explain such love, it's quite plausible that no answer is forthcoming. The same can be said, as I noted above, for my love of my kids. Why do I love them? I just do.

The main problem with the volitional view is that it is counterintuitive.[13] If no reason rooted in the beloved can be given for love, then there is no reason why a lover loves the beloved instead of someone else. This result doesn't accommodate the deep and enduring nature of love or the active feature of love. Remember, love is active *and* passive. The volitional view captures the passive side of love well, but it fails to account for other features of love, including the need for action-guiding reasons for love, reasons often grounded in certain qualities of the beloved.

According to the *quality view*, the answer to the question "Why do you love me?" is "Because you have valuable qualities *x*, *y*, and *z*." Such qualities might include physical beauty, an attractive personality, a compassionate disposition, and the like. This view also gets some things right. I do give reasons why I love my wife (her beauty, character, personality) and often praise what I love about her to my friends.

But there are problems with the quality view too. One is that the perceived value of qualities in the beloved changes over time. This threatens to make love fragile, not deep and enduring. Another problem has to do with the particularity of love. For if my love for a particular person is based on their qualities, it seems like I ought to love some other person too, as long as they have the same valued qualities x, y, and z as my beloved does. In fact, if some other person has valued qualities x, y, and z to a greater degree than my beloved does, it seems like I ought to love that other person *more* than my beloved. These counterintuitive results render the quality view problematic.

The *relational view* answers the question "Why do you love me?" with "Because I value you and my relationship to you." So, I love my kids because I have a history, a relationship, with them and perceive that relationship as valuable. The same goes for my wife and friends. This view also gets things right. The history I have with my kids or wife or friends helps explain the constancy and particularity of my love, even if there are other individuals who possess similar valuable qualities.

There are problems with the relational view, however. This view can't accommodate love at first sight, one-sided love, or committed relationships in which a person is valued and the relationship is valued, yet there is no desire for union (more on this below).

Finally, there is the *emotional view*. This is perhaps the most popular view in culture, the view described above as "confluent love." This is the view of love as passion and of marriage as an emotional union. In the Mariah Carey song "We Belong Together (Remix)," Jadakiss raps, "Feel you in my stomach like you a part of my belly." While this line seems somewhat awkward out of context, it aptly captures the gut-level hunger of love. "Why do you love me?" "Because you make me feel a certain way." The emotional view identifies that gut feeling as the essence of love. Of course, the emotional view has its defenders within the philosophical literature too.

There is much to appreciate about the emotional view. Love, including sexual love, is full of emotions and pleasures. The emotional view accommodates these facts, but it runs too far with them. The problem is that emotions alone are not able to bear the weight of love. Emotions come and go, but love is supposed to remain—especially in certain relationships such as between a parent and child, husband and wife, and certain friends—even if there are no longer positive emotions associated with the love.

We've briefly assessed the volitional, quality, relational, and emotional views of love. What I want you to see is that none of these theories singlehandedly accommodates the five features we noted above regarding love. This doesn't mean there's no satisfactory account of love, but it does mean that we'll need a more complex account of love than any of these views suggest. It's time to invite another guest from the distant past to join us.

Thomas Aquinas was a thirteenth-century theologian and monk, and who knows more about romance than celibate monks from the Middle Ages? Aquinas wrote extensively on love, and I think his account hits our target. For now, I'll just note two components of his account of love, as summarized by Eleonore Stump.[14] First, Aquinas says that love is primarily love of persons.[15] Love of something outside that category (such as the love of coffee or a painting or a pet) is understood as, at least in part, bound up in a person's love of himself or herself. So, a person who loves coffee or a painting or a pet is someone who *desires* that thing *as a good for himself or herself.* In this light, we can see how all the things we love ultimately consist in the love of either ourselves or someone else. Second, Aquinas notes that love consists in two interconnected desires: the desire for the well-being or flourishing of the beloved and the desire for union with the beloved.[16] Notice that in this reasoning, loving a person means desiring not merely that person's being but their *well-being.* Moreover, the type of union in view here is far deeper than sexual union. Sex comes cheap and easy; union and closeness are richer and more difficult.

Aquinas's account seems to capture widely held intuitions about love. To say love is just chemistry, as the materialist does, or just about sex, as much of popular culture does, seems rather shallow and off the mark. We don't want just to survive but to thrive, and Aquinas's account highlights that love is a great good. It captures Pieper's assertion that the most fundamental affirmation in love is "It is good that you are." Aquinas's account of love as the desire for union seems right too. Love is a coming together, a uniting of two distinct selves into a complex whole without removing the individuality of each self.

This longing to be united is powerfully expressed in Gail Caldwell's moving memoir on friendship, *Let's Take the Long Way Home*. She and her friend Caroline discovered each other later in life, and Caldwell describes the early days of their friendship: "Finding Caroline was like placing a personal ad for an imaginary friend, then having her show up at your door funnier and better than you had conceived. Apart, we had each been frightened drunks and aspiring writers and dog lovers; together, we became a small corporation."[17] Each remained a distinct individual—but a better individual—because of the other. Their loving friendship united them into a larger, complex whole, a "small corporation" ready to face the world.

Sadly, their time was cut short when Caroline was diagnosed with cancer. One day, near the end, Caroline managed to sneak out of the hospital. She longed to walk through the woods with Caldwell and their dogs or to row on the Charles River as they once did. As Caroline stood on the banks watching rowers pass by, she called her friend. Caldwell reports the call: "'I miss *us*,' she told me on the phone that morning. 'I miss our lives together.'"[18] Caroline was lamenting the disruptive nature of cancer as it robbed her of time together with a beloved friend, and soon it would rob the beloved of her presence altogether. Love not only affirms our goodness; it unites us to goodness so that we can thrive on the journey of life and death.

According to Aquinas, then, there are two answers to the question "Why do you love me?" The first is "Because it's good." And

the second is "Because it's you."[19] This twofold answer highlights
the interconnectedness of the two desires of love. In loving my son
Joshua or my wife Ethel or my friend Mike, I desire their well-
being—because that is a great and valuable good—and I desire
them. My love would be deficient if I desired only their well-being
but not each of them.

We should note that while love's two desires are connected,
they are different in character. The desire for the well-being of
the beloved does not depend on anything intrinsic to the beloved,
whereas the desire for union does.[20] The kind of union desired
depends on the kind of relationship in view. In romantic love,
the desired union will include sexual union, whereas in parental
love, it will not. In this way, the desire for union is responsive to
the relational characteristics of the beloved. This captures love's
complex nature and the multiple ways in which it can be directed.
The desire for union is also responsive to the intrinsic qualities of
the beloved, which are among the factors one considers when de-
termining what character and extent of the union are appropriate
to a relationship. Stump offers this illustration:

> In order to unite with the beloved, the lover must share something
> of himself with her. What he can share and the degree to which he
> can share it, however, will be dependent on her as well as on him.
> A man who is a composer may want to share his labor and joy in
> composition with his much-loved sister; but if she is tone-deaf
> and musically illiterate, what he is able to share with her will be
> different from what he could share with her if she herself were a
> musician. The union appropriate for him to desire with her will
> thus be shaped by intrinsic characteristics of hers and by his per-
> ception of those characteristics. To this extent, his love of her will
> be responsive to her, or to what he sees of her.[21]

Let's recap: according to Aquinas love is both responsive to
the beloved (given the desire for union with the beloved) and not
responsive to the beloved (given the desire for the good of the beloved as well as the kind of relationship in view).[22] It is active and

passive, complex, multiply directed, deep and abiding (depending on the kind of relationship in view), and of great value. It captures what is right about each of the contemporary (single-answer) accounts of love canvassed above and folds them into a richer, more complex whole.[23] We've discovered, I submit, a love worth having. It's also something we all want, and want deeply. I want to be loved and to love in the way Aquinas describes. I'll bet you do too. Let's stipulate that, with Aquinas's help, we've accurately described the nature of love. Let's also make an empirical claim: this kind of love is a feature of the world. Hopefully you've experienced this love. The next question is this: What story of the world best explains the reality of love?

The Argument from Love

In graduate school, my philosophy professor J. P. Moreland often arrived at our metaphysics class singing, "Let's get metaphysical, metaphysical!" to the tune of Olivia Newton-John's 1981 hit song "Physical." Sitting down to write this section, staring at a blank computer screen, J. P.'s voice—and his rendition of the song—came to my mind. "Let's get metaphysical, metaphysical!" Okay, J. P., you're right. "It's gettin' hard, this holdin' back." It's time to get metaphysical.

Consider the following argument, which we can call *the argument from love*:

> The existence of love is not surprising given theism.
> The existence of love is very surprising given naturalism.
> Therefore, by the likelihood principle, the existence of love strongly supports theism over naturalism.

Arguments are helpful as we journey to discover the true story of the world. They clarify our thinking and help us see connections. They guide us on our quest for truth. I think the argument from love is a good argument. Love, understood as the desire for the well-being of and union with the beloved, strongly supports theism over naturalism. Let's consider each step of the argument.

The argument begins with the claim that the existence of love is not surprising given theism. At least two reasons support this claim. First, according to theism, God is perfectly loving. God is defined as a personal being worthy of worship. Arguably, being essentially loving is entailed by being worthy of worship. If God were not in fact loving, or were loving but not *essentially* loving, then God would be morally and/or metaphysically deficient and not worthy of our worship. The Christian Scriptures, of course, affirm God's essential loving nature.[24] We read, for example, that "God is love" (1 John 4:8). On theism, love is at the heart of reality; it's eternal and thus prior to nature. Second, according to theism, God created the universe out of love. We might ask why God created the universe. God didn't need anything. So why create? To spread his joy, delight, and love. Love is by nature diffusive; it wants to be shared, spread, enjoyed, gifted. So God creates a "riotous diversity" of creatures.[25] God creates a universe full of *persons* capable of entering into loving relationships with others. Love is why we exist. In sum, according to theism, love is prior to nature; it is at the heart of reality; and it is the reason we exist. On theism, love is not surprising.

On naturalism, the existence of love is late and (as far as we know) local. Moreover, love is an emergent property of the universe. It is not fundamental. Love is not at the heart of reality. Naturalism tells us that love is in large part erotic and irrational, if Freud is correct, and for survival and reproduction, if Darwin is correct.[26] The desires of love are for sexual union and the *being* of others, but—at least initially, and never fundamentally—not for the *well-being* of others.[27] As the atheist philosopher Michael Ruse describes, most of the natural world has little use for long-term love—with the exception of humans (and perhaps birds).[28] On evolutionary accounts of love, we never crave the beloved for their own sake; love is always, in the end, for the propagation of the species. The fact that we do find deep and enduring love, as defined by Aquinas, is very surprising on naturalism.

The *likelihood principle*, a standard principle of inductive reasoning, states that for two competing hypotheses, a set of observations strongly supports one hypothesis over the other "precisely when the first hypothesis confers on the observations a higher probability than the second one does."[29] Therefore, given the likelihood principle, the existence of love strongly supports theism over naturalism.

A Love That Pursues

Back to *The Bachelor* and *The Bachelorette*. Many of us watch these shows because we hope to find an enduring and satisfying love. Our hopes and longings are instructive, providing a clue about the nature of reality. As Alvin Plantinga writes, "Human erotic love is a sign of something deeper, something so deep that it is uncreated, an original and permanent and necessarily present feature of the universe."[30] Our obsession with love and sex also reveals a deep truth about our quest for authenticity: *we can't name ourselves.* We find ourselves together, in community. We are not meant to be radical individuals—atoms in the void—that occasionally bump and grind in an otherwise lonely universe. We were made for more. We were made for Another. On the Christian story, God creates us to know him primarily and others secondarily as we live out our God-given purpose on this good and beautiful earth. Yet we've screwed things up. We've run from God, and we run from ourselves and others too. It would have been easier for God to give up on us. Thankfully, he didn't. Rather, God pursued us. He pursues you and me now. This is the deep, enduring, and satisfying love we long to be united with: a love that seeks the good of another no matter what, a love that seeks to be united with the other even when the other is unlovable. What is your name? *Beloved.* God says to you, right now, "It's good that you exist; it's good that you are in this world!" And he doesn't write this on computer paper. He demonstrates this love to us in the most extraordinary way, as we'll see in our final chapter. But first we will look at another powerful clue: the pervasive and alluring beauty found in the world.

10

Beauty

I think an ordinary paper company like Dunder Mifflin was a great subject for a documentary. There's a lot of beauty in ordinary things. Isn't that kinda the point?

—Pam Halpert, *The Office*

Beauty is the last thing which the thinking intellect dares to approach, since only it dances as an uncontained splendor around the double constellation of the true and the good and their inseparable relation to one another.

—Hans Urs von Balthasar, *The Glory of the Lord*

It's time to let you in on a secret. When I teach, I don't always reveal to my students what I want them to learn. The readings and lecture topics—the kinds of things you might find on a syllabus—are the "primary text" of the course. I want my students to learn the primary text. But almost always, I want to impart something more. Let's call this the "subtext" of a class.

Imparting subtext is more difficult. It involves imagination, emotion, and will. It requires that I give something of myself to my students. In valuing head and heart, reason and imagination, truth and goodness and beauty, the hope is that I might gift knowl-edge *and understanding*. I do this because we are not merely ra-tional animals. We are desiring animals, moral animals, relational animals, and imaginative animals. I seek to teach in a way that respects what it means to be fully human, blending reason with imagination.

You may have already guessed, but the same goes for this book. There is the primary text: the words written and the arguments made. I've sought to walk the path of reason. But I've sought to walk this path without ever leaving the imagination behind. (Hence my personification of Lady Nature and Lady Philosophy as well as my judicious use of other guides from the past and pres-ent.) In fact, the book's central metaphor, hiking stones, requires us to engage our imagination. Just as hiking cairns—small piles of stones stacked together—shepherd hikers toward a summit, we've been noticing clues and stacking them into a pile as we journey to discover the true story of the world. We've walked some of the well-trodden paths, the lowlands where there are dirt and rocks and insects and trees. We've walked the more difficult terrain of the human species and the human heart, exploring along the way the cartography of desire. Now, in the final two chapters, we'll journey into more rarified air as we consider beauty and religion, art and faith.

The stones are stacking up. We are still on the path. But as we near the summit, the hiking is more difficult; the way, more mys-terious. In this chapter, we'll explore the mysterious yet evocative domain of the imagination and its quest, often through the arts, for beauty.

Oscar Wilde's novel *The Picture of Dorian Gray* helps us see the mysterious yet evocative interplay of beauty, art, imagination, and understanding. Basil Hallward has painted a masterpiece, a portrait of his alluring and beautiful young friend Dorian Gray. The representation is so perfect that it is difficult to distinguish the person from the painting. Basil has captured, it seems, beauty itself. The young Gray is unaware of his beauty until it is pointed out by Basil's friend Lord Henry. "You have a beautiful face, Mr. Gray. Don't frown. You have." Lord Henry quickly moves from the beauty of Dorian Gray to theorizing about beauty itself:

> And Beauty is a form of Genius—is higher, indeed, than Genius, as it needs no explanation. It is of the great facts of the world, like sunlight, or spring-time, or the reflection in dark waters of that silver shell we call the moon. It cannot be questioned. It has its divine right of sovereignty. It makes princes of those who have it. You smile? Ah! When you have lost it you won't smile. . . . People say sometimes that Beauty is only superficial. That may be so. But at least it is not so superficial as Thought is. To me, Beauty is the wonder of wonders. It is only shallow people who do not judge by appearances. The true mystery of the world is the visible, not the invisible.[1]

This is high, if somewhat confusing, praise of beauty. Beauty is "of the great facts of the world," "the wonder of wonders," the only "true mystery of the world." These seem correct; beauty is something of great value, evocative yet mysterious. But Lord Henry also asserts that beauty "cannot be questioned," "needs no explanation," and "is not so superficial as Thought is." These are confusing claims. It would seem that beauty, like anything else, needs an explanation. And it's not clear what Lord Henry, or Wilde, meant in saying that beauty is "not so superficial" as thought.

Wilde also raises important questions about art. Dorian is young and beautiful, but Lord Henry points out that in time, Dorian's beauty will fade, whereas the picture will forever remain a "perfect type."[2] In a kind of Faustian bargain, Dorian impulsively and sincerely wishes that he would be forever young and the picture would grow old. He would give anything, even his soul, for eternal youth. His wish is granted. A mystical transaction takes place. Dorian, the person, remains young and beautiful. The painting grows decrepit, reflecting the changing state of his soul. The changing nature of the painting, as a living picture of Dorian Gray's soul, suggests that art is in some sense revelatory.

Art reveals truths about the world and human nature or, perhaps, helps us understand our experience of the world. On the other hand, as Dorian Gray plunges into a life of sensual pleasure, it seems that art's chief value is the pleasure it brings. Art, Lord Henry suggests at the end of the book, is "simply a method of procuring extraordinary sensations."[3]

In order to discover what beauty reveals about the true story of the world, we'll consider four questions that *The Picture of Dorian Gray* raises but leaves unanswered: What is beauty? What is art? What is the relationship between beauty, art, and understanding? What does beauty reveal about ultimate reality? On this leg of our journey we'll be joined by some old favorites, including Aquinas, as well as by the modern-day iconoclast Banksy.

The Nature of Beauty

Recall Lord Henry's claim that beauty is "of the great facts of the world." Let's unpack that. There are physical facts, truths, about the world: for example, facts about the mass of an electron, or the number of chairs in a room, or the temperature in Florida today. These are facts or truths about physical reality or some part of it. More controversially, there are moral facts of the world too. There are truths about values and obligations that are "of the great facts of the world": for example, honesty is a virtue, murder is wrong, and vanity is deadly (which is nicely illustrated by Wilde's novel). But here is a more controversial claim: *just as there are physical and moral facts, there are also aesthetic facts.* Facts about beauty are part of the furniture of the world. We can unpack this by switching from language about facts to language about *things*: there are beautiful things in the world, and they are part of the inventory of the world. Lord Henry pointed to sunlight, springtime, and the moon's reflection on dark waters. We could add to this list a well-planned urban park, the awe-inspiring majesty of the Rocky Mountains or a Texas sunset, the elegance of a dance move or a batter's swing, the grandeur of Bach's Toccata and Fugue in

D Minor, the sublimity of Coleridge's "The Rime of the Ancient Mariner," the sophistication of Einstein's field equations, the simplicity of the law of gravity, and the fittingness of an act of mercy.

An objection can be raised to this last claim: beauty is not "in the world," some maintain, but rather "in the eye of the beholder." In this view, while beauty might *appear* to be "in things," in reality beauty exists merely in the minds of humans. It is part of the subjective landscape of reality. If this statement regarding the subjectivity of beauty is true, then there is a place for beauty, but it is not of the "great facts of the world"; rather, it is one of the great facts of *the human experience of* the world. David Hume thought beauty belongs solely to the realm of human experience: "Beauty is no quality in things themselves: It exists merely in the mind which contemplates them; and each mind perceives a different beauty. One person may even perceive deformity, where another is sensible of beauty; and every individual ought to acquiesce in his own sentiment, without pretending to regulate those of others."[4] There is truth in Hume's claim—but something amiss too. It is undeniable that beauty is perceived or beheld by minds. But it does not follow that beauty exists *only* in minds.

I offer two arguments for the claim that beauty is an objective feature of the world. The first is *the argument from aesthetic agreement and disagreement*. Consider the list of beautiful things two paragraphs above. While our judgments can and probably do differ on some of these items, notice also that there is substantial agreement. I suspect, but you'll need to confirm for yourself, that you largely agree with me about the items included in the list of beautiful things. This agreement is best explained by positing objective beauty—that is, beauty independent of the human mind—in beautiful things.[5] Moreover, if aesthetic judgments are merely expressions of personal preference, then disagreement would be pointless. But it sure seems like we can be mistaken in our aesthetic judgments (as my wife often reminds me), and we often disagree with the aesthetic judgments of others. The first is impossible and the second unreasonable if all judgments of beauty exist only in the mind. Peter Forrest forcefully presses this implausible consequence of aesthetic relativism:

> "How ugly the stars are tonight! How trivial the pounding of the waves on the beach! And is it not crass to be thrilled by mountains? The rain forest and the wild-flowers are quite repulsive. And as for sunsets. . . ."
>
> If a full-blown relativism in aesthetics was correct, then those responses would be unusual but not in any way improper. But my reaction is that anyone who fails to appreciate the beauty of this universe is defective. Natural beauty has as much claim to be an objective feature of this universe as do the colors, sounds, and so forth on which it is based.[6]

The wide agreement on matters of beauty and the possibility of genuine disagreement provide good reasons to think, contrary to Hume, that beauty resides in things themselves, not merely in the mind that contemplates beautiful things.

A second argument for the claim that beauty is an objective feature of the world is known as *the indispensability argument*.[7] In science and philosophy, theories are judged to be probably true or false in light of their possession or lack of possession of certain theoretical virtues, such as simplicity, elegance, empirical adequacy, coherence, and explanatory scope and power. Notice that each of these virtues picks out aesthetic properties. Theories with the most theoretical virtues—that is, aesthetic properties— are judged to be better or more probably true. But every theory is judged in terms of one or more of these aesthetic features. Beauty, it seems, is "allied with truth."[8] When it comes to theory construction and evaluation—the kinds of theory building we do in philosophy and science and the kind of theory building we are doing in this book—beauty is our guide. We can't do without aesthetic concepts and terms. Thus, since (as we believe) there are true theories to be discovered, we can't do without beauty either.

We've made an important discovery about the nature of beauty: beauty is a real feature of the world! Beauty is independent of the human mind; it is one "of the great facts of the world." Yet—with a nod toward the subjectivist—it must be beheld or perceived by a mind. Beauty is not "in the eye of the beholder"; rather, beauty— real, objective, in-the-world beauty—is beheld by the eye or the ear or nose or, more generally, the mind.

There are two other features of beauty to notice by attending to the "feel" or the "what it is like" of aesthetic experience. First, *the perception of beauty is an invitation to reconsider the world and a guide to help us find our place in the world.* Elaine Scarry describes the mysterious structure of perception at the moment one stands in the presence of beauty as follows: "The beautiful thing seems—is—incomparable, unprecedented; and that sense of being without precedent conveys a sense of the 'newness' or 'newbornness' of the entire world. . . . It is the very way the beautiful thing fills the mind and breaks all frames that gives the 'never before in the history of the world' feeling."[9] Beauty arrests and stills. It captivates and fills. It nourishes and gives life. There is a kind of weightiness or glory or excellence—or, as we'll put it below, *transcendence*—to beautiful things that demands attention, serving as a "small wake-up [call] to perception."[10] The experience of beauty moves us too. We "continually revise [our] location," according to Scarry, "in order to place [ourselves] in the path of beauty."[11] Beauty, then, functions as a kind of greeting, perhaps from another world—an invitation.[12] Beauty whispers in our ears: "Welcome. Take my hand as we journey together to the home you've always longed for."

Second, *the experience of beauty is inexhaustibly pleasurable.* Beauty is not equated with pleasure, but all experiences of beauty are pleasurable. And the pleasure of beauty is unlike other pleasures. As Scarry writes, "Many human desires are coterminous with their object. A person desires a good meal and—as though by magic—the person's desire for a good meal seems to end at just about the time the good meal ends. But our desire for beauty is likely to outlast its object because, . . . unlike all other pleasures, the pleasure we take in beauty is inexhaustible. No matter how long beautiful things endure, they cannot out-endure our longing for them."[13] I'm craving a hamburger. When I eat that hamburger, as pleasurable as it will be, the craving will be gone. But the pleasure of standing before the beauty of the majestic royal palms in my front yard or before the cresting ocean waves at the Jupiter Inlet beach fulfills my longing for beauty without extinguishing the longing for these (and other) beautiful things. The delight of standing before beauty nourishes and sustains me in a way that hamburgers never will.

By attending to the phenomena of beautiful things and our experience of beautiful things, we've discovered three features of beauty itself: beauty has an objective and subjective component, it demands our attention in order to guide us home, and it is inexhaustibly pleasurable. Thomas Aquinas helpfully captures these features of beauty. Regarding the subjective side of beauty, Aquinas notes that "the 'beautiful' is something pleasant to apprehend."[14] Regarding the objective side of beauty, Aquinas provides criteria for identifying beautiful things: "For beauty includes three conditions, 'integrity' or 'perfection,' since those things which are impaired are by the very fact ugly; due 'proportion' or 'harmony'; and lastly, 'brightness' or 'clarity,' whence things are called beautiful which have a bright color."[15] Beautiful things exhibit three qualities: *wholeness* (integrity or perfection), such that everything is as it should be, creating in us a sense of rest and peace; perfect *harmony* (proportion), such that every part of a beautiful thing brings out the best in every other part, creating in us a sense of joy and at-homeness; and *radiance* (brightness or clarity), communicating something transformative even as it is veiled in mystery.[16] The theologian John Navone describes the disclosive and evocative power of beautiful things: "Beauty discloses or radiates the truth and goodness of things; therefore, it entails communication, communion, and community."[17] Likewise, the philosopher Roger Scruton notes that "beauty demands to be noticed; it speaks to us directly like the voice of an intimate friend."[18]

Art, Beauty, and Understanding

In October 2018, Banksy destroyed his *Girl with Balloon* as the auctioneer's gavel pounded the podium at Sotheby's. As it sold for $1.4 million, onlookers watched with shock, awe, and confusion as the print was sliced into strips by a shredder hidden in the work's frame. Within days, the shredded work of art found new life and a new name: *Love Is in the Bin.* The buyer went through with the purchase, realizing that she would end up with her own piece of art history.[19] Banksy serves as a perfect guide for the next part of our journey.

What is the nature of art? What distinguishes art from nonart? It will be helpful to have some clear examples. I stipulate, and hope you'll agree with me, that clear cases of artwork include Banksy's *Girl with Balloon*, Jackson Pollock's *Night Mist*, Claude Monet's *Gardens of the Villa Moreno*, Paul Cézanne's *Portrait of Alfred Hauge*, and Georgia O'Keeffe's *Red Flower*.[20] What is equally clearly *not* artwork? Surveying my desk as I contemplate a list, I'd include paper clips, rulers, #10 envelopes (business edition), and plastic water bottles. I think you'll agree with me, but if not, make your own lists. I think it will include similar items on each side of the ledger. What about Banksy's *Love Is in the Bin*? On the one hand, it seems like art. The buyer still paid the $1.4 million, anticipating that the work's value will increase in time. On the other hand, it is important to remember that *Love Is in the Bin* is a *destroyed* piece of art. It seems odd to think that destroying what is clearly a work of art in some clever way is sufficient for the creation of a new work of art. Even so, I happily include it on the "artwork" side of the ledger.

Setting aside *Love Is in the Bin* for the moment, now that we've identified some clear examples of art and nonart, we might ask, What property do all works of art share in common that all nonart lacks? Defining the essence of art is often thought to be "the central problem of aesthetics."[21] According to *essentialism*, then, there is an essence to art, and the job of the philosopher of art is to specify what that essence is by specifying the feature that all works of art share. There have been many proposals for this critical feature of art: that it has significant form or beauty (or more broadly, aesthetic properties); that it is pleasurable to apprehend, representative of reality, expressive of human feeling, expressive of human intuition, or purposive without purpose, and more.[22] There are at least two problems with essentialism.[23] First, for any proposed feature, there are clear and recognized works of art that do not possess that feature. For example, poetry and representational paintings possess significant form, but it is not clear that dramas such as film or opera can. Likewise, it is easy to see how a poem expresses human emotion, but it is not obvious how a string of sounds in instrumental music could be said to be expressive (not just of human emotions, but of anything, since discrete sounds, strictly speaking, are not *about* anything). Second, the essentialist assumes that art is a fixed concept, but sociologically and historically this is false. Art is a socially embedded activity. What might have counted as art in the past or in another culture might not count as art today or across cultures.

For at least these reasons, recently philosophers of art have sought nonessentialist definitions. Two prominent nonessentialist accounts of art are *institutionalism* and *historicism*. According to institutionalism, art is whatever the art world says it is. According to historicism, an object counts as art if it stands in the appropriate historical relation to other artworks it resembles. Both views are problematic. I'll share one problem with each view.[24]

Institutionalism suffers from the problem of established authorities. Who exactly, we might ask, are the established authorities in the art world? Is it gallerists, museum curators, critics, auction houses, patrons of art, or the artists themselves? These groups of stakeholders often disagree with each other. Consider Banksy's work. Some, including the experts at Sotheby's, consider his work art; others consider it vandalism. Or consider Marcel Duchamp's *Fountain*. Initially, art critics rejected his urinal as art, but eventually they changed their minds. The same can be said for graffiti art, which is widely regarded as a legitimate art form today but wasn't in the 1970s. Duchamp's urinal and Banksy's graffiti—either they are art or they are not. Over time, gallerists, museum curators, critics, auction houses, patrons, and artists disagree and change their minds, and this implies that they can be wrong. But if these authorities can be wrong, then it seems they must appeal to someone or something distinct from the art world to judge a work as art or nonart. If so, then institutionalism is false.

Historicism either collapses into essentialism or institutionalism or is explanatorily vacuous.[25] If *Love Is in the Bin* is art because it is historically related to *Girl with Balloon*, and *Girl with Balloon* is art because it has a historical relationship to some other artwork, and so on down the line, we will eventually arrive at rock bottom—at "first art" that has no relation to any earlier artwork. We might ask about this first artwork, What makes *it* art? If we point to some feature of the artwork that is sufficient for it to count as art, the view collapses into essentialism. If we point to some relation the first art has with the art world at that time, the view collapses into institutionalism. Either way, historicism inherits the problems of either essentialism or institutionalism, as discussed above. Alternatively, the defender of historicism could say that the first work of art just *is* art, period. End of story. No criteria or relational feature would be needed to dub the first art as genuine art. But then two worries arise. First, if there is no justification for first art, it seems we've lost our justification for judging any object in that historical line as art. Second, if we can dub first art as art without appeal to ancestry, why can't we do that for *any* object? The view becomes vacuous.

It's time to take stock. I've argued, albeit briefly, that none of the prominent theories of art are sufficient to specify the nature of art. This doesn't mean there isn't a workable theory of art. I think the lesson, rather, is that there is no *value-neutral* theory of art. There is no workable, purely *descriptive* account of the nature of art. Our primary question then becomes, What is the *value* of art? If we can answer that question, then we can specify how we *ought* to demarcate art from nonart as well as a normative (as opposed to purely descriptive) theory of art. The philosopher Gordon Graham describes the dialectic: "Consequently, this distinction between art and non-art is not a reflection of a reality independent of our thinking about art. . . . However, to accept this does not carry the implication that we have to cease making the distinction. It only means that we cannot interpret the distinction descriptively; there is nothing to prevent us interpreting it *normatively*. That is to say, applying the distinction between art and non-art does not signal a *discovery*, but a *recommendation*."[26]

The upshot is that the phrase "work of art" is both descriptive and evaluative. When we denote an object or performance as art, we not only say what it is; we also give the object or performance some evaluative status.

What is the chief value of art? I'll report my agreement with Graham (and others): the chief value of art is *cognitive*.[27] Art enhances, or has the capacity to enhance, our *understanding* of the world. Consider again Banksy's *Love Is in the Bin*. What does it reveal? Ironically, Banksy is demonstrating our lack of rigor and care in perceiving. We no longer see the world in its proper light, as enchanted, sacred, mysterious. Rather, we have reduced people and things, including art, to market value. *Girl with Balloon*, a work with questionable aesthetic value, sold for $1.4 million based on the reputation of the artist. So did *Love Is in the Bin*. Almost immediately, the new work of art was assessed in terms of its market value. The art enthusiasts have missed the point. The real value is not *in* the thing but in what we long for *through* the thing: goodness, truth, beauty, and engagement with reality itself.

The artist is a border crosser, walking those aesthetic surfaces of the world that mark the line between the visible and the invisible, the world as experienced and reality as it is, pointing, for those who have eyes to see, to truth and meaning.[28] There are many beautiful things in the natural world. But artwork adds to the world what Elaine Scarry calls an additional "site of beauty."[29] The artist functions as a kind of prophet and guide, shocking us to engage reality by presenting to us works of art that reveal the meaning of the world, often in beautiful and tantalizing and pleasurable ways. Let beauty, and now the beauty as revealed in art, "serve as small wake-up calls to perception."[30] Behold beauty. See it—in the mind, in the things of this world, in art—afresh. Let it lead you home. It's time to consider what beauty reveals about the true story of the world.

The Argument from Beauty

What does beauty reveal about ultimate reality? Paul Draper, whom we met in chapter 8, thinks that beauty provides *some* evidence for theism, even if that evidence is ultimately outweighed by other features of the world: "I agree that beauty supports theism, but maintain that the overall pattern of good and evil in the world is much more probable on naturalism than on theism. . . . So the ability of theism to explain beauty and our enjoyment of it is a relatively small advantage for theism. Arguments from evil against theism are much more powerful than the argument from beauty in favor of theism."[31]

Others see a much tighter connection between beauty and God. Elaine Scarry nicely captures the view of many artists, philosophers, and theologians throughout the centuries: "One can see why beauty—by Homer, by Plato, by Aquinas, by Dante (and the list would go on, name upon name, century by century, page upon page . . .)—has been perceived to be bound up with the immortal, for it prompts a search for a still earlier precedent, and the mind keeps tripping backward until it at last reaches something that has no precedent, which may very well be immortal."[32]

It seems, at least initially, that beauty provides evidence for God. But how strong is that evidence? For Draper, the evidence from beauty for theism is outweighed by the evidence from evil for naturalism. Fair enough. But as we saw, Draper's argument fails. It is not the case that evil supports naturalism. It is also not the case that the fact of evil outweighs, and thus removes, the "relatively small advantage" that beauty provides for theism. Draper's olive branch to theism understates the evidential force of beauty for theism. (As I type, I'm reminded of colloquialisms that I've said to my kids not a few times: "Go big, or go home" and "In for a penny, in for a pound." I suppose it's now obvious, at this point on our journey, that I'm "all in" for theism. Stay with me. It's worth it.)

Part of the problem is that Draper hasn't grasped adequately the nature and significance of beauty. It is not just the bare facts of beauty and our enjoyment of it that cry out for explanation. To find our way, we've got to state as clearly as possible our key findings related to beauty. I'll organize them into two claims, two pieces of evidence, in need of explanation:

E_1: The world is *saturated* with beautiful things.[33]
E_2: Beautiful things possess a *transcendent* quality.[34]

Our first piece of evidence, E_1, focuses attention on the fact that beauty is an objective, valuable, deep, and pervasive feature of the world. Beauty is found everywhere, and abundantly: in the mathematical laws that describe the physical universe as a whole, in the starry heavens, in the medium-sized things and people on earth, and within the microscopic (e.g., cells, DNA strands, and ice crystals). Beauty is not an accidental property of a small slice of the universe. It is one of the great and central facts of the world. It saturates our world and imbues it with value. Our second piece of evidence, E_2, focuses attention on the radiant, evocative, and delightful nature of beauty. Beauty awakens. It calls. It sets us on a journey. It is pleasing—inexhaustibly pleasing in a way that suggests something more, something beyond.

I now offer the following argument from beauty to God, similar in form to the argument from love considered in the previous chapter:

Facts E_1 and E_2 are not surprising given theism.
Facts E_1 and E_2 are very surprising given naturalism.
Therefore, by the likelihood principle, the facts E_1 and E_2 strongly support theism over naturalism.

If my version of the argument from beauty is successful, the result is that beauty provides strong support for theism (not weak support, as Draper claims). Let's consider each premise.

Why are facts E_1 and E_2 unsurprising given theism? For a simple reason: Any universe created by a personal being worthy of worship (recall our definition of God in the book's introduction) will be a *good* universe, a universe full of value and valuable things. Beauty is a value, and beautiful things are valuable things. Thus, any world created by God will be full of—saturated with— beautiful things. Moreover, a good God (an entailment from our concept of God) would want to communicate something of himself to creatures. (Goodness is "diffusive" of itself; it wants to be shared, expressed, communicated.) It is not surprising, then, that God creates a world that points to him, and does so in a delightful way. In fact, on theism, *everything* points to God because everything is good and beautiful. (More on this in a minute.)

But when applied to naturalism, facts E_1 and E_2 are very surprising. Regarding E_1, consider an analogy with art. As Mark Wynn notes (following F. R. Tennant), works of art are rarely beautiful without artistic intent (and sometimes artwork fails to be beautiful *with* artistic intent).[35] If naturalism is true, then there is no divine artist to create a beautiful universe. Hence, from the standpoint of naturalism it is very surprising that the universe is saturated with beauty. Moreover, as we've noted, beauty is valuable—objectively so. But the existence of objectively valuable facts is difficult to square with naturalism (as argued in chapter 5 when discussing moral values). Regarding E_2, naturalism makes the radiant, evocative nature of beauty puzzling. As Peter Forrest writes, "Beautiful things and people suggest to us that there is something infinitely more beautiful."[36] But if naturalism is true, this suggestive quality of beauty turns out to be a sham, awakening us to something—infinite beauty—that doesn't exist. Thus, the value of beauty turns out to be questionable on naturalism, and the fact that beautiful things possess a transcendent quality is very surprising.

Can an evolutionary explanation for the perception of beauty render E_1 and E_2 unsurprising to those who hold to naturalism? I doubt it. On the evolutionary story, beauty is not an objective thing, but a subjective illusion. Natural selection has programmed us to perceive certain things as beautiful because they aid our survival and reproduction: the perception of *human* beauty is natural selection's way of promoting breeding; the perception of *natural* beauty is natural selection's way of promoting our attention, or our ancestors' attention, to environments conducive to life (such as lush landscapes full of fruit trees, shrubs, and water); and the perception of *artistic* beauty is just natural selection's way (to select one among many possible stories) of promoting group cohesion conducive to cooperation and survival.[37] Unfortunately for the naturalist, none of these evolutionary accounts explains all cases of the perception of beauty. Our perception of human beauty is not always connected to sexual attraction. We can recognize the beauty of someone of the same sex or someone old without being sexually attracted to that person. The perception of natural beauty is not wedded to environments conducive to life. We recognize the beauty of a desert landscape or an Arctic icescape even though such environments are hostile to survival. The perception of artistic beauty is difficult to square with the Darwinian narrative too. Music, for example, has the power to bring people together (e.g., when we sing the national anthem before a baseball game) and to incite violence and destruction (e.g., Charles Manson's claim that the Beatles' song "Helter Skelter" inspired a killing spree). More generally, beautiful artwork is neither necessary for group cohesion nor sufficient. Much of our aesthetic experience seems useless, neither an adaption nor a by-product of an adaption conducive to survival. Worse, some aesthetic experiences might even contribute to our demise; we perceive lions and tigers as beautiful, but in this case, beauty's call is not that we should then go and pet them. In sum, evolutionary accounts of the perception of beauty fail to undercut the claim that E_1 and E_2 are very surprising given naturalism. The conclusion of the argument from beauty, then, given the likelihood principle, is that facts E_1 and E_2 strongly support theism over naturalism.

The Divine Artist

Facts about beauty provide *evidence* for God's existence. Beauty is another clue, a stone to stack on our cairns that mark the way. Like a key that frees prisoners from a dungeon, beauty transports us from the ordinary to the extraordinary, from the mundane to the transcendent. We've learned that there is something beyond this world, something of infinite value—something, as Peter Forrest hinted at, "infinitely more beautiful" than finite beauty. This is an amazing discovery! What we have longed for all along in our enjoyment of beautiful things is the source of beauty. And that source, as we've now learned, is God. Our final question, then, is this: What is the relationship between God—Beauty itself—and creaturely beauty? Once again, Aquinas offers the critical insight: "The beauty of a creature is nothing other than the likeness of divine beauty participated in things."[38] On this theistic account of beauty, God is Fundamental Beauty and creatures are derivatively beautiful in virtue of their participation in divine beauty. Creatures are beautiful because they share in some aspect or dimension of divine beauty.

Beauty teaches us important truths about God, the world, and our place in it: God is a Divine Artist; the world is a work of art; and as a work of art, the world points to and helps us understand God, the sacred realm, and our place in the divine economy. Recall that the chief value of art is *cognitive*—art helps us understand reality. But then everything, as a work of art, points to and illuminates the divine in some way. Nothing is ordinary—even an "ordinary paper company like Dunder Mifflin" is extraordinary. Beauty saturates our world and teaches us about God and the things of God. We can even go further, given our theistic account of beauty: in perceiving beautiful things, we indirectly perceive God himself.[39] As C. S. Lewis describes, "The books or the music in which we thought the beauty was located will betray us if we trust in them; it was not *in* them, it only came *through* them, and what came through them was longing."[40]

Listen to beauty's call. Do you hear it? God, the Divine Artist, is calling you home.

11

Religion

The life of man is a story; an adventure story; and in our vision
the same is true even of the story of God.

—G. K. Chesterton, *The Everlasting Man*

I am the living bread that came down from heaven. Whoever
eats this bread will live forever. This bread is my flesh, which I
will give for the life of the world.

—Jesus, in John 6:51

Andy and Lance are an odd pair of friends. Andy is tall, lanky,
and gloomy. Lance is short, balding, and quick-witted. On
the surface, both are unimpressive. Andy can't find steady work;
he works odd jobs as a temp agency employee. Lance works a
dead-end job as a forklift operator. A deeper look at their lives,
however, reveals much of value. Andy and Lance are united in
friendship by their shared passion for metal detecting. They are
detectorists, spending their free time walking the beautiful fields
surrounding the small British town of Danebury in northern Essex.
Armed with metal detectors and their knowledge of the area and
its history, they patiently search, along with other members of the

illustrious Danebury Metal Detecting Club, for valuable Roman or Saxon artifacts. Almost always, they only find junk: toy cars, ring pulls, nails, buttons, rusted barbed wire fencing.

Things seem to be changing for the better when they are granted permission to detect on Farmer Bishop's land, which is rumored to be the ancient burial site of a Saxon king. Andy and Lance believe they are closing in on their quarry. Still, the gold continues to elude them. Their hope soars when Andy's fiancé, Becky, takes a fresh look at a map of the area surrounding Bishop's farm. She reminds them that the landscape would have looked different during Saxon times and argues that another location on the map might have been a more fitting burial site in that era. Armed with this new perspective, Lance, Andy, Becky and another member of the detecting club set out with renewed excitement. As Lance's metal detector beeps over what they hope will prove to be the Saxon burial site, the others stop and watch. Lance eagerly thrusts his spade into the ground. Moments later, with disappointment, he pulls from the ground another piece of junk. They walk away in disgust, with the buried hoard of gold and precious stones a mere inch beneath Lance's hole.

This season 1 ending to the British comedy *Detectorists* reminds us of two important points as we near the terminus of our quest. First, sometimes we need another's perspective to help us see more clearly. Many of us need a new posture too: openness to transcendence. The clues point us in the right direction, but we need faithful guides, too, to lead the way and help us understand. Second, we don't want to give up the search too soon. Inspired by wonder, we've embarked on a journey with, as John Gardner explains, "the feeling that at the deepest level the world and man's true self are one." We hope to make sense of Life, the Universe, and Everything, driven by the conviction—or at least the hope— that "beauty and goodness, which are natural to the human heart, lie somehow also at the center of the physical universe."[1] I believe we are on the verge of discovering that treasure. To borrow from *Detectorists*, our spade is in the ground and we're inches away from pay dirt. World and desire have converged, pointing to a story alive and understanding and inviting.

This final chapter will be the most personal. I'll be your guide, sharing in more detail my own quest to discover the true story of the world. We've considered ten clues—stones—that point to some version of the religious story as the true story of the world. We have good reason to think, or so I've argued, that God exists. As I've employed the term, God is understood as an immaterial personal being worthy of worship. This leads to some version of theism as the true story of the world.

The word *religion* comes from the Latin *religare*, which means "to bind or connect." Religion, understood as the human search to unite with the divine, is our last clue. Wherever there is culture, there is religion. Humans, it seems, are inherently religious. What best explains this religious impulse? It's time to be bold: people are inherently religious because we've been created by God to know God. We are *creatures* who can only make sense of our lives in relation to the Creator. Here is the treasure I've discovered: *Christianity is the religion founded by God; Christianity is the true story of the world.* All the clues converge, pointing to Jesus and the gospel story as the true and satisfying story. In this closing chapter, I'll argue for this claim in three steps. First, I'll establish that, at most, only one religion can be true. Second, I'll share the evidence I've discovered in support of the claim that Christianity is the true religious story. Finally, I'll conclude by showing that Jesus and the gospel story are the treasure we've been seeking all along.

There Can Be Only One True Religion

I begin with a simple point of logic. Two mutually exclusive claims cannot both be true at the same time and in the same sense. This is called the law of noncontradiction. We've discovered this law of logic by the light of reason. I see it. I think you do too. Consider the following sentences: "I am typing. I am not typing." Notice that at most only one of these sentences can be true. If it is true that

I am typing, then it is false that I am not typing (and vice versa). Do you see the truth of the law of noncontradiction?[2]

Let's apply this insight to various religions. Notice that religions make contradictory claims about reality. Nontheistic religions such as Hinduism and Buddhism teach that God or the divine is not personal, whereas theistic religions teach that God is personal. God is either personal or impersonal; both can't be true. I've argued that the clues point to theism. This means, as we apply the law of noncontradiction, that nontheistic religions are false. (This claim is consistent with the claim that various teachings within any religion can be true. Religions, as total descriptions of ultimate reality, include claims about the nature of God, humans' fundamental problem, and the solution to that fundamental problem. Religions that make claims about God, humans' problem, or the solution to humans' problem that are inconsistent with the truth are false religions. Still, it is possible for a false religion to make other claims that are true, even if it goes wrong as a total description of ultimate reality. For example, many world religions make the same basic ethical claims, and truly make those claims.)

Various theistic religions contradict each other also. For example, Christianity claims that Jesus is divine, whereas Islam and Judaism claim that Jesus is not divine. Either Jesus is divine or he is not, so it can't be the case that Christianity, Judaism, and Islam are all true. Either Christianity is true (in which case, Judaism and Islam are false) or Christianity is false (in which case, either Judaism or Islam may be true). I use "either" in that statement because Judaism and Islam make contradictory claims about reality. So, at most, there can only be one true religion.

Imagine listing all the great religions on a whiteboard: Christianity, Islam, Judaism, Buddhism, Hinduism—and we can even throw in religious pluralism (the claim that all religions are equally valid paths to God) and atheism (now understood as a kind of quasi religion). If we were to record next to the name of each religion humans' fundamental problem, God's solution, and the prescribed means of "salvation," each column on our whiteboard would be full of contradictory claims. This exercise helps us see that at most, only one religion is true. (It could also turn out that they are all false and that some other religious story is the one true story.) This is because all the great religions as listed contradict each other. Given the law of noncontradiction, they can't all be right (again, this is not to speak of secondary beliefs within each religious tradition, many of which are true and in agreement with each other). There can only be one true religion.

Christianity Is the True Story of the World

We now arrive at my crucial claim: *Christianity is the true story of the world*. To see why I think this claim is true, I want to share a bit of my story.

I grew up somewhat religious. When I was younger, I occasionally played the piano at church, and for a year or two I was a member of the handbell choir. I was confirmed into the Lutheran church in seventh grade. For the most part, especially as time went on, church was relegated to the margins of life, along with any belief in God. During my senior year in high school, my friend Sean and I were casually chatting in a restaurant. Our conversation turned to the question of God. For some reason unknown to me, I mentioned to Sean that I was religious. He was a bit surprised, given my lifestyle at the time. I was surprised at my answer too. I rarely, if ever, thought about God. If pressed, I'd say I believed in God. I had not arrived at that belief through any rigorous intellectual process. Rather, I thought just about everyone believed in God in roughly the same way we all believe in the other side of the moon: everyone knows it's there, but it makes little difference to our lives. Sean accepted my religious declaration as a point of interest to be noted and then filed away. As we moved on, though, my declaration reverberated in my head. I'm religious? What did I mean by this? Why did I even say that? I wasn't particularly religious. But deep within my heart, it seems, I thought I ought to be.

Fast-forward to my freshman year in college. I went to a school in southern Ohio known for beautiful people, pristine redbrick buildings, and academic rigor. I loved it. It was time to make my mark on the world—and to have a little fun along the way. Everything was going according to plan until two guys knocked on my door one afternoon. "Are you interested in talking about spiritual things?" My mind raced. How could I get them to leave? I recalled my earlier conversation with Sean. Maybe I should give these guys a few minutes. I am, after all, religious. "Sure, come on in." They did. And my life was forever changed.

They explained that they were Christians—followers of Christ. They wanted to tell me the "good news"—the gospel message about Jesus. No problem, I thought. I'm religious. I've gone to church. I know about Jesus. But still, I wondered, why were these somewhat normal looking college students at my door talking about Jesus? It wasn't even Sunday. This seemed weird to me. Religion is for Christmas and Easter and maybe a few other Sundays if you can manage to get out of bed. They summarized the basic message of Christianity, as best I can recall, something like this:

God loves you and wants you to live a full and meaningful life. But you are imperfect—sinful—and thus separated from God. In fact, the "wages of sin" is death—spiritual separation from God for eternity. But God, rich in love, has provided a way for you to be reconciled with God. God the Father sent his one and only Son, Jesus, to die on a Roman cross to pay that penalty for your sins. If you were to believe in Jesus Christ and trust in him and his sacrifice on the cross, you would be forgiven of your sin and reconciled to God. You would enter into a personal relationship with God and have eternal life. All you need to do is confess your sin, believe in Jesus, and ask him to come into your life.

As I listened, two nagging thoughts began to enter my awareness. First, why had I never heard this story? I'd heard all the words before: Jesus, sin, cross, forgiveness, faith. But I'd missed the central message of the Christian story. I was perplexed. Second, I wondered, What if what they are saying is true? In relation to being a Christian or not being a Christian, I kind of saw myself in the middle. I do not think they confronted me with the law of noncontradiction, but they did say something like, "That's not a real option—at least biblically speaking. You either personally respond to Christ or you don't." Uncomfortable. I didn't know what to say. Suddenly I realized that being religious wasn't enough. Going to church didn't make me a Christian. What God required was a personal response of faith, a response I had not yet made.

The next part of the story is somewhat hazy. I did my best to get rid of them. Since they were in my room, and I was now late for calculus, I looked for the path of least resistance to get them to leave. It seemed as though the best way was to pray with them and, in their words, "ask Jesus into my life." So there I was, in my dorm room, pretending to pray along with these two students, faking my conversion. After our prayer, with excitement on their faces and relief on mine, they drove me to calculus class.

I had not become a Christian that day. My words, and my prayer, were not sincere. But the event had awakened me. I needed to discover the truth about Jesus and the gospel. I needed to discover if Christianity was the true story of the world.

For the next few months, I began to seriously investigate the claims of and evidence for Christianity. I talked to my friend Mike, who had earlier identified himself as a Christian, about the Bible. I went to a weekly class that was examining the evidence for Christianity at a local church. I was shocked. The evidence for Christianity is strong. After a year of talking, investigating, and reading the Bible and many books on Christianity, I again bent my knee and offered a prayer to God. This time it was sincere. I believed Jesus was divine, the Son of God, and I placed my faith in him for the forgiveness of my sins. I had discovered the true story of the world. I realized then and still believe now that Jesus and the gospel story are what my heart, and every human heart, longs for most deeply.

The Evidence for Christianity

What is the evidence for Christianity that I found so compelling? Three strands of evidence were crucial to my discovery: the historical trustworthiness of the biographies of Jesus (also called *the Gospels*), Jesus's claim to be divine, and the evidence for the resurrection. I will summarize these lines of evidence in this section.[3] I invite you to look at the evidence in greater depth yourself, as I did.[4]

First, *the four biographies of Jesus—Matthew, Mark, Luke, and John—are trustworthy for purposes of history*. To see why we can trust the biographies of Jesus, consider eyewitness accounts in general. Most evenings Ethel will recount her day to me. She'll share what she did at work, who she talked to, and what she saw and experienced. Yesterday, as reported by Ethel, she saw Krista. I believe that Ethel saw Krista, and I believe that based on her testimony. Notice that Ethel is *able* and *willing* to tell the truth about what she saw—and, further, that I have no reason to doubt her report. Krista and Ethel work in the same building. They see each other often. Thus, she is able to tell the truth about Krista. Moreover, Ethel is willing to tell the truth about Krista (and many other things too). I know this because I know Ethel. She doesn't suffer from hallucinations, she wears contact lenses and can see clearly, and she values truth and honesty. If she says she saw Krista, I believe her.

Likewise, the authors of the biographies of Jesus were *able* and *willing* to tell the truth about Jesus. They were able because (1) they were eyewitnesses or associates of eyewitnesses to the life of Jesus, and (2) there was a short gap between the recording of the events and the actual events recorded (within ten to fifteen years, in some cases). Further, we have good reason to think the authors were willing to tell the truth because their writings possess many marks of authenticity. To cite one example, in the Gospels we find reports about Jesus or his followers that might be embarrassing to them, such as Jesus cursing a fig tree (Mark 11:12–14) or failing to know the time of his return (13:32). If the Gospel authors were making up fake or embellished stories, they wouldn't include embarrassing details. They certainly wouldn't die for a lie, as almost all the disciples did (with the exception of John). The biographies of Jesus have all the marks of genuine history. They record real people, real places, and real events.

Second, *Jesus claims to be divine*. Recall again my encounter with the two students in my dorm room. One of the passages they shared with me was John 14:6: "Jesus answered, 'I am the way and the truth and the life. No one comes to the Father except through me.'" This passage bothered me. I realized Jesus was no ordinary man. If I were to walk around proclaiming to be "the way and the truth and the life," I'd either be condemned as a liar or locked up as a lunatic. Yet people came to believe Jesus was Lord. He didn't literally walk around saying, "I am God." That would have been too direct and difficult to understand in the Jewish culture. Rather, as N. T. Wright notes, Jesus did and said the kinds of things that only God would say or do.[5] For example, Jesus forgave sins (Mark 2:2–12), received worship (Matt. 28:17), and claimed equality with God the Father (John 10:30). As C. S. Lewis argues, when considering the life and words of Jesus, there are only three possibilities: he is a liar, a lunatic, or Lord.[6] But it is not plausible to think Jesus knowingly lied. He had nothing to gain from dying for a lie, yet he went to his death on a Roman cross without recanting his claims. Likewise, it is not plausible to think Jesus was a lunatic. Rather, Jesus is described as a lucid, well-balanced man who sustained deep, abiding relationships with others and lived a morally exemplary life. The best explanation for Jesus's words and actions is that he is Lord. Further, a nondivine Savior can't really save us from anything. We don't need more instructions on how to live our best life; we need God to forgive and heal us. Human beings make good prophets but not good messiahs. Jesus claimed to be divine.

Finally, and crucially, *Jesus backs up his claim to be divine by rising from the dead*. I quickly realized during that freshman year of investigation that if I was to refute Christianity, I would have to refute the resurrection account. So, I dove into the evidence for the resurrection—and to my surprise, I was blown away by how compelling it is. There is, as the historian John Dickson observes, "a resurrection-shaped 'dent' in the historical record."[7] Three facts, in particular, are best explained by the resurrection: the fact that the tomb of Jesus was found empty three days after his crucifixion, the fact that Jesus appeared to many people over a period of many days after the resurrection, and the fact of the origin of the disciples' belief in Jesus's resurrection itself. These facts, among others, are widely accepted. Naturalistic attempts to explain them, or explain them away, are implausible (e.g., that the appearances of Jesus were mass hallucinations, or that the disciples or Romans or Jews stole the body). Thus, there are good reasons to think Jesus physically rose from the dead. If it is true, then Jesus's claim to be divine is validated. Christianity is the religion founded by God. Hence, Christianity is the true story of the world!

Christianity Is the Best Possible Story

We've reached the summit. The cairns and guides have led us to this place. We've heard from atheists and skeptics—Darwin, Dennett, Sartre, Hume, Voltaire, Draper, and many more—and we've carefully considered their case. And we've had fun along the way, weaving story, art, and the imagination into our time together. Here at the summit, we're surrounded by a great cloud of witnesses—Lady Nature, Lady Philosophy, Boethius, Aquinas, Pascal, Lewis, Chesterton, and many more—all pointing to Jesus and the gospel as the true story of the world. Let's fill in the details a bit to help us see more clearly the beauty of the Christian story.

In chapter 1, I described the religious story in terms of a three-act play: *God—alienation—union*. The Christian story is a more fine-grained version of this religious story. My favorite ways of framing the Christian story include *home—away—home again* and *tragedy—comedy—fairy story*.[8] Perhaps the clearest story arc to help us grasp the Christian story, however, is in terms of *creation—fall—redemption—restoration.* I'll unpack the brilliance and beauty of the Christian story in terms of this four-act play, highlighting our clues as they point to Jesus.

In the beginning there was the eternal triune God—Father, Son, and Holy Spirit—existing in unity and diversity: a perfect community of love. This divine love spread itself in joy and delight into *creation*, as the living God brought into being a universe full of order, beauty, abundance, and life [**universe, life, love**]. In order to display and communicate his perfect goodness, God playfully and artistically created a world full of a great diversity of finite creatures—substances—possessing various powers and perfections [**species, morality, beauty**]. Humans are the pinnacle of God's creative activity, made in the divine image to be God's representatives on earth [**humans**]. Humans receive all things from God, and as divine representatives—kings and queens, priests and priestesses—they are charged to steward and regift all things back to God [**meaning, happiness**].

The highest good for humans is relationship with God [**happiness**]. In order to relate to God and others, humans were given free will. This power to choose gives humans the ability to be self-determiners of their actions, character, and life story. This freedom of the will is a great good, but it also creates the possibility of evil, pain, and suffering. Humanity's first couple—Adam and Eve—misused their creaturely freedom, attempting to meet their needs on their own instead of with God's help and guidance. This single act of disobedience resulted in the *fall* of humanity. Because of sin—morally culpable wrongdoing before God—humanity is now alienated from God, others, and self. The fall changed everything. The world has been turned upside down. All physical, social, and cultural structures are broken and corrupted [**pain**].

The penalty for sin is spiritual death—eternal separation from God. Worse, rebellious humans can do nothing on their own to reconcile with God. There is no way to earn salvation through human effort [**religion**]. But God did not give up on humans. He pursued them. In love, God sent his one and only Son, Jesus, to *redeem* humankind from sin, death, and alienation. Taking on a human nature, Jesus, the eternal, divine Son, became fully human too. He entered human history, living a perfect life as he proclaimed hope and healing to the world. He willingly died on a cross—taking all sin, pain, and suffering upon himself—so that humanity could be reconciled to God and the world could be healed. In an awe-inspiring display of love, Jesus gave himself "for the life of the world" (John 6:51). Three days later, Jesus physically rose from the dead, appeared to many people at many places, and then ascended back to the Father. Salvation and eternal life are possible, but cannot be earned. Salvation is a gift from God. All we can do is receive it. We do so by placing our faith in Jesus. Each person is saved by grace through faith (i.e., ventured trust) in Jesus. In this, Christianity is utterly unique among all world religions.

In the end, God will make all things new again. The world will be *restored*. Redeemed humans will reign with God in this universe forever. In the renewed creation, people will once again enjoy perfect harmony with God, themselves, and the world. We'll worship God and enjoy his unmediated presence, and we'll meaningfully work and relate too. We'll join with God in that eternal dance of mutual love and joy and delight. All will be well. And all will be right.

This is a great story. It's the best kind of story, full of drama, intrigue, tragedy, comedy, and fairy tale. But it's not just a great story. I think it's the greatest possible story. Just as Anselm famously defined God as the greatest possible *being*, Christianity is the greatest possible *story*.[9] And it is true! Christianity unites into a satisfying whole our longings for truth, goodness, and beauty, locating the source of all things in Christ. In Christianity alone do reason and romance, philosophy and story blend perfectly together. As G. K. Chesterton colorfully wrote,

The sanity of the world was restored and the soul of man offered salvation by something which did indeed satisfy the two warring tendencies of the past; which had never been satisfied in full and most certainly never satisfied together. It met the mythological search for romance by being a story and the philosophical search for truth by being a true story. . . . The more deeply we think of the matter the more we shall conclude that, if there be indeed a God, his creation could hardly have reached any other culmination than this granting of a real romance to the world. Otherwise the two sides of the human mind could never have touched at all; and the brain of man would have remained cloven and double; one lobe of it dreaming impossible dreams and the other repeating invariable calculations.[10]

We've discovered a story that is true to the way the world *is* and true to the way the world *ought* to be. We've traveled far and wide, through time and through the human heart, and all the clues point to Jesus and the gospel story. Our quest has led us to this moment and to this place. The world has revealed its secret, its gold.[11] Our hope was well founded. There is beauty and goodness at the center of the physical universe because Jesus is at that center. Jesus is the beauty of all beautiful things, the good of all good things, and the truth to which all created things point. As Pascal describes, "Jesus Christ is the object of all things, the centre towards which all things tend." Thus, "whoever knows him knows the reason for everything."[12] Jesus is the point of it all, including the point of the Christian story. When you get Jesus, you get everything your heart desires: meaning, purpose, love, identity, happiness, and rest.

Our journey of discovery has come to an end. We've traveled together as far as we can on that quest.[13] A new and unending adventure is before you, however: the *journey of faith*. You won't want to walk alone on that journey either. God has gifted to us the Bible, a kind of "enchanted map," as well as many fellow travelers—the church—to help us on the journey of faith.[14] But you alone must take that first step. The decision is yours to make. It's the same decision I was confronted with in my freshman dorm room: *What do you make of Jesus Christ?*

As we end our journey of discovery, I want to return to the question posed at the beginning of the book: *Who am I?* I argued that we cannot answer the question of identity until we discover the true story of the world. Locate your life in the true story and you'll receive your true name.[15] Jesus invites you to come, to place your faith in him, and to find your true home: "Yet to all who did receive him, to those who believed in his name, he gave the right to become children of God" (John 1:12). The choice is yours. I've shown you what I've discovered. May you receive Jesus and take on your new name: *child of God*.

Acknowledgments

To Rick James, thanks for being the consummate encourager. You not only read the entire manuscript but offered insight and humor that resulted in a much better final product. I hope this book serves as a useful tool for Cru staff and students. Thanks to Shane O'Neill, Brandon Rickabaugh, Jonathan Ashbach, Michael Keas, Courtney McLean, Ross Inman, and Paul Copan for reading a part of the manuscript or offering advice, feedback, and wisdom. Your friendship and help are much appreciated! I wrote the four chapters exploring the origins of the universe, life, species, and humans while a visiting scholar during the 2019–2020 academic year at the Carl F. H. Henry Center for Theological Understanding at Trinity Evangelical Divinity School. Thanks to Tom McCall, Geoffrey Fulkerson, Joel Chopp, Matthew Wiley, Jordan Wessling, Craig Bartholomew, Craig Keener, and Brian Matz for offering feedback as these chapters developed. I'm grateful to Palm Beach Atlantic University for the privilege of teaching and the space to research and write on these weighty topics of perennial concern. Thanks to Kenneth Crane—a fellow traveler and artist who helps us see the world better—for the magical cover design and chapter illustrations. I'm grateful to my editor at Brazos Press, Katelyn

Beaty: thank you for your steady hand, for your insightful comments on an earlier version of the manuscript, and for making all the needed fixes along the way. Finally, I couldn't do much without my family. To my wife, Ethel, I am glad that you exist! (To the reader: see the chapter on love to understand the joke.) But seriously, Ethel, you are a gift from God to me. I'm grateful for you and love the life we have together. And to Austin, Madeleine, Travis, Joshua: I love each of you deeply. I'm proud to be your dad. Thanks for letting me share bits and pieces of our journey in this travelogue. I look forward to many more adventures as we go.

Notes

Introduction: The Search

1. I'm echoing one of my favorite lines from Thornton Wilder's play *Our Town* (New York: HarperCollins, 1998), 46.

2. Hannah Arendt, *The Human Condition* (Chicago: University of Chicago Press, 1958), 181.

3. Arendt, *Human Condition*, 186.

4. Neil deGrasse Tyson, *Astrophysics for People in a Hurry* (New York: Norton, 2017), 33.

5. Sean Carroll, *The Big Picture: On the Origins of Life, Meaning, and the Universe Itself* (New York: Dutton, 2016), 3.

6. George Bernard Shaw, quoted in John Navone, *Seeking God in Story* (Collegeville, MN: Liturgical Press, 1979), 63. I've not been able to independently locate this quote or confirm that Shaw actually said it.

7. Lawrence Krauss, *The Greatest Story Ever Told—So Far: Why Are We Here?* (New York: Atria Books, 2017).

8. Bertrand Russell, *Why I Am Not a Christian, and Other Essays on Religion and Related Subjects* (New York: Touchstone, 1957), 107.

9. Hereafter, following convention, I'll refer to God with the masculine pronoun without taking a position on God's gender (or whether God has a gender at all).

10. See Anselm, *Proslogion* 2.

11. Roderick M. Chisholm, *The Foundations of Knowing* (Minneapolis: University of Minnesota Press, 1982), chap. 5.

12. Antony Flew, "The Presumption of Atheism," *Canadian Journal of Philosophy* 2, no. 1 (1972): 29–46.

13. R. Douglas Geivett, "A Pascalian Rejoinder to the Presumption of Atheism," in *God Matters: An Anthology*, ed. Christopher Bernard and Raymond Martin (New York: Longman, 2002), 172.

14. Alan of Lille, *Plaint of Nature*, trans. James J. Sheridan (Toronto: Pontifical Institute of Mediaeval Studies, 1980), 112.

15. Navone, *Seeking God in Story*, 160.

Chapter 1 The Universe

1. Douglas Adams, *The Hitchhiker's Guide to the Galaxy*, 25th anniv. ed. (New York: Harmony Books, 2004), 223.

2. Adams, *Hitchhiker's Guide to the Galaxy*, 223, 227.

3. Adams, *Hitchhiker's Guide to the Galaxy*, 228.

4. Adams, *Hitchhiker's Guide to the Galaxy*, 236.

5. Adams, *Hitchhiker's Guide to the Galaxy*, 237.

6. Adams, *Hitchhiker's Guide to the Galaxy*, 237.

7. Adams, *Hitchhiker's Guide to the Galaxy*, 237, 238.

8. Joshua Rasmussen, *How Reason Can Lead to God: A Philosopher's Bridge to Faith* (Downers Grove, IL: IVP Academic, 2019), 24.

9. Rasmussen, *How Reason Can Lead to God*, 22. The tile example is Rasmussens's example, not mine.

10. Alan of Lille, *Plaint of Nature*, trans. James J. Sheridan (Toronto: Pontifical Institute of Mediaeval Studies, 1980), 121.

11. Alan of Lille, *Plaint of Nature*, 144.

12. The remainder of this paragraph summarizes the discussion by William Lane Craig and James D. Sinclair in "The *Kalam* Cosmological Argument," in *The Blackwell Companion to Natural Theology*, ed. William Lane Craig and J. P. Moreland (Malden, MA: Blackwell, 2012), 125.

13. Michael A. Strauss, "The Expansion of the Universe," in *Welcome to the Universe: An Astrophysical Tour*, by Neil deGrasse Tyson, Michael A. Strauss, and J. Richard Gott (Princeton: Princeton University Press, 2016), 212.

14. J. Richard Gott, "The Shape of the Universe and the Big Bang," in Tyson, Strauss, and Gott, *Welcome to the Universe*, 368–69.

15. Adams, *Hitchhiker's Guide to the Galaxy*, 143.

16. The idea of starting with numbers familiar to us and then progressing to less familiar numbers is from Neil deGrasse Tyson, "The Size and Scale of the Universe," in Tyson, Strauss, and Gott, *Welcome to the Universe*, 17–25.

17. Steven Bertoni, "This Is How Hostess Makes 1 Million Twinkies A Day," *Forbes*, April 15, 2015, https://www.forbes.com/sites/stevenbertoni/2015/04/15/this-is-how-hostess-makes-1-million-twinkies-a-day/#26e69929fb58.

18. Rich Duprey, "15 Fascinating Things You Probably Didn't Know about McDonald's Corp.," The Motley Fool, October 11, 2016, https://www.fool.com/investing/2016/10/11/15-fascinating-things-you-probably-didnt-know-abou.aspx.

19. Or "Eat Mor Chikin," as the ubiquitous cows found on Chick-fil-A billboards implore. The figures about hamburgers are slightly modified from Tyson's calculations in "Size and Scale of the Universe," 18.

20. Martin Rees, *Just Six Numbers: The Deep Forces That Shape the Universe* (New York: Basic Books, 2000), 6.

21. Victor J. Stenger, "Faith in Anything Is Unreasonable," in *Is Faith in God Reasonable? Debates in Philosophy, Science, and Rhetoric*, ed. Corey Miller and Paul M. Gould (New York: Routledge, 2014), 67.

22. Alan of Lille, *Plaint of Nature*, 118.

23. Roger Penrose, "Time-Asymmetry and Quantum Gravity," in *Quantum Gravity 2: A Second Oxford Symposium*, ed. C. J. Isham, R. Penrose, and D. W. Sciama (Oxford: Clarendon, 1981), 249.

24. Robin Collins, "The Teleological Argument," in Craig and Moreland, *Blackwell Companion to Natural Theology*, 220.

25. For a helpful discussion of the ratio of matter to antimatter in the early universe, the cosmological constant, and the initial density problem (the so-called flatness problem), see Geraint F. Lewis and Luke A. Barnes, *A Fortunate Universe: Life in a Finely Tuned Cosmos* (Cambridge: Cambridge University Press, 2016), 157–67, 204–8.

26. Brian Schmidt, foreword to Lewis and Barnes, *Fortunate Universe*, xi.

27. The gravitational constant G has a value of 6.67×10^{-11} m^3 kg^{-1} s^{-2}.

28. Collins, "Teleological Argument," 212.

29. Lewis and Barnes, *Fortunate Universe*, 108–9.

30. Lewis and Barnes, *Fortunate Universe*, 109.

31. For a discussion and defense of the principle of sufficient reason, see Alexander R. Pruss, "The Leibnizian Cosmological Argument," in Craig and Moreland, *Blackwell Companion to Natural Theology*, 26–60.

32. This principle is suggested by Angus Ritchie, *From Morality to Metaphysics: The Theistic Implications of Our Ethical Commitments* (Oxford: Oxford University Press, 2012), 145.

33. These physical models fall into three basic families: *quantum fluctuation models* that give rise to baby universes emerging from an eternally existing primordial vacuum, *string scenarios* in which universes result from the collision of two three-dimensional membranes eternally expanding and collapsing, and *chaotic inflation models* that give rise to "droplet universes" that bubble out from an eternal and ever-expanding inflation field. For a nice summary of these models, see William Lane Craig, *Reasonable Faith: Christian Truth and Apologetics* (Wheaton: Crossway, 2008), 131–41.

34. William Lane Craig, "Graham Oppy on the *Kalām* Cosmological Argument," in *The Kalām Cosmological Argument: Philosophical Arguments for the Finitude of the Past*, ed. Paul Copan with William Lane Craig, vol. 1, (New York: Bloomsbury Academic, 2018), 168.

35. Craig, "Graham Oppy on the *Kalām* Cosmological Argument," 168.

36. For a summary of the three basic multiverse proposals, see Jeffrey Koperski, *The Physics of Theism: God, Physics, and the Philosophy of Science* (Malden, MA: Wiley-Blackwell, 2015), 85–88.

37. For a more detailed discussion of both of these problems, see Koperski, *Physics of Theism*, 86.

38. There are *philosophical* reasons to think such multiverse scenarios might be true. We could, following the philosopher David Lewis, postulate causally isolated universes in order to ground our modal discourse (i.e., language about what is possible or impossible), or we could postulate some principle, such as the principle of plenitude, such that *anything that could exist must exist*. I'll just report that I'm unpersuaded that we need to adopt Lewis's modal realism to explain our modal discourse. Even if something like the plenitude principle is employed to generate every logically possible or mathematically consistent universe, there are no good reasons to think such a principle would have causal powers to bring about the multiverse. That would require an agent. For David Lewis's defense of concrete modal realism, see his *On the Plurality of Worlds* (Malden, MA: Blackwell, 1986). For a fascinating discussion of the history of the principle of plenitude and how it has figured in Western thought, see Arthur O. Lovejoy, *The Great Chain of Being* (Cambridge, MA: Harvard University Press, 1936).

39. As Timothy O'Connor summarizes, the inflationary universe generator requires "e.g., that the original small space giving rise to the droplet universes conform to Einstein's equation of general relativity and have a high energy density in its inflation field, and it presupposes other framework physical principles that structure the theory." Timothy O'Connor, *Theism and Ultimate Explanation: The Necessary Shape of Contingency* (Malden, MA: Wiley-Blackwell, 2012), 106.

Chapter 2 Life

1. Philip K. Dick, *Do Androids Dream of Electric Sheep?*, in *Four Novels of the 1960s: The Man in the High Castle, The Three Stigmata of Palmer Eldritch, Do Androids Dream of Electric Sheep?, Ubik*, ed. Jonathan Lethem, Library of America (New York: Library of America, 2007), 575.

2. Lesley A. DuTemple, *The Complete Idiot's Guide to Life Science* (Indianapolis: Macmillan, 2000), 4.

3. For a helpful overview of the debate over the definition of life, see Mark A. Bedau, "The Nature of Life," in *The Philosophy of Artificial Life*, ed. Margaret A. Boden (Oxford: Oxford University Press, 1996), 332–37.

4. David S. Oderberg, "Synthetic Life and the Bruteness of Immanent Causation," in *Aristotle on Method and Metaphysics*, ed. Edward Feser (New York: Palgrave Macmillan, 2013), 213.

5. David S. Oderberg, *Real Essentialism* (New York: Routledge, 2007), 180.

6. Oderberg, *Real Essentialism*, 194. Immanent causation is often contrasted with *transient* causation, in which the effect terminates in something outside the agent.

7. Edward Feser, *Aristotle's Revenge: The Metaphysical Foundations of Physical and Biological Science* (Neunkirchen-Seelscheid, Germany: Editiones Scholasticae, 2019), 378.

8. For more on the concept of substance, see James K. Dew Jr. and Paul M. Gould, *Philosophy: A Christian Introduction* (Grand Rapids: Baker Academic, 2019), chap. 9.

9. There are inanimate substances too—atoms, molecules, and perhaps other higher level composite objects—but we'll primarily concern ourselves in this chapter and the next two with *living* substances.

10. Another way certain common features or properties can be blocked is through artificial crossing of organisms of different kinds, resulting in sterile hybrids. See Oderberg, *Real Essentialism*, 178–79.

11. DuTemple, *Complete Idiot's Guide to Life Science*, 70–72.

12. Michael J. Benton, *The History of Life: A Very Short Introduction* (Oxford: Oxford University Press, 2008), 35.

13. Oderberg, *Real Essentialism*, 184.

14. This older scheme is not exactly right, of course, for bacteria and other prokaryotes are neither animals nor plants. To be thorough, I'd add another level below plants for these wily creatures. For simplicity, I'll stick to the main kinds of substances as noted by Aristotle.

15. Oderberg nicely summarizes the claim I'm making here: "The fact that phylogeny (the study of origins) has invaded, and now permeates, morphology (the study of the form and functions of an organism or its species) has led to classifications that from a metaphysical point of view do not represent reality." Oderberg, *Real Essentialism*, 189.

16. Where do creatures assigned to the Monera, Protista, and Fungi kingdoms (from the five-kingdoms taxonomy) and Archaea and Bacteria (from the three-domains model) *essentially* belong? Monera, protista, archaea, and bacteria are all sensory animals; fungi are vegetative animals. For a helpful discussion of how to map the modern "tree of life" taxonomies onto the essentialist taxonomy suggested here, see Oderberg, *Real Essentialism*, 183–93; and Feser, *Aristotle's Revenge*, 391–400.

17. Kori Rumore and Jonathan Berlin, "Serial Stowaway: 22 Airport Incidents Involving Marilyn Hartman," *Chicago Tribune*, March 18, 2021, https://www.chicagotribune.com/data/ct-serial-stowaway-timeline-of-incidents-htmlstory.html#nt=latestnews&rt=floating-rail.

18. Sean Carroll, *The Big Picture: On the Origins of Life, Meaning, and the Universe Itself* (New York: Dutton, 2016), 270.

19. Daniel C. Dennett, *From Bacteria to Bach and Back: The Evolution of Minds* (New York: Norton, 2017), 26–27.

20. James Tour, "An Open Letter to My Colleagues," *Inference: International Review of Science* 3, no. 2 (August 2017), https://inference-review.com/article/an-open-letter-to-my-colleagues.

21. Portions of this section were published earlier in the *Southwestern Journal of Theology*. Thanks to the editor of the journal for permission to reproduce some of that essay here. For the original essay, see Paul M. Gould, "God, Atheism, and the Origins Debate," *Southwestern Journal of Theology* 60, no. 2 (2018): 137–54.

22. Robert C. Bishop, Larry L. Funck, Raymond J. Lewis, Stephen O. Moshier, and John H. Walton, *Understanding Scientific Theories of Origins: Cosmology, Geology, and Biology in Christian Perspective* (Downers Grove, IL: IVP Academic, 2018), 203.

23. The Late Heavy Bombardment was a period of almost 300 million years, occurring between 4.1 and 3.8 billion years ago, when a large number of asteroids collided with the earth, causing it to remain molten.

24. M. R. Walter, R. Buick, and J. S. R. Dunlop, "Stromatolites 3,400–3,500 Myr Old from the North Pole Area, Western Australia," *Nature* 284 (April 1980): 443–45.

25. A. P. Nutman, V. C. Bennett, C. R. L. Friend, M. J. Van Kranendonk, and A. R. Chivas, "Rapid Emergence of Life Shown by Discovery of 3,700-Million-Year-Old Microbial Structures," *Nature* 537 (September 2016): 535–38.

26. Some scientists argue that carbon-isotope studies based on large-scale deposits of carbon found in the form of graphite in ancient rocks point to an even earlier date for life's origin on earth: 3.8 billion years ago! If these studies are correct, life appeared *literally*

immediately after the end of the Late Heavy Bombardment period. See Bishop et al., *Understanding Scientific Theories of Origins*, 368.

27. Gerald Rau, *Mapping the Origins Debate: Six Models of the Beginning of Everything* (Downers Grove, IL: IVP Academic, 2012), 84.

28. For a transcript and streamable recording of a 1996 lecture by Stephen Hawking on whether life originated in outer space, see "Life in the Universe," https://www.hawking.org.uk/in-words/lectures/life-in-the-universe.

29. Bishop et al., *Understanding Scientific Theories of Origins*, 365.

30. I'm summarizing a helpful discussion of the typical approach by synthetic chemists as described in Bishop et al., *Understanding Scientific Theories of Origins*, 387–88.

31. For a helpful survey of the current state of origin-of-life studies with respect to the ingredients problem, see Bishop et al., *Understanding Scientific Theories of Origins*, 365–88.

32. For a review of the difficulties in synthetically creating even some of the precursors to just a few of the many molecules within the building block class, see James Tour, "Animadversions of a Synthetic Chemist," *Inference: International Review of Science* 2, no. 2 (May 2016), https://inference-review.com/article/animadversions-of-a-synthetic-chemist.

33. Doug Axe describes functional coherence as "the hierarchical arrangement of parts needed for anything to produce a high-level function—each part contributing in a coordinated way to the whole." Douglas Axe, *Undeniable: How Biology Confirms Our Intuition That Life Is Designed* (New York: HarperCollins, 2016), 144.

34. Rau, *Mapping the Origins Debate*, 88.

35. Genes are regions of chromosomes found within a cell that are themselves long molecules of double-stranded DNA, molecules made up of four *kinds* of nucleotide bases that are well suited for the storage and transmission of information.

36. Stephen C. Meyer, *Darwin's Doubt: The Explosive Origin of Animal Life and the Case for Intelligent Design* (New York: HarperOne, 2013), 163.

37. Axe, *Undeniable*, 57.

38. Michael Denton, *Evolution: A Theory in Crisis* (London: Burnett Books, 1985), 323, quoted in Axe, *Undeniable*, 31.

39. Stephen C. Meyer, *Signature in the Cell: DNA and the Evidence for Intelligent Design* (New York: HarperOne, 2009), 212.

40. Bishop et al., *Understanding Scientific Theories of Origins*, 397.

41. Axe, *Undeniable*, 126. It is beyond physical representation because there are only 10^{80} elementary particles in the universe. Thus, a single 80-character line of text would suffice to write out the number of elementary particles in the universe, and the total number of physical events over the universe's history would only require another half line (10^{116}) (Axe, *Undeniable*, 125). William Dembski calculates the maximum number of physical events that could have taken place in the history of the universe to be 10^{140}, determined by multiplying the number of elementary particles (10^{80}), the amount of time since the Big Bang (10^{17} seconds), and the maximum number of events that could occur between elementary particles given the speed of light (10^{43} events per second). See Meyer, *Signature in the Cell*, 216–17.

42. Axe, *Undeniable*, 132–34.

43. Some have attempted to increase the probability of assembling life from nonlife by arguing that the assembly of the necessary proteins for life was gradual. This is implausible due to the relatively short amount of time available for life to arise between the end of the Late Heavy Bombardment era and the emergence of living organisms (i.e., between 100 to 320 million years). For other ideas about how to raise the probabilities, many of which are highly speculative, see Bishop et al., *Understanding Scientific Theories of Origins*, 397–98. There is also the related question of which came first—the chicken (the protein) or the egg (RNA or DNA). The current front-runner among origin-of-life theories is that RNA came first, and from the first RNA strands DNA and proteins developed. For a helpful discussion of the RNA-first proposal, see Bishop et al., *Understanding Scientific Theories of Origins*, 398–409.

44. Thomas Aquinas, *The Treatise on the Divine Nature: Summa Theologiae I.1–13*, trans. Brian J. Shanley, OP (Indianapolis: Hackett, 2006), 24.

Chapter 3 Species

1. Candice Millard, *The River of Doubt: Theodore Roosevelt's Darkest Journey* (New York: Anchor Books, 2005).

2. David M. Raup, *Extinction: Bad Genes or Bad Luck?* (New York: Norton, 1992), 3–4.

3. Estimates vary wildly regarding how many species of living organisms there are today. A 2011 study estimates that there are 8.7 million species on the earth (plus or minus 1.3 million). With less than 2 million species cataloged by biologists, the majority of species on earth await discovery. See Camilo Mora, Derek P. Tittensor, Sina Adl, Alastair G. B. Simpson, and Boris Worm, "How Many Species Are There on Earth and in the Ocean?," *PloS Biology* 9 (August 2011), https://journals.plos.org/plosbiology/article?id=10.1371/journal.pbio.1001127.

4. Alister E. McGrath, *A Fine-Tuned Universe: The Quest for God in Science and Theology* (Louisville: Westminster John Knox, 2009), 157.

5. Michael J. Benton, *The History of Life: A Very Short Introduction* (Oxford: Oxford University Press, 2008), 39.

6. Benton, *History of Life*, 45.

7. Benton, *History of Life*, 56–59.

8. Stephen C. Meyer, *Darwin's Doubt: The Explosive Origin of Animal Life and the Case for Intelligent Design* (New York: HarperCollins, 2013), 71–72.

9. This is called the Ordovician period. See Benton, *History of Life*, 57.

10. Benton, *History of Life*, 71.

11. Benton, *History of Life*, 88.

12. Benton, *History of Life*, 93; see also Robert M. Hazen, *The Story of Earth: The First 4.5 Billion Years, from Stardust to Living Planet* (New York: Penguin Books, 2012), 248–49.

13. Benton, *History of Life*, 102, 118–19.

14. Benton, *History of Life*, 140.

15. Benton, *History of Life*, 144–45.

16. The metaphor of a world gradually waking up is from Thomas Nagel, *Mind and Cosmos: Why the Materialist Neo-Darwinian Conception of Nature Is Almost Certainly False* (Oxford: Oxford University Press, 2012), 117.

17. I'm reminded of C. S. Lewis's description of Aslan's creation of Narnia. As the animals burst forth in Narnia, "there was so much cawing, cooing, crowing, braying, neighing, baying, barking, lowing, bleating, and trumpeting." C. S. Lewis, *The Magician's Nephew* (New York: HarperCollins, 1955), 123.

18. "I am fully convinced that species are not immutable." Charles Darwin, *On the Origin of Species: A Facsimilie of the First Edition* (Cambridge, MA: Harvard University Press, 2003), 6.

19. Darwin, *Origin of Species*, 420.

20. Elliott Sober, *Philosophy of Biology*, 2nd ed. (Boulder, CO: Westview, 2000), 151.

21. David S. Oderberg, *Real Essentialism* (New York: Routledge, 2007), 219.

22. Oderberg, *Real Essentialism*, 224.

23. David S. Oderberg, "The Great Unifier: Form and the Unity of the Organism," in *Neo-Aristotelian Perspectives on Contemporary Science*, eds. William M. R. Simpson, Robert C. Koons, and Nicholas J. Teh (New York: Routledge, 2018), 212; Denis Walsh, "Evolutionary Essentialism," *British Journal for the Philosophy of Science* 57 (2006): 430.

24. *Objection:* We don't need essences to explain inheritability and resemblance between individual organisms of the same species; we can explain the phenomena by appeal to DNA and the genetic code alone. *Reply to objection:* The information contained within the genetic code is necessary but not sufficient for inheritability and resemblance for at least two reasons. First, there is biological information found in organisms that is not encoded within DNA and the genetic code—i.e., epigenetic information—that plays a key role in their development and morphological structure. Second, while DNA does direct protein synthesis, the properties of individual proteins do not fully determine the assembly of an organism's higher-level structures. There are other sources of information that help arrange individual proteins into groups of proteins, groups of proteins into cell parts, cell parts into cells, cells

into tissues, tissues into organs, and so on (Meyer, *Darwin's Doubt*, 276). My claim is that essences nicely explain why within an organism there are multiple sources of information that work together in a highly coordinated manner to guide the development of organisms as well as the inheritance of recurrent traits in an organism's offspring.

25. Oderberg, *Real Essentialism*, 234.

26. Robert C. Koons, "Thermal Substances: A Neo-Aristotelian Ontology of the Quantum World," *Synthese* 198 (2019), https://doi.org/10.1007/s11229-019-02318-2.

27. Portions of this section were published earlier in the *Southwestern Journal of Theology*. Thanks to the editor of the journal for permission to reproduce some of that essay here. For the original essay, see Paul M. Gould, "God, Atheism, and the Origins Debate," *Southwestern Journal of Theology* 60, no. 2 (2018): 137–54.

28. Sean Carroll, *The Big Picture: On the Origins of Life, Meaning, and the Universe Itself* (New York: Dutton, 2016), 226.

29. Carroll, *Big Picture*, 273.

30. Gerald Rau, *Mapping the Origins Debate: Six Models of the Beginning of Everything* (Downers Grove, IL: IVP Academic, 2012), 102.

31. I'm interested, then, in the question of *macroevolution*, the idea that *distinct* species evolved through Darwinian processes. *Microevolution*—the idea of change within species—while uncontroversial, cannot account for the biological diversity found on earth.

32. Meyer, *Darwin's Doubt*, 158.

33. For a helpful summary of the development of the modern evolutionary synthesis, see Robert C. Bishop, Larry L. Funck, Raymond J. Lewis, Stephen O. Mishier, and John H. Walton, *Understanding Scientific Theories of Origins: Cosmology, Geology, and Biology in Christian Perspective* (Downers Grove, IL: IVP Academic, 2018), 474–91.

34. Meyer, *Darwin's Doubt*, ix.

35. Stephen C. Meyer, "Neo-Darwinism and the Origin of Biological Form and Information," in *Theistic Evolution: A Scientific, Philosophical, and Theological Critique*, ed. J. P. Moreland, Stephen C. Meyer, Christopher Shaw, Ann K. Gauger, and Wayne Grudem (Wheaton: Crossway, 2017), 111–12.

36. Douglas Axe, *Undeniable: How Biology Confirms Our Intuition That Life Is Designed* (New York: HarperCollins, 2016), 97. As Axe summarizes, "Evolutionary theory ascribes inventive power to natural selection alone. However, because selection can only home in on the fitness signal from an invention after that invention already exists, it can't actually invent."

37. Axe, *Undeniable*, 103.

38. Jack L. King and Thomas H. Jukes, "Non-Darwinian Evolution," *Science* 164, no. 3881 (1969): 788, quoted in Meyer, *Darwin's Doubt*, 173.

39. Hugo De Vries, *Species and Varieties: Their Origin by Mutation* (Chicago: Open Court, 1904), 4, quoted in Axe, *Undeniable*, 220.

40. While I need not argue for the stronger claim here, Axe argues that accidental invention by random mutation is physically impossible. See Axe, *Undeniable*, 87–162.

41. In chap. 2, the number 10^{74} was used to specify the ratio of functional to nonfunctional proteins of any length. Here, 10^{77} expresses the ratio of functional to nonfunctional proteins of 150 amino acids in length (Meyer, "Neo-Darwinism and the Origin of Biological Form and Information," 116). For the original results, see Douglas Axe, "Estimating the Prevalence of Protein Sequences Adopting Functional Enzyme Folds," *Journal of Molecular Biology* 341 (2004): 1295–1315.

42. Meyer, "Neo-Darwinism and the Origin of Biological Form and Information," 117.

43. Meyer, "Neo-Darwinism and the Origin of Biological Form and Information," 118.

44. Gerd B. Müller and Stuart A. Newman, "Origination of Organismal Form: The Forgotten Cause in Evolutionary Theory," in *On the Origin of Organismal Form: Beyond the Gene in Developmental and Evolutionary Biology*, ed. Gerd B. Müller and Stuart A. Newman (Cambridge, MA: MIT Press, 2003), 7.

45. Meyer, *Darwin's Doubt*, 326. The endosymbiotic origin of mitochondria and plastids from bacteria in a eukaryotic cell would be an exception. For if endosymbiotic theory is

the best explanation for the origin of mitochondria and plastids, then the functions of the precursor bacterium did in fact pass on. The context of Meyer's quote is a discussion of Michael Lynch's theory of neutral or "non-adaptive" evolution, a non-Darwinian theory that relegates natural selection to a largely insignificant role. For more on endosymbiotic theory, horizontal gene transfer, and whole-genome duplication, see Bishop et al., *Understanding Scientific Theories of Origins*, 513–22, in which the coauthors take a much rosier view of the creative power of these newly proposed mechanisms than I do. As I shall argue below, however, even if I'm wrong, it doesn't follow that the origin of species can be wholly explained without appeal to God. Either way, the origin of species points to the reality of an intelligent cause.

46. Meyer, *Darwin's Doubt*, 326.

47. Meyer, *Darwin's Doubt*, 331.

48. Meyer, *Darwin's Doubt*, 307.

49. Meyer, *Darwin's Doubt*, 329. For a detailed critique of many leading non-Darwinian mechanisms currently proposed by evolutionary biologists, including evolutionary development theory ("evo-devo"), see 291–335.

50. This summarizes the argument made in Walsh, "Evolutionary Essentialism," 424–48.

51. Walsh, "Evolutionary Essentialism," 444. *Phenotypic plasticity* refers to the ability of individual organisms to respond to a large array of phenotype variation in response to environmental factors.

52. For more on the role of essences in evolution, see also Stephen J. Boulter, "Can Evolutionary Biology Do Without Aristotelian Essentialism?," *Royal Institute of Philosophy Supplement* 70 (2012): 83–103; and Christopher J. Austin, "Aristotelian Essentialism: Essence in the Age of Evolution," *Synthese* 194 (2017): 2539–56.

53. For a book-length argument moving from the complex and "functionally coherent" activities of living organisms to a divine mind, see Axe, *Undeniable*. As he colorfully states, "I can only see these ingenious creeping, climbing, swimming, soaring, blooming, burrowing, luring, lunging, spinning, sporulating, fleeing, and fighting inventions as having come from the mind of God. To me nothing else makes sense" (185).

Chapter 4 Humans

1. Louisa May Alcott, *Little Women* (New York: Bantam Books, 1983).

2. Alcott, *Little Women*, 10.

3. Alcott, *Little Women*, 11.

4. Alcott, *Little Women*, 11.

5. Josef Pieper, *Faith, Hope, Love* (San Francisco: Ignatius, 2012), 91–92.

6. William Lane Craig has recently argued that *Homo heidelbergensis* were the earliest biological humans and thus all those who descended from them (Neanderthals, Denisovans, *Homo sapiens*) are (or were) human too. See William Lane Craig, *In Quest of the Historical Adam: A Biblical and Scientific Exploration* (Grand Rapids: Eerdmans, 2021).

7. Douglas Adams, *The Hitchhiker's Guide to the Galaxy*, 25th anniv. ed. (New York: Harmony Books, 2004), 269.

8. Yuval Noah Harari, *Sapiens: A Brief History of Humankind* (New York: Harper-Perennial, 2015), 3.

9. Harari, *Sapiens*, 5.

10. There is not a single line of descent from the great apes to modern humans, however. For example, *Homo sapiens* is not a direct descendant of either *Homo erectus* or Neanderthals, although there is genomic evidence to suggest that *Homo sapiens* interbred with Neanderthals and Denisovans. It is postulated that *Homo sapiens* and Neanderthals share a common ancestor in *Homo heidelbergensis* and that *Homo sapiens* and *Homo erectus* share a common ancestor with *Homo habilis*, possibly the first *Homo* species to emerge from the Australopithecines species. For more on the possible relationships between various species in the *Homo* lineage, see Robert C. Bishop, Larry L. Funck, Raymond J. Lewis, Stephen O. Mishier, and John H. Walton, *Understanding Scientific Theories of Origins: Cosmology,*

Geology, and Biology in Christian Perspective (Downers Grove, IL: IVP Academic, 2018), 577–79. See also Craig, *In Quest of the Historical Adam.*

11. Johan De Smedt and Helen De Cruz, *The Challenge of Evolution to Religion* (New York: Cambridge University Press, 2020), 32.

12. Contemporary biology affirms *monophylogeny*, the view that humans today are of the same biological type. *Homo sapiens* have been the only humans for roughly ten thousand to forty thousand years. For helpful summaries of the science supporting monophylogeny, see Alan R. Templeton, "Human Races: A Genetic and Evolutionary Perspective," *American Anthropologist* 110, no. 3 (1998): 632–50; and Alan R. Templeton, "Biological Races in Humans," *Studies in History and Philosophy of Biological and Biomedical Sciences* 44 (2013): 262–71. I was first alerted to these references from S. Joshua Swamidass, *The Genealogical Adam and Eve: The Surprising Science of Universal Ancestry* (Downers Grove, IL: IVP Academic, 2019), 128.

13. Harari, *Sapiens*, 12.

14. Harari, *Sapiens*, 13.

15. Harari, *Sapiens*, 20–21.

16. Harari, *Sapiens*, 21, 33.

17. Harari, *Sapiens*, 37.

18. Harari, *Sapiens*, 78.

19. Harari, *Sapiens*, 79.

20. Harari, *Sapiens*, 244.

21. For a sophisticated discussion of one "deck stacking" noninterventionist approach to the origins of life, species, and humans, see Michael J. Murray, "Natural Providence (or Design Trouble)," *Faith and Philosophy* 20, no. 3 (2003): 307–27. For an account of human origins that accepts evolutionary science and, on the basis of that science, rejects a historical first couple, see Dennis R. Venema and Scot McKnight, *Adam and the Genome: Reading Scripture after Genetic Science* (Grand Rapids: Brazos, 2017). Unfortunately for Venema and McKnight, some of the arguments made against the possibility of a first pair of humans are demonstrably fallacious; see S. Joshua Swamidass, "Three Stories on Adam," Peaceful Science, August 5, 2018, http://peacefulscience.org/three-stories-on-adam/.

22. Swamidass, *Genealogical Adam and Eve.*

23. For a nice overview of the scientific case *against* the evolutionary account of human origins, including the standard evolutionary account of the fossil evidence as summarized earlier in this chapter, see J. P. Moreland, Stephen C. Meyer, Christopher Shaw, Ann K. Gauger, and Wayne Grudem, eds., *Theistic Evolution: A Scientific, Philosophical, and Theological Critique* (Wheaton: Crossway, 2017), 431–521.

24. On this second option, it is possible to reconcile the genetic evidence (including the current genetic diversity in the human population) with the thesis that there was an original human pair, created uniquely by God between fifty thousand and one million years ago, from which all other humans descend. On one version of this model of human origins defended by the organization Reasons to Believe, Adam and Eve are the *genetic* and *genealogical* ancestors of all humans and uniquely created by God between fifty thousand and two hundred thousand years ago. See Fazale Rana with Hugh Ross, *Who Was Adam? A Creation Model Approach to the Origin of Humanity*, 2nd ed. (Covina, CA: RTB Press, 2015). See also a series of blog posts by the molecular biologist Anjeanette Roberts: "How Can Christians Disagree over Adam and Eve?," December 19, 2019, https://reasons.org/explore/blogs/theorems -theology/how-can-christians-disagree-over-adam-and-eve; "Mosaic Eve: Mother of All (Part 1)," January 16, 2020, https://reasons.org/explore/blogs/theorems-theology/mosaic-eve -mother-of-all-part-1; and "Mosaic Eve: Mother of All (Part 2)," January 23, 2020, https:// reasons.org/explore/blogs/theorems-theology/mosaic-eve-mother-of-all-part-2. For a sole progenitor model with a later date for the first pair of humans (around five hundred thousand years ago), see Ann Gauger, "Not a Simple Question," *Making Note of the Moments* (blog), November 25, 2019, https://anngauger.blog/2019/11/25/not-a-simple-question/. Craig (see *In Quest of the Historical Adam*) suggests that humanity's first pair were members of *Homo heidelbergensis* living between one million and seven hundred fifty thousand years ago.

25. For a decent multiple-views book on the question of human origins, including the young earth perspective, see *Four Views on the Historical Adam*, ed. Matthew Barrett and Ardel B. Caneday (Grand Rapids: Zondervan, 2013).

26. "The difference in mind between man and the higher animals, great as it is, certainly is one of degree and not kind." Charles Darwin, *The Descent of Man* (New York: Heritage, 1972), 109.

27. George Gaylord Simpson, *The Meaning of Evolution* (New Haven: Yale University Press, 1967), 345.

28. As the science popularizer Neil deGrasse Tyson states, "We are participants in a great cosmic chain of being, with a direct genetic link across species both living and extinct. . . . We are one with the rest of nature, fitting neither above nor below, but within." *Astrophysics for People in a Hurry* (New York: Norton, 2017), 199, 201.

29. G. K. Chesterton, *The Everlasting Man* (San Francisco: Ignatius, 2008), 36.

30. Consider the story of Nim Chimpsky, a chimpanzee that was taught sign language from 1973 to 1978 in order to determine if the closest human ancestor (according to evolutionary theory) possessed the capacity for language. The lead investigator in Project Nim, Herbert S. Terrace of Columbia University, concluded that chimpanzees are not capable of stringing together words into meaningful sentences. The best Nim could come up with were nonsense sentences such as "Give orange me give eat orange me eat orange give me eat orange give me you." Dava Sobel, "Researcher Challenges Conclusion that Apes Can Learn Language," *New York Times*, October 21, 1979, https://www.nytimes.com/1979/10/21/archives/researcher-challenges-conclusion-that-apes-can-learn-language.html. Thanks to Joshua Swamidass, *Genealogical Adam and Eve*, 128, for alerting me to the story of Nim.

31. Chesterton, *Everlasting Man*, 36.

32. Chesterton, *Everlasting Man*, 38.

33. As Chesterton put it in *Everlasting Man*, "Man is not merely an evolution but rather a revolution" (26).

34. Daniel C. Dennett, *From Bacteria to Bach and Back: The Evolution of Minds* (New York: Norton, 2017), 3.

35. Dennett, *From Bacteria to Bach and Back*, 53.

36. Dennett, *From Bacteria to Bach and Back*, 148.

37. Dennett, *From Bacteria to Bach and Back*, 170.

38. Dennett, *From Bacteria to Bach and Back*, 171.

39. Dennett, *From Bacteria to Bach and Back*, 209.

40. Dennett, *From Bacteria to Bach and Back*, 211.

41. Dennett, *From Bacteria to Bach and Back*, 260.

42. Dennett, *From Bacteria to Bach and Back*, 87.

43. J. P. Moreland, *The Soul: How We Know It's Real and Why It Matters* (Chicago: Moody, 2014), 28.

44. Moreland, *Soul*, 27–28.

45. Richard Swinburne, *Are We Bodies or Souls?* (Oxford: Oxford University Press, 2019), 12.

46. Thomas Nagel, "Is Consciousness an Illusion?," *New York Review of Books* 64, no. 4 (March 9, 2017): 33.

47. Kevin Kimble and Timothy O'Connor, "The Argument from Consciousness Revisited," in *Oxford Studies in Philosophy of Religion*, ed. Jonathan L. Kvanvig, vol. 3 (Oxford: Oxford University Press, 2011), 132.

48. David Bentley Hart, "The Illusionist," *New Atlantis* 53 (Summer/Fall 2017): 121.

49. I'm speaking loosely in the main text. More technically, the Hard Problem is that of explaining how facts about nonconscious things (physical properties and events) entail or explain facts about conscious things (the phenomenal properties and subjects). Thanks to Brandon Rickabaugh for helping me think through the Hard Problem. The term was coined by the philosopher David Chalmers in "Facing up to the Problem of Consciousness," *Journal of Consciousness Studies* 2, no. 3 (1995): 200–219.

50. Hart, "Illusionist," 114, 113.

51. Interestingly, in light of the serious problems with a purely materialistic account of mental phenomena, a growing minority of philosophers are now positing forms of *panpsychism*, the view that consciousness is a fundamental feature of reality, part of the ground floor, such that the fundamental particles of physics (whatever they turn out to be) have conscious experiences. This recent move, I think, shows the strength of the argument from mental phenomena to minds. For more, see Brandon Rickabaugh, "The Primacy of the Mental: From Russellian Monism to Substance Dualism," *Philosophia Christi* 20, no. 1 (2018): 31–41.

52. For a helpful overview of the argument from consciousness to God, see J. P. Moreland, "The Argument from Consciousness," in *The Blackwell Companion to Natural Theology*, ed. William Lane Craig and J. P. Moreland (Malden, MA: Wiley-Blackwell, 2012), 282–343; and Kimble and O'Connor, "Argument from Consciousness Revisited."

53. Perhaps God front-loaded proto-conscious properties into the initial conditions of the world and set the world in motion such that minds would arise at the proper time. Alternatively, perhaps God directly created minds at the moment of human origins.

Chapter 5 Morality

1. "Alcatraz Escape Attempts," Alcatraz History, accessed December 10, 2021, https://www.alcatrazhistory.com/escapes1.htm. Although, check out the movie *The Rock*, in which we learn that at least Sean Connery's (fictional) character managed to escape Alcatraz and live to tell the story (and fight some rogue Marines who threatened to blow up much of San Francisco).

2. See, e.g., John Krasinski, "Some Good News," YouTube video, 15:43, March 29, 2020, https://www.youtube.com/watch?v=F5pgG1M_h_U.

3. For a compelling story of injustice in America and one lawyer's fight for prison reform, see Bryan Stevenson, *Just Mercy: A Story of Justice and Redemption* (New York: Random House, 2014).

4. Boethius, *The Consolation of Philosophy*, trans. W. V. Cooper (Ex-classics Project, 2009), 8, https://www.exclassics.com/consol/consol.pdf.

5. Boethius, *The Consolation of Philosophy*, trans. Victor Watts (New York: Penguin Books, 1999), 3–4.

6. Boethius, *Consolation of Philosophy* (Watts), 7.

7. Boethius, *Consolation of Philosophy* (Watts), 16.

8. Boethius, *Consolation of Philosophy* (Watts), 20.

9. Bill Bryson, *A Walk in the Woods: Rediscovering America on the Appalachian Trail* (New York: Broadway Books, 1998), 207.

10. James K. A. Smith, *On the Road with Saint Augustine: A Real-World Spirituality for Restless Hearts* (Grand Rapids: Brazos, 2019), 12.

11. William Golding, *Lord of the Flies* (New York: Penguin Books, 2016), 176.

12. Golding, *Lord of the Flies*, 180.

13. While I won't consider it here, there is another version of subjectivism, sometimes called *relativism*, such that moral facts are indexed to the beliefs or preferences of society or culture. The problems that infect subjectivism infect cultural relativism too, so I set it aside. For more on subjectivism and relativism, see Russ Shafer-Landau, *Whatever Happened to Good and Evil?* (Oxford: Oxford University Press, 2004).

14. These problems with subjectivism are discussed in detail in chaps. 3, 4, and 5, respectively, of Shafer-Landau, *Whatever Happened to Good and Evil?*

15. Joshua Rasmussen, *How Reason Can Lead to God: A Philosopher's Bridge to Faith* (Downers Grove, IL: IVP Academic, 2019), 138–40.

16. C. S. Lewis, *Miracles* (New York: Touchstone, 1996), 49.

17. Erik J. Wielenberg, *Robust Ethics: The Metaphysics and Epistemology of Godless Normative Realism* (Oxford: Oxford University Press, 2014).

18. Wielenberg, *Robust Ethics*, 50–56.

19. William Lane Craig, "William Lane Craig's Opening Speech," in *A Debate on God and Morality*, ed. Adam Lloyd Johnson (New York: Routledge, 2020), 33–35. Although Wielenberg replies to Craig's basic objection, I think that he ultimately fails to explain why

moral facts supervene on certain physical facts. The story becomes, as Craig dubs it, a kind of "Voodoo Metaphysics" (35).

20. David Baggett, "Psychopathy and Supererogation," in Johnson, *Debate on God and Morality*, 147.

21. For a nice back-and-forth on what is now called the Evolutionary Argument against Naturalism, see Johnson, *Debate on God and Morality*. See also Alvin Plantinga, *Where the Conflict Really Lies: Science, Religion, and Naturalism* (Oxford: Oxford University Press, 2011), chap. 10.

22. C. Stephen Evans, *Natural Signs and the Knowledge of God: A New Look at Theistic Arguments* (Oxford: Oxford University Press, 2010), 120–21.

23. Thomas Nagel, *Mind and Cosmos: Why the Materialist Neo-Darwinian Conception of Nature Is Almost Certainly False* (Oxford: Oxford University Press, 2012), 67, 92. See also John Leslie, *Universes* (New York: Routledge, 1989); and Philip Goff, "The Universe Knows Right from Wrong," *Nautilus*, September 9, 2020, http://nautil.us/issue/89/the-dark-side/the-universe-knows-right-from-wrong.

24. Angus Ritchie, *From Morality to Metaphysics: The Theistic Implications of Our Ethical Commitments* (Oxford: Oxford University Press, 2012), 186.

25. Ritchie, *From Morality to Metaphysics*, 186.

26. Or alternatively, moral obligations are grounded in God's commands. While many theists are attracted to some version of divine command theory, I lean more toward a so-called natural law account. I tend to think that many moral obligations are grounded in certain (necessary) facts about human flourishing, and others (especially contingent moral obligations, obligations that would be supererogatory if God had not commanded them, such as the command to obey the Sabbath) are grounded in God's command. Importantly, either way, objective moral obligations are grounded in the divine being, either in virtue of the divine willing to create finite essences or through divine commands.

27. Bertrand Russell, *Why I Am Not a Christian* (New York: Touchstone, 1957), 107.

Chapter 6 Meaning

1. I follow Joshua Seachris in thinking that the question of life's meaning is a request for a narrative that makes sense of our life's existence and deep existential concerns. See Joshua Seachris, "The Meaning of Life as Narrative: A New Proposal for Interpreting Philosophy's 'Primary' Problem," *Philo* 12, no. 1 (2009): 5–23.

2. Seachris calls these competing intuitions the "staying-power intuition" and the "scarcity intuition." See Joshua Seachris, "Death, Futility, and the Proleptic Power of Narrative Ending," *Religious Studies* 47 (2011): 142.

3. Owen Flanagan, *The Really Hard Problem: Meaning in a Material World* (Cambridge, MA: MIT Press, 2007), xii.

4. Wilfrid Sellars, "Philosophy and the Scientific Image of Man," in *Science, Perception and Reality* (New York: Humanities, 1963), 1, quoted in Flanagan, *Really Hard Problem*, 5.

5. The phrase "contextualizing pursuits" comes from Seachris, "Meaning of Life as Narrative," 9.

6. Jean-Paul Sartre, *Nausea* (New York: New Directions, 2007), vi.

7. Sartre, *Nausea*, 23.

8. Sartre, *Nausea*, 38.

9. Sartre, *Nausea*, 36.

10. Sartre, *Nausea*, 37.

11. Sartre, *Nausea*, 38.

12. Sartre, *Nausea*, 122.

13. Sartre, *Nausea*, 128.

14. Bertrand Russell, *Why I Am Not a Christian* (New York: Touchstone, 1957), 107.

15. This example and analogy are from Seachris, "Meaning of Life as Narrative," 13.

16. Alex Rosenberg, *The Atheist's Guide to Reality: Enjoying Life without Illusions* (New York: Norton, 2011). Rosenberg uses the term "Nice Nihilism" to refer to the idea

that even though *moral* nihilism is true (i.e., there are no objective moral values), it is a rather tame or mild or pleasant or nice kind of nihilism. Darwinian processes have selected a nice morality in order to aid human survival: hence, "Nice Nihilism." I think the same label can apply to Rosenberg's discussion of *meaning* nihilism, so I'll adopt it here for that sphere of human life too.

17. Rosenberg, *Atheist's Guide to Reality*, 205.

18. Rosenberg, *Atheist's Guide to Reality*, 313.

19. Rosenberg, *Atheist's Guide to Reality*, 315.

20. Wendy Syfret, "Sunny Nihilism: 'Since Discovering I'm Worthless My Life Has Felt Precious,'" *The Guardian*, December 17, 2019, https://www.theguardian.com/lifeandstyle /2019/dec/18/sunny-nihilism-since-discovering-im-worthless-my-life-has-felt-precious.

21. Jia Tolentino, "Love, Death, and Begging for Celebrities to Kill You," *New Yorker*, June 21, 2019, https://www.newyorker.com/culture/cultural-comment/love-death-and-beg ging-for-celebrities-to-kill-you.

22. Syfret, "Sunny Nihilism." Of course, if there is Nice Nihilism, there could also be something like "Mean Nihilism"—perhaps this is suggested to us by the Joker as well. Some people just want to watch the world burn.

23. Flanagan, *Really Hard Problem*, 4.

24. Flanagan, *Really Hard Problem*, 107.

25. Flanagan, *Really Hard Problem*, 37.

26. Flanagan, *Really Hard Problem*, 203.

27. Flanagan, *Really Hard Problem*, 37. This is Flanagan's way of describing the six spaces of meaning as we find ourselves in the early twenty-first century.

28. Seachris, "Death, Futility, and the Proleptic Power of Narrative Ending." The dating example is from Seachris.

29. Blaise Pascal, *Pensées*, trans. A. J. Krailsheimer (New York: Penguin Books, 1995), 45.

30. C. S. Lewis, *The Problem of Pain* (New York: HarperCollins, 2001), 152.

Chapter 7 Happiness

1. William Kent Krueger, *This Tender Land* (New York: Atria, 2019).

2. Krueger, *This Tender Land*, 249.

3. I know no one has uttered "galas" since the 1950s, but the alliteration was totally worth it.

4. Boethius, *The Consolation of Philosophy*, trans. Victor Watts (New York: Penguin Books, 1999), 48.

5. Boethius, *Consolation of Philosophy*, 20.

6. I'm allowing myself some creative license here. Obviously, *Consolation of Philosophy* is a work of Boethius throughout, and Lady Philosophy is just a personification of wisdom employed by Boethius (and now me) to explore deep, perennial questions about life, happiness, and God.

7. Boethius, *Consolation of Philosophy*, 52.

8. For more on the moral guilt associated with affluence, see Rachel Sherman, *Uneasy Street: The Anxieties of Affluence* (Princeton: Princeton University Press, 2017).

9. Richard Eckersley, "The Mixed Blessings of Material Progress: Diminishing Returns in the Pursuit of Happiness," in *The Exploration of Happiness*, ed. Antonella Delle Fave (New York: Springer, 2013), 241. Eckersley's reference to "a dark side of the American dream" is from Tim Kasser and Richard M. Ryan, "A Dark Side of the American Dream: Correlates of Financial Success as a Central Life Aspiration," *Journal of Personality and Social Psychology* 65, no. 2 (1993): 410–22.

10. Boethius, *Consolation of Philosophy*, 53.

11. David Foster Wallace, *This Is Water* (New York: Little, Brown, 2009), 103.

12. David Brooks, *The Second Mountain: The Quest for a Moral Life* (New York: Random House, 2019), 12. The report can be accessed at https://mcc.gse.harvard.edu/reports /children-mean-raise.

13. Boethius, *Consolation of Philosophy*, 56.

14. Boethius, *Consolation of Philosophy*, 56.

15. Brooks, *Second Mountain*, 22.

16. The phrase is from the Danish novelist Matias Dalsgaard as discussed in Brooks, *Second Mountain*, 24.

17. Brooks, *Second Mountain*, 24.

18. Boethius, *Consolation of Philosophy*, 58.

19. Boethius, *Consolation of Philosophy*, 59.

20. Boethius, *Consolation of Philosophy*, 41.

21. Boethius, *Consolation of Philosophy*, 42.

22. Boethius, *Consolation of Philosophy*, 59.

23. Boethius, *Consolation of Philosophy*, 58.

24. Jim Carrey and Dana Vachon, *Memoirs and Misinformation* (New York: Knopf, 2020), 159.

25. Jim Carrey, "Jim Carrey at MIU [Maharishi International University]: Commencement Address at the 2014 Graduation," YouTube video, 26:08, May 30, 2014, https://www.youtube.com/watch?v=V80-gPkpH6M&t=1s. For a transcript, see https://www.rev.com/blog/transcripts/jim-carrey-commencement-speech-transcript-2014-at-maharishi-university-of-management. The material quoted can be found by watching (or reading) beginning at the 18:30 mark.

26. Robert Nozick, *Anarchy, State, and Utopia* (New York: Basic Books, 1974), 42.

27. Nozick, *Anarchy, State, and Utopia*, 43.

28. John Stuart Mill, *Utilitarianism* (Indianapolis: Hackett, 2001).

29. Boethius, *Consolation of Philosophy*, 43.

30. Blaise Pascal, *Pensées*, trans. A. J. Krailsheimer (New York: Penguin Books, 1995), 19.

31. On the tragic early death of those who recklessly pursue pleasure, see the discussion around the so-called 27 Club, a "club" composed of famous musicians such as Jimmy Hendrix, Janis Joplin, Jim Morrison, and Kurt Cobain, all of whom tasted the riches of life but died tragic deaths from drugs or by suicide at age twenty-seven. For more, see https://en.wikipedia.org/wiki/27_Club. Thanks to Shane O'Neill for alerting me to the Twenty-Seven Club and to Anthony Kiedis and Larry Sloman's book *Scar Tissue* (New York: Hachette Books, 2004).

32. Kiedis with Sloman, *Scar Tissue*, 206–7.

33. Boethius, *Consolation of Philosophy*, 60.

34. Boethius, *Consolation of Philosophy*, 63.

35. Boethius, *Consolation of Philosophy*, 68–73.

36. The phrase "road-hunger" comes from James K. A. Smith, *On the Road with Saint Augustine: A Real-World Spirituality for Restless Hearts* (Grand Rapids: Brazos, 2019), 5.

37. Smith, *On the Road with Saint Augustine*, 5.

38. Wallace, *This Is Water*, 100–102.

39. C. S. Lewis, *The Weight of Glory* (New York: HarperCollins, 2001), 36–42.

Chapter 8 Pain

1. Voltaire, *Candide*, trans. Burton Raffel (New Haven: Yale University Press, 2005), 2.

2. Voltaire, *Candide*, 129.

3. Eleonore Stump, *Wandering in Darkness: Narrative and the Problem of Suffering* (Oxford: Oxford University Press, 2010), 6–8.

4. The phrase "destroyer of optimism" is from Philip Littell's introduction to Voltaire, *Candide* (n.p.: Millennium, 2014), 7.

5. Richard M. Gale, "Evil as Evidence against God," in *Debating Christian Theism*, ed. J. P. Moreland, Chad Meister, and Khaldoun A. Sweis (Oxford: Oxford University Press, 2013), 197.

6. David Hume, *Dialogues concerning Natural Religion and the Posthumous Essays*, ed. Richard H. Popkin (Indianapolis: Hackett, 1980).

7. Hume, *Dialogues concerning Natural Religion*, 63.

8. In other words, I'm arguing that being free is incompatible with being determined. This view of freedom is called incompatibilism or libertarian freedom. For more on the debate between compatibilist and incompatibilist conceptions of freedom, see Robert Kane, *A Contemporary Introduction to Free Will* (Oxford: Oxford University Press, 2005).

9. For a sophisticated discussion of the basic argument that I've sketched above, see Alvin Plantinga's discussion of the Freewill Defense in his *The Nature of Necessity* (Oxford: Clarendon, 1974), 164–95. Before moving on, you might wonder: Could not God create significantly free creatures that never, as a matter of fact, do evil? C. S. Lewis is helpful here: "We can, perhaps, conceive of a world in which God corrected the results of this abuse of free will by His creatures at every moment: so that a wooden beam became soft as grass when it was used as a weapon, and the air refused to obey me if I attempted to set up in it the soundwaves that carry lies or insults. But such a world would be one in which wrong actions were impossible, and in which therefore, freedom of the will would be void: nay, if the principle were carried out to its logical conclusion, evil thoughts would be impossible, for the cerebral matter which we use in thinking would refuse its task when we attempted to frame them." C. S. Lewis, *The Problem of Pain* (New York: HarperOne, 2001), 24.

10. Hume, *Dialogues concerning Natural Religion*, 66.

11. Hume, *Dialogues concerning Natural Religion*, 74.

12. Hume, *Dialogues concerning Natural Religion*, 75.

13. Paul Draper, "Pain and Pleasure: An Evidential Problem for Theists," *Noûs* 23 (1989): 331–50; reprinted in *God and the Problem of Evil*, ed. William L. Rowe (Malden, MA: Blackwell, 2001), 180–202. References are from the essay as contained in the Rowe volume.

14. Draper, "Pain and Pleasure," 181.

15. Draper formalizes this claim as follows, where "O" stands for a statement reporting all the observed facts about pain and pleasure in the world: "C: $P(O/HI)$ is much greater than $P(O/theism)$." Draper, "Pain and Pleasure," 182. In English, C reads as the probability of the observed facts about pain and pleasure in the world is much greater on the assumption of HI than on the assumption of theism.

16. For the details, see Draper, "Pain and Pleasure," 183–89.

17. Draper, "Pain and Pleasure," 188.

18. Hume, *Dialogues concerning Natural Religion*, 74.

19. Alvin Plantinga, "On Being Evidentially Challenged," in *The Evidential Argument from Evil*, ed. Daniel Howard-Snyder (Bloomington: Indiana University Press, 1996), 253–54. The qualifier "so it seems to me" is appropriate since Draper employs the notion of epistemic probability in his argument.

20. I'm trying to simplify the discussion without losing any of the rigor of Draper's argument. More accurately, Draper's claim is that P (O3/HI & O1 & O2) >! P (O3/theism & O1 & O2) where "O3" represents the observed biologically gratuitous pleasure and pain in the world, "O1" represents the observed biologically useful pleasure and pain of sentient moral creatures, and "O2" represents the observed biologically useful pleasure and pain of sentient nonmoral creatures (Draper, "Pain and Pleasure," 188–89). I've omitted the "plus the observed biologically useful pleasure and pain" from my discussion in the chapter text, but the reader should understand it to be part of the background information when considering the evidential value of biologically gratuitous pleasure and pain.

21. Plantinga, "On Being Evidentially Challenged," 256.

22. Richard Otte, "Evidential Arguments from Evil," *International Journal for Philosophy of Religion* 48 (2000): 3.

23. Otte, "Evidential Arguments from Evil," 8.

24. For a more detailed discussion of the Bible's first book and what we can learn about God, evil, and suffering from it, see Paul M. Gould, "Genesis and the Problem of Evil: Philosophical Musings on the Bible's First Book," in *Cambridge Companion to Genesis*, ed. Bill Arnold (Cambridge: Cambridge University Press, 2022), chap. 13. For a much fuller account of what we can learn about evil from the biblical narrative, see Stump, *Wandering in Darkness*.

25. J. R. R. Tolkien, *The Return of the King* (New York: Del Rey, 2012), 337–38.

211

26. See Psalm 35:27b, "The Lord be exalted, who delights in the well-being of his servant."

27. See Psalm 37:4, "Take delight in the Lord, and he will give you the desires of your heart."

28. As Stump puts it, given the aim of flourishing (understood as union with God), and given the fact that flourishing is a degreed concept, the reason for suffering is either *surrender* (for the nonbeliever in God) or *growth* (for the believer in God): "The benefit for the suffering whose aim is the sufferer's surrender to God's love is the warding-off the worst things for human beings. The benefit for the suffering whose aim is growth in internal integration in the cooperative process of sanctification is the increased closeness to God and the correlative increase in human flourishing and glory." Stump, *Wandering in Darkness*, 396–97.

29. For details of how this might look, see Stump, *Wandering in Darkness*, 446–48.

30. There is much more, of course, that can and should be said. Stump limits her discussion, as I have, to fully functioning adult humans. Elsewhere, I've tried to extend this theodicy in outline form to include non–fully functioning humans, infants, and animals; see Gould, "Genesis and the Problem of Evil."

31. As C. S. Lewis famously wrote, "God whispers to us in our pleasures, speaks in our conscience, but shouts in our pain: it is His megaphone to rouse a deaf world." Lewis, *Problem of Pain*, 91.

Chapter 9 Love

1. Green Day, "Boulevard of Broken Dreams," from *American Idiot*.

2. Amy Kaufman, "Why People Are So Obsessed with *The Bachelor*, according to the Woman Who Wrote a Book on It," interview by Samantha Cooney, *Time*, March 4, 2018, https://time.com/5168186/bachelor-book-interview/. See Amy Kaufman, *Bachelor Nation: Inside the World of America's Favorite Guilty Pleasure* (New York: Dutton, 2018).

3. Mark Regnerus, *Cheap Sex: The Transformation of Men, Marriage, and Monogamy* (Oxford: Oxford University Press, 2017), 10.

4. Regnerus, *Cheap Sex*, 177.

5. Regnerus, *Cheap Sex*, 9.

6. Alex Rosenberg, *The Atheist's Guide to Reality: Enjoying Life without Illusions* (New York: Norton, 2011), 3.

7. Dante Alighieri, *The Divine Comedy*, vol. 3, *Paradiso*, trans. Robert M. Durling (Oxford: Oxford University Press, 2012), canto 33, p. 667.

8. Josef Pieper, *Faith, Hope, Love* (San Francisco: Ignatius, 1986), 164.

9. For a nice discussion of these four kinds of love, see C. S. Lewis, *The Four Loves* (New York: Harcourt Brace Jovanovich, 1988).

10. For a more detailed survey of contemporary accounts of love, see Esther Engels Kroeker, "Reasons for Love," in *The Routledge Handbook of Love in Philosophy*, ed. Adrienne M. Martin (New York: Routledge, 2019), 277–87; and Bennett Helm, "Love," in *The Stanford Encyclopedia of Philosophy*, ed. Edward N. Zalta, last modified August 11, 2017, https://plato.stanford.edu/archives/fall2017/entries/love/.

11. Harry Frankfurt, "Moral Normativity and the Necessities of Love," in Martin, *Routledge Handbook of Love in Philosophy*, 337.

12. Adele's song, from the album 25, is aptly titled "Why Do You Love Me."

13. Eleonore Stump, *Wandering in Darkness: Narrative and the Problem of Suffering* (Oxford: Oxford University Press, 2010), 87.

14. Stump, *Wandering in Darkness*, 90–92.

15. Stump, *Wandering in Darkness*, 91.

16. Stump, *Wandering in Darkness*. Regarding the desire for the good of the beloved, see, e.g., Thomas Aquinas, *Summa Theologiae* I-II, Q. 26, A. 4: "I answer that, As the Philosopher says (Rhet. ii, 4), 'to love is to wish good to someone.' Hence the movement of love has a twofold tendency: towards the good which a man wishes to someone (to himself or to another) and towards that to which he wishes some good. Accordingly, man has love of

concupiscence towards the good that he wishes to another, and love of friendship towards him to whom he wishes good" (https://www.newadvent.org/summa/2026.htm#article4). Regarding the desire for union, see, e.g., Aquinas, *Summa Theologiae* I-II, Q. 66, A. 6, where in a discussion of the theological virtues (faith, hope, and love), Aquinas states, "But the love of charity is of that which is already possessed: since the beloved is, in a manner, in the lover, and, again, the lover is drawn by desire to union with the beloved" (https://www.newadvent.org/summa/2066.htm#article6).

17. Gail Caldwell, *Let's Take the Long Way Home: A Memoir of Friendship* (New York: Random House, 2010), 13.

18. Caldwell, *Let's Take the Long Way Home*, 130.

19. According to Stump, the first answer is Aquinas's answer, and the second is an extension from Aquinas's position. See Stump, *Wandering in Darkness*, 527n57.

20. Stump, *Wandering in Darkness*, 96–97.

21. Stump, *Wandering in Darkness*, 99.

22. Stump describes the differing kinds of relationships as "offices of love." Each office of love specifies the kind of love appropriate to a kind of relationship. Thus, the kind of love appropriate for a priest to feel toward a parishioner is distinct from the kind of love appropriate for a wife to a husband, or parent to a child, although there will be overlap in many cases. The offices of love help us see how love can be changeless regardless of the intrinsic qualities of the beloved (in the case of parent love, for example) yet how love can also vary within certain kinds of relationships (for example, friendship love that changes as the intrinsic qualities of the beloved change). For more on the offices of love, see Stump, *Wandering in Darkness*, 98–99.

23. For more on how Aquinas's account of love captures what is right and avoids what is wrong about contemporary views, see Stump, *Wandering in Darkness*, 102–4.

24. Interestingly, there is also an argument from the nature of perfect love to the triune God of Christianity. The idea is that perfect love requires mutual sharing of love between persons as well as mutual cooperation in the sharing of love between two persons with a third. Thus, it is reasoned, God must be more than one person but no more than three. Perfect love entails that God is exactly three persons! For a more detailed discussion of this argument originally formulated by Richard of St. Victor (c. 1110–73), see Richard Swinburne, *Was Jesus God?* (Oxford: Oxford University Press, 2008), 28–34.

25. The phrase "riotous diversity" is from Andrew Davison, *Participation in God: A Study in Christian Doctrine and Metaphysics* (Cambridge: Cambridge University Press, 2019), 33.

26. As Sigmund Freud wrote, "The nucleus of what we mean by love naturally consists (and this is what is commonly called love, and what the poets sing of) in sexual love with sexual union as its aim" (*Group Psychology and the Analysis of the Ego*, trans. James Strachey [London: The International Psycho-analytical Press, 1922], 37). Regarding Darwinism, Edward O. Wilson claims that love is an emotion produced by the hypothalamus and limbic system, both features of the human anatomy "engineered [by natural selection] to perpetuate DNA" (Edward O. Wilson, *Sociobiology: The New Synthesis* [Cambridge: Belknap, 1975], 3).

27. There are naturalistic evolutionary accounts of deep and enduring agape love, most often appealing to "reciprocal altruism." Others, such as Friedrich Nietzsche, reject the need to explain long-term love and altruism, arguing that the true driving force in all human action is not sexual craving but "the will to power." See Jerry L. Walls, "The Argument from Love and from the Meaning of Life," in *Two Dozen (or So) Arguments for God: The Plantinga Project*, ed. Jerry L. Walls and Trent Dougherty (Oxford: Oxford University Press, 2018), 309–11.

28. Michael Ruse, "Love and Evolution," in *The Oxford Handbook of Philosophy of Love*, ed. Christopher Grau and Aaron Smuts (Oxford: Oxford University Press, forthcoming); published online, September 2017, https://doi.org/10.1093/oxfordhb/9780199395729.013.13, 8.

29. Elliott Sober, "Philosophy of Biology," in *The Blackwell Companion to Philosophy*, ed. Nicholas Bunnin and Eric Tsui-James, 2nd ed. (Malden, MA: Blackwell, 2003), 322.

30. Alvin Plantinga, *Warranted Christian Belief* (Oxford: Oxford University Press, 2000), 321, quoted in Walls, "The Argument from Love and from the Meaning of Life," 318.

Chapter 10 Beauty

1. Oscar Wilde, *The Picture of Dorian Gray* (Mineola, NY: Dover, 1993), 16.

2. Wilde, *Picture of Dorian Gray*, 159.

3. Wilde, *Picture of Dorian Gray*, 157.

4. David Hume, "Of the Standard of Taste," in *Essays Moral, Political, and Literary*, ed. Eugene F. Miller (Indianapolis: Liberty Fund, 1987), 230.

5. One could raise an evolutionary objection at this point: aesthetic agreement is best explained by evolution. I'll address the challenge from evolution below.

6. Peter Forrest, *God without the Supernatural: A Defense of Scientific Theism* (Ithaca, NY: Cornell University Press, 1996), 133–34.

7. In this paragraph I'm summarizing a longer argument in Eddy M. Zemach, *Real Beauty* (University Park: Pennsylvania State University Press, 1997), 64–67.

8. Elaine Scarry, *On Beauty and Being Just* (Princeton: Princeton University Press, 1999), 52.

9. Scarry, *On Beauty and Being Just*, 22–23.

10. Scarry, *On Beauty and Being Just*, 81.

11. Scarry, *On Beauty and Being Just*, 7.

12. Scarry, *On Beauty and Being Just*, 25–26.

13. Scarry, *On Beauty and Being Just*, 50.

14. Thomas Aquinas, *Summa Theologiae* I-II, Q. 27, A. 1, https://www.newadvent.org/summa/2027.htm#article1.

15. Aquinas, *Summa Theologiae* I, Q. 39, A. 8, https://www.newadvent.org/summa/1039.htm#article8.

16. This sentence summarizes the helpful exposition of Aquinas's three aspects to beautiful things in Barbara Nicolosi, "The Artist," in *For the Beauty of the Church: Casting a Vision for the Arts*, ed. W. David O. Taylor (Grand Rapids: Baker Books, 2010), 106–9.

17. John Navone, *Toward a Theology of Beauty* (Collegeville, MN: Liturgical Press, 1996), vii.

18. Roger Scruton, *Beauty: A Very Short Introduction* (Oxford: Oxford University Press, 2011), xi.

19. "Latest Banksy Artwork 'Love Is in the Bin' Created Live at Auction," Sotheby's (website), October 11, 2018, https://www.sothebys.com/en/articles/latest-banksy-artwork-love-is-in-the-bin-created-live-at-auction.

20. All of the artworks listed, with the exception of the Banksy work, can currently be found at the Norton Museum of Art, West Palm Beach, Florida.

21. As stated by the philosopher Clive Bell, "The Aesthetic Hypothesis," in *The Philosophy of Art: Readings Ancient and Modern*, ed. A. Neil and A. Ridley (New York: McGraw Hill, 1995), 100, quoted in Gordon Graham, *Philosophy of the Arts: An Introduction to Aesthetics*, 3rd ed. (New York: Routledge, 2005), 222.

22. For a discussion of each of these proposed features of artworks, see Graham, *Philosophy of the Arts*, 221–24; and Robert Stecker, *Aesthetics and the Philosophy of Art: An Introduction* (Landham, MA: Rowman & Littlefield, 2005), 85–86.

23. Both problems are discussed in detail in Graham, *Philosophy of the Arts*, 224–28.

24. For a more detailed critique of institutionalism and what I'm calling historicism, see Graham, *Philosophy of the Arts*, 229–30; and Stecker, *Aesthetics and the Philosophy of Art*, 92–100.

25. My discussion is modeled after comments made by Stecker, *Aesthetics and the Philosophy of Art*, 99–100.

26. Graham, *Philosophy of the Arts*, 244.

27. For a detailed defense of what is called *aesthetic cognitivism*, see Graham, *Philosophy of the Arts*, 52–75.

28. In my use of the phrase "aesthetic surfaces of the world," I'm riffing on Scarry's claim that "the surfaces of the world are aesthetically uneven" (Scarry, *On Beauty and Being Just*, 110).

29. Scarry, *On Beauty and Being Just*, 114. The artist Barbara Nicolosi claims that "beauty is the terrain of real artists, and one way to recognize them is if they dwell in this terrain." Nicolosi, "Artist," 106, emphasis omitted.

30. Scarry, *On Beauty and Being Just*, 81.

31. Paul Draper, "Seeking but Not Believing," in *Divine Hiddenness: New Essays*, ed. Daniel Howard-Snyder and Paul K. Moser (Cambridge: Cambridge University Press, 2002), 204.

32. Scarry, *On Beauty and Being Just*, 30.

33. The language of "saturation" is from F. R. Tennant's work on the argument from beauty; see F. R. Tennant, *Philosophical Theology*, vol. 2 (Cambridge: Cambridge University Press, 1930), 91, quoted in Mark Wynn, *God and Goodness: A Natural Theological Perspective* (New York: Routledge, 1999), 19–20.

34. The language of "transcendent" is from Forrest, *God without the Supernatural*, 135.

35. Wynn, *God and Goodness*, 20.

36. Forrest, *God without the Supernatural*, 135.

37. This paragraph is inspired by the unpublished work of Jonathan Ashbach; I thank him for allowing me to read his manuscript "Rediscovering the Aesthetic Argument: A Phenomenological Presentation." For an excellent book-length discussion of evolutionary accounts of beauty and aesthetic appreciation, see John D. Barrow, *The Artful Universe Expanded*, 2nd ed. (Oxford: Oxford University Press, 2011).

38. Aquinas, *Exposition of On the Divine Names* 4.5, quoted in Andrew Davison, *Participation in God: A Study in Christian Doctrine and Metaphysics* (Cambridge: Cambridge University Press, 2019), 343.

39. Ryan West and Adam C. Pelser, "Perceiving God through Natural Beauty," *Faith and Philosophy* 32, no. 3 (2015): 293–312.

40. C. S. Lewis, *The Weight of Glory* (New York: HarperOne, 2001), 30.

Chapter 11 Religion

1. John Gardner, "Wonder," *NEA Journal* (February 1957), 73, quoted in Sam Keen, *Apology for Wonder* (New York: Harper & Row, 1969), 20.

2. The medieval philosopher Avicenna reportedly took a rather harsh stance on anyone who fails to see the truth of the law of noncontradiction: "Anyone who denies the law of noncontradiction should be beaten and burned until he admits that to be beaten is not the same as not to be beaten, and to be burned is not the same as not to be burned." Alas, this quote seems to be a commentator's gloss on Avicenna. The actual quote reads, "By resolving the difficulty [arising] from [the existence] of contrary syllogisms [encountered by] the perplexed, we are able to guide him. As for the obdurate, he must be subjected to the conflagration of fire, since 'fire' and 'not fire' are one. Pain must be inflicted on him through beating, since 'pain' and 'no pain' are one. And he must be denied food and drink, since eating and drinking and the abstention from both are one [and the same]. This principle, which we have defended against those who deny it, is the first principle of demonstrative proofs. It is incumbent on the first philosopher to defend it." Avicenna, *The Metaphysics of "The Healing,"* trans. Michael E. Marmura (Provo, UT: Brigham Young University Press, 2005), 43. Thanks to John Doncevic, the university librarian at Palm Beach Atlantic University, for unraveling this Gordian knot. For we learn that Avicenna was actually much harsher than the popular internet quote suggests: those who deny the law of noncontradiction should be beaten, burned, *and* starved! I'll not recommend the path of Avicenna, but if you don't see the truth of the law of noncontradiction, I recommend something even more torturous: enroll in a philosophy class at the local university.

3. I go into greater detail regarding these three lines of evidence, along with my coauthors, in Paul M. Gould, Travis Dickinson, and R. Keith Loftin, *Stand Firm: Apologetics and the Brilliance of the Gospel* (Nashville: B&H Academic, 2019), 69–125.

4. For introductions to the historical evidence regarding the Bible, Jesus, and the resurrection, I recommend the following, in increasing level of difficulty: Josh McDowell and Sean McDowell, *Evidence That Demands a Verdict: Life-Changing Truth for a Skeptical World* (Nashville: Nelson, 2017); William Lane Craig, *Reasonable Faith: Christian Truth and Apologetics*, 3rd ed. (Wheaton: Crossway, 2008), chaps. 5–8; and N. T. Wright, *The Resurrection of the Son of God*, Christian Origins and the Question of God 3 (Minneapolis: Fortress, 2003).

For a nice introduction to the skeptical challenge to these claims regarding the Bible, Jesus, and the resurrection, see Bart D. Ehrman, *Misquoting Jesus: The Story behind Who Changed the Bible and Why* (New York: HarperOne, 2007), and Bart D. Ehrman, *How Jesus Became God: The Exaltation of a Jewish Preacher from Galilee* (New York: HarperOne, 2015).

5. N. T. Wright, *The Challenge of Jesus: Rediscovering Who Jesus Was and Is*, 2nd ed. (Downers Grove, IL: IVP Books, 2015), 122.

6. See especially C. S. Lewis, "The Shocking Alternative," in *Mere Christianity* (New York: HarperOne, 2001), 47–52; and C. S. Lewis, "What Are We to Make of Jesus Christ?," in *God in the Dock: Essays on Theology and Ethics*, ed. Walter Hooper (Grand Rapids: Eerdmans, 1970), 157–60. In *Stand Firm*, my coauthors and I argue that there are actually five possibilities regarding Jesus: he is lama (i.e., a great moral teacher), legend (i.e., nonexistent), liar, lunatic, or Lord (Gould, Dickinson, and Loftin, *Stand Firm*, 92–106).

7. John Dickson, *Life of Jesus: Who He Is and Why He Matters* (Grand Rapids: Zondervan, 2010), 157.

8. For more on the Christian story, understood in terms of *home—away—home again*, see Paul M. Gould, *Cultural Apologetics: Renewing the Christian Voice, Conscience, and Imagination in a Disenchanted World* (Grand Rapids: Zondervan, 2019), 208–10. Thanks to my friend Stephen Kirk for his teaching on the Christian story using the metaphor of the home. See also Frederick Buechner, *Telling the Truth: The Gospel as Tragedy, Comedy, and Fairy Tale* (New York: HarperCollins, 1977).

9. Alvin Plantinga argues that the best possible story includes atonement, and maybe incarnation, and thus the best possible story will also include pain and suffering. See Alvin Plantinga, *Where the Conflict Really Lies: Science, Religion, and Naturalism* (Oxford: Oxford University Press, 2011), 58–59; and Alvin Plantinga, "Supralapsarianism, or 'O Felix Culpa,'" in *Christian Faith and the Problem of Evil*, ed. Peter van Inwagen (Grand Rapids: Eerdmans, 2005).

10. G. K. Chesterton, *The Everlasting Man* (San Francisco: Ignatius, 2008), 248.

11. I'm riffing on C. S. Lewis's claim that the world feels haunted by transcendence: "Until you step off the plane of the picture into the large dimensions of death you cannot see the gold. But we have reminders of it. To change our metaphor, the blackout is not quite complete. There are chinks. At times the daily scene looks big with its secrets." *The Problem of Pain* (New York: HarperCollins, 2001), 153. I also recommend to you, once again, the British comedy series *Detectorists*. Without spoiling the show, I can only say that the series finale nicely illustrates the beauty of the gospel, as treasure rains down from on high as a kind of divine gift.

12. Blaise Pascal, *Pensées*, trans. A. J. Krailsheimer (New York: Penguin Books, 1995), 141.

13. And it is a *quest*. As the Catholic philosopher Mark Dooley reminds us, "Understanding who you are, and where you belong, requires a long detour through the residue of history and culture" (*Moral Matters: A Philosophy of Homecoming* [New York: Bloomsbury, 2015], 48).

14. The description of the Bible as an "enchanted map" is from James K. A. Smith, *On the Road with Saint Augustine: A Real-World Spirituality for Restless Hearts* (Grand Rapids: Brazos, 2019), 175.

15. Pastor Timothy Keller writes, "The question of identity is not 'who am I?' but 'whose am I?'. . . . Only if God names us, and we serve him, will we be free from enslavement because he grants us love on the basis of Jesus' performance, not ours. If he names us—if we are his—we can finally rest in our identity as his child." Timothy Keller, *Preaching: Communicating Faith in an Age of Skepticism* (New York: Viking, 2015), 138–39.